3·99 36/13A

MAPPING DIFFERENCE

Mapping Difference
The Many Faces of Women in Contemporary Ukraine

Edited by

Marian J. Rubchak

Berghahn Books
New York • Oxford

First published in 2011 by

Berghahn Books

www.berghahnbooks.com

©2011 Marian J. Rubchak

Library of Congress Cataloging-in-Publication Data

Mapping difference : the many faces of women in contemporary Ukraine / edited by
Marian J. Rubchak.
    p. cm.
Includes bibliographical references and index.
ISBN 978-0-85745-118-7
 1. Women—Ukraine. 2. Women—Ukraine—Social conditions—21st century.
3. Feminism—Ukraine. I. Rubchak, Marian J.
HQ1665.45.M37 2011
305.409477'090512—dc22

2010029875

British Library Cataloguing in Publication Data

A catalogue record for this book is available from the British Library

Printed in the United States on acid-free paper.

ISBN: 978-0-85745-118-7 Hardback

Contents

Figures

Tables

Foreword

The collection of essays that you are about to read represents a unique and unprecedented effort to bring together the views of Ukrainian and North American scholars on issues relating to gender and gender politics in Ukraine today. At this pivotal juncture of the country's transformation, the issue of gender and gender parity looms large, and the stakes for the women involved are enormous. And yet gender remains a terribly unexplored topic and therefore, in those rare instances when it is taken into consideration, it is often misunderstood or misappropriated. This volume aims to shore up this lacuna in our knowledge of Ukrainian women's lives and the dynamics that shape the joys and challenges that color them. By offering rich insights into the historical, political, and social forces that structure the choices Ukrainian women have and the decisions they make in their everyday lives, these essays constitute a valuable addition to the literature on contemporary Ukraine.

The portrait of the status of women—and gender issues after socialism more generally—that evolves from these essays is perplexing and contradictory. No single individual illustrates the paradoxes of gender in Ukraine today better than Yulia Tymoshenko, one of the country's most visible and successful *berehyni*, a mythical matriarchal goddess figure. She is the former prime minister of Ukraine, legendary for her power, independence, and maverick opinions. She was previously a successful businesswoman, which earned her wealth and influence, and one of two leaders of the Orange Revolution, which garnered respect. These accomplishments have combined to position her well to become a contender for the Ukrainian presidency (at the time of this writing she announced her candidacy). And yet, like many other women in Ukraine with far less monetary and cultural capital, she does not consider herself a feminist. She does not even particularly identify with legislative initiatives that could positively impact women, although she clearly must have confronted numerous gender-based barriers, prejudices, and stereotypes as she moved up the ladder to take her place among the elite of the Soviet Union, and now among the most powerful in Ukraine. Such is the puzzling state of feminism in Ukraine today. It is precisely these types of counterintuitive paradoxes that the essays in this volume address with critical acumen and analyze with fresh perspectives.

To solve the puzzle of explaining how gender is understood in postsocialist societies, these scholars move beyond the frequent laments and binary images of women in Ukraine, either as oppressive, dictatorial, and domineering or oppressed, passive, and decorative. By shedding light on the dynamics that have shaped the status of women, such as rhetorical practices, migration, media images, and educational conventions, to name a few, these essays illuminate the issues and problems that particularly confront women as well as the sources that have helped to generate them. We gain an understanding of the fluidity of the challenges women face today, and an acute awareness of the pitfalls and potential promises that mark the path of gender politics and hamper those that chose to pursue them.

Most notably, these authors illustrate for us the enormous variety in understandings of gender and of gender-based problems and how these understandings vary by region, profession, generation, and other social factors. The inclusion of a variety of disciplines and methodologies from different national traditions allows the collection as a whole to offer a mosaic portrait of the lives of women in Ukraine. Most of all, I am grateful to these authors for providing fresh perspectives on gender politics that focus on the experiences and testimonies of women themselves in Ukraine today. By doing so, these authors are able to present lively and animated snapshots of the humanity and struggles of Ukrainian women. By reading this collection, we gain an understanding of how these dynamics are interrelated and mutually reinforcing. For example, one essay details the issue of massive outmigration of women to regions beyond the post-Soviet space for long-term employment, economic tourism, or worse as part of human trafficking. Such widespread and prolonged migration has radically altered the workforce and family life in Ukraine, prompting some women who stayed behind in Ukraine to become advocates for the weak and powerless, often the oldest or youngest members of society. Views of daily life in the near and far abroad are refracted back to Ukraine through the media in gender-biased language (genderlect) in divergent ways, contributing to the regional variations in understandings of gender-based identities. It is these interconnections that these essays illustrate so vividly.

All in all, this collection fills a gap in the scholarly and popular literatures on gender issues at a time when the topic is of growing importance. These authors not only help us to understand the idea of discrimination and preferential treatment but also its sources. They are to be commended for offering concrete suggestions as to how the standing, status, and well-being of women in contemporary Ukrainian society can be improved by curbing patronizing language, occupational segregation, and the overall asymmetrical status between the genders, which contributes unnecessarily to the downward mobility of women. By offering analyses of gender-based issues, policies, and problems as well as specific recommendations as to how imbalances and injustices can be reordered more fairly, the ambitions and applications of this volume are boundless. It is a rare volume indeed that accomplishes so much.

Catherine Wanner

Acknowledgments

One of the most gratifying experiences in producing a volume of collected works such as this is the opportunity it presents for sharing information and working with a diverse community of such talented scholars. I wish especially to acknowledge my innumerable friends and acquaintances in Ukraine who gave so generously of their time and expertise as work on this collection proceeded. One person, in particular, deserves special thanks—my gracious friend, colleague, and frequent hostess in Kyiv, Tamara Melnyk. She has shared invaluable material on gender issues with me over the years, included me in numerous gender related events whenever I was in Kyiv, and took special pains to host informal feminist gatherings in her home, where many inspirational conversations took place. Larysa Kobelyans'ka, coordinator of UN-sponsored programs on gender education, also merits special thanks for her efforts in arranging invitations to a host of high-level events on women's issues. I wish also to express my appreciation to Oksana Kis' for alerting me to important developments, relevant to my research, as they unfolded in Ukraine. To my colleague Sarah Phillips I owe my appreciation for her careful reading of the manuscript and insightful suggestions. I have incurred many more debts along the way; to everyone who so generously contributed time and effort—I thank you.

Multiple fellowships and grants from IREX (International Research and Exchanges Board) and the Senior Scholar Program of the Fulbright Foundation funded many of my research trips to Ukraine, where the idea for this collection was born. The Shevchenko Scientific Society, New York branch, generously offered the necessary funds to complete this collection in its late stage. I am also indebted to Valparaiso University for its unwavering support of my scholarship over the years, including a Senior Research Professorship after I left the classroom, the terms of which provide the means to continue my research.

On a somewhat different note, I am grateful to my grandson Adrian Byramji, who was always on hand to offer technical support. When my temperamental computer consigned this entire collection to the dustbin of cyberspace, he retrieved it from obscurity.

Finally, I wish to express my appreciation to Anna Gutsol of FEMINA, in Kyiv, for permission to use images of its women protesting against sexual exploitation and other forms of social injustice. I am also grateful to Cambridge University Press for permission to reprint, in modified form, Laada Bilaniuk's "Gender, Language Attitudes, and Language Status in Ukraine," *Language in Society* 32 (2003): 47–78.

This collection is dedicated to the late Natalka Chukhim, cherished friend and colleague, whose untimely passing left such a void in my life and in Ukraine's community of gender scholars.

CHAPTER I

Turning Oppression into Opportunity

An Introduction

Marian J. Rubchak

> Women hold up half the sky
> —Chinese proverb

In their introductory chapter to *Living Gender under Communism*, Janet Johnson and Jean Robinson note that the Soviet era had witnessed gender, which was "simultaneously promoted in the rhetoric on motherhood and denied in the rhetoric on the 'woman question' and women's equality" (2007).[1] There are parallels to be drawn here between Soviet discourse and that of today's Ukraine. Much of the latter's rhetoric on women projects the image of an empowered *berehynia* (guardian) as progenitor, custodian of family values, and national identity,[2] whereas women's true equality remains contested.

Notwithstanding such correlations between then and now, significant differences also remain to be explored. With Ukraine's chain of historical memory having been deliberately obscured during the Soviet era, the nation lost almost three-quarters of a century in its evolution to an open democratic society. In 1991 independence unsealed the communist borders, eliminated Soviet proscriptions, and revealed a gateway for contacts with the west. The ensuing exchange released a flow of information, and resources for establishing, coordinating, and sustaining gender-friendly programs, while fostering conditions in which new gender formations might materialize and multiply. In this postcommunist space, weaker, often contradictory social pressures on negotiating gender and disseminating its message have replaced the dictatorial state regulations that once circumscribed personal agency (Johnson and Robinson 2007: 8–9). Yet, neotraditional societal values, foregrounding the idea that women are products of nature, without any intervention from culture and society, impose their own constraints on the dynamics of gender construction. This volume explores such contradictory impulses—individual freedom to determine one's gender, and societal impediments to a multiplicity of new gender constructions.

An early indicator of the shifting mood of opinion on women's rights might have been observed in the ranks of the intellectual elite with the appearance of an article titled "Does Ukrainian Literary Scholarship Need a Feminist School?" in 1991.[3] It was the product of one of Ukraine's earliest post-Soviet proponents of feminism, Solomea Pavlychko. Two years later her initiative provided the stimulus for a team of talented women to launch the country's first self-styled "feminist" magazine titled *Piata Pora* (Fifth Season). It created a sensation, yet for all of its bold initiative—and it *was* bold for the time and the place—this "feminist" journal did not lack for paradoxes. Articles on equal rights and opportunities intermingled with references to women in essentialist roles, and warnings about the dangers of publicly active women losing their femininity. This caution, versions of which I heard repeatedly during my numerous visits to Ukraine, brought to mind something I read in an article written by Dmytro Vydrin, titled: "Woman, Glamour and Politics." In a discussion devoted to female politicians, the author argued: "When a man enters politics he leaves behind his principles, but when a woman enters politics she leaves behind her womanhood" (2007). In the second issue, published in March 1993, *Piata Pora* continued to exhibit the unmistakable signs of evolving into yet another traditional women's magazine. In an attempt to sustain their agenda of publishing a "feminist" journal, its editors featured articles on notable women in history and female contributions to literature and art, yet alongside these pieces examples of neotraditional values competed for space. Whatever the initial intent of the journal's founders, it soon became obvious that this "grand feminist experiment" was fated for extinction. They had managed to bring out a second issue, but in so doing the founders exhausted their financial resources and were unsuccessful in attracting further funding. Despite this setback, their dream of spreading the feminist "gospel" did not die with the journal's demise.

In May 1994, for the first time Ukrainian readers were able to read serialized selections in translation from Simone de Beauvoir's *The Second Sex*. They were published in the widely circulated magazine *Ukraina,* prior to the release of a two-volume edition of the entire translated work later that year (13–14).[4] It was hoped that this celebrated feminist publication would soon become the cornerstone of an east-west feminist ideological bridge. As Tatiana Zhurzhenko noted in her contribution to this volume, however, that cornerstone had already been laid—not in Ukraine, but in the North American Ukrainian diaspora. There, studies on Ukrainian feminism had a somewhat earlier start, with the publication of *Feminists Despite Themselves,* by Martha Bohachevsky-Chomiak, in 1988, followed by writings of others. Those early works returned an important piece of history to Ukraine, and scholarly collaboration was eagerly anticipated as a result. It quickly became apparent however, that at least for a time this would be a dichotomous relationship, with feminism being viewed through a bifocal lens, until the respective sides were able to reconcile their dissimilar historical and cultural experiences.

The following year, 1995, as if to send a signal that a genuine window of opportunity for mainstreaming gender politics was finally opened, women in Ukraine prepared to participate in the Fourth World Congress on Women in Beijing. Meanwhile, pressed by skillful negotiations on the part of a resolute group of female activists, the Ukrainian government scheduled a path-breaking event in Kyiv on 12 July 1995. For the first time in the nation's history the parliament (*Verkhovna Rada*) convened a special hearing on discrimination against women. Although billed as an historical breakthrough in elevating women's issues to the highest political level, in point of fact the hearing functioned as a "showcase" of the country's progress in complying with the 1979 UN Convention "On Eliminating All Forms of Discrimination against Women," one of several international women's rights treaties to which Soviet Ukraine was a signatory. As Tatiana Zhurzhenko reminds us: "the Ukrainian government, bound by its international obligations, found itself compelled to cooperate with Ukrainian women's groups in developing national programs" (2004: 37). Dignitaries from Ukraine and abroad were in attendance at this historic public show of compliance.

The majority of speakers were female activists, members of women's associations, NGOs, and the government. In the course of their appeals for gender equality, a number of them characterized authentic Ukrainian women as irrevocably bound to gender-specific roles irrespective of their public accomplishments. Their presentations underscored the persistence with which most of Ukraine's women embrace the traditional model of separate spheres yet, all too comfortable with this accommodation, they simply collude in their own subordination. Their extremely low numbers in Ukraine's post-Soviet leadership positions, and virtual confinement to traditional female agendas when they do come to office, attest to the continuing tenacity of patriarchal values in Ukraine. Although the dominant discourse on women's issues offers the illusion of empowered womanhood, in fact it functions as an effective agent of acculturation to values designed to serve a male power structure. This deception carries immense appeal for Ukrainian women, however; it lulls them into a false sense of their superior worth, even as it relegates them to the status of a second sex.

During the hearing, many of the participants pressed their demands for justice with phrases such as: "allowing women to be women," accompanied by references to women as reproducers of the nation, its culture, and its moral values. The Janus-like attribute of their calls for special concessions on the one hand, and demands for equal rights and opportunities on the other, created an uneasy discursive alliance throughout the proceedings. It also evoked ridiculous relics of the pervasive sexism, causing men to declare that "women cannot cook soup with one hand and run the affairs of a country with the other." One male legislator went so far as to suggest that gender injustice might be eliminated if women were to elect appropriate men to advocate on their behalf (*Ukrainian Observer,* 26 March 2007).[5]

On 9 June 2004, large segments of a second hearing sounded like "déjà-vu all over again." The same maternalist language, the same tired references to women's "beauty and charm" heard nine years earlier, reverberated throughout the hall. To be fair, faint echoes of new concerns also found their way into the discourse—appeals for ending violence against women, and certain practical suggestions for resolving the gender justice impasse. Unfortunately for the women's cause, the latter continue to resist implementation.

Although these initial attempts at securing equal rights proved disappointing, not all of the women's demands went unnoticed, as a third hearing on 21 November 2006 confirmed. Contrary to the first two women-dominated sessions, on this occasion both speakers and guests consisted of men and women in roughly equal numbers. Two discrete subjects were scheduled for deliberation: violence against women during the morning session, and equal rights and opportunities in the afternoon. Except for a single digression, when a lone female participant resurrected the tired old canard of the women's "natural" moral superiority,[6] most of morning's proceedings concentrated on the alarming rise in the volume of female trafficking, and domestic violence against women.[7] Participants also took the opportunity to register their formal support of an amendment on equal rights and opportunities to Ukraine's constitution, ratified at the beginning of the year.[8]

So far so good, I thought, as I looked around at the mixed assembly that morning. Did this indicate that a gender-parity threshold had finally been reached? I thought it might, but my optimism was short lived. What had seemed to represent genuine progress veiled a strong undercurrent of persistent male indifference to women's rights. As if to underscore this, most of the men who attended the morning session drifted away during the midday break.

Can greater female participation in public life supply a remedy? A small minority of women have begun to establish their presence in various public offices, although their long-standing exclusion from positions of authority still inhibits the ability of most to affect public policy in any significant way. The periodic renaming and downgrading of the one ministerial agency with any formal connection to women's issues provides us with a credible indicator of their continuing marginalization at these highest levels. In 1995, following the Beijing conference, a Presidential Committee on Women, Maternity, and Childhood was formed in Ukraine, after which it became the Ministry of Family and Youth. The ministry's sponsorship of such promising events as bringing together government administrators, legislators, and activists in a series of consciousness-raising workshops, training sessions, and seminars resulted in failure to make any substantive gains. This led to a serial reorganization into less influential bodies. In 2005, the committee rose once again to the level of a ministry, named the Ministry of Children, Family, and Youth. In 2006, in yet another name change the body became known as the Ministry of Family, Youth, and Sport, but this time it featured only a gender subset and a disproportionate emphasis on sport.[9] Apart from political appointments to government offices representing the interests of family and children, the potential for women becoming full partners in the political mainstream remained an elusive dream.

An excerpt from the presidential greeting on International Women's Day in 2008 indicates what an uphill struggle for gender parity women in transitional Ukraine continue to face:

> My dear Ukrainian women, I greet you with this spring celebration, a celebration of women's beauty which blooms in today's Ukraine. In my heart I hold only the most tender feelings toward you, as do millions of men in their hearts—men bewitched by you, devoted to you, and grateful for your love. I wish you happiness, love, and offer my assurance that everything in your lives will come out right. ... We love, respect, and thank you—our mothers, our wives, our beloveds, our friends, our daughters—all of the most important women in our lives. ... On this joyful day of celebrating love and hope I greet you, our most enticing, most beautiful women in the world![10]

So much for progress. For his part, in 2009 Deputy Lytvyn greeted the women with:

> A woman's mission is to bear and raise children, to be the *Berehynia* [still with us] of the family hearth. No less vital in this day and age is her participation in community life, engagement in business, and show of professionalism in all that she does.

> Without you, our beloved women, there would be less light, love, and warmth. You fill our days with brilliant color and help us men to grow finer, inspiring us to noble deeds. You give us strength to become better, more caring, and self-assured—qualities requiring that special feminine tact, intuition, tolerance, and endurance—those amazing traits which men so often tend to lack.

> Accept our most profound appreciation, beloved women, for your maternal generosity, intelligence, and support. From the depths of our hearts we wish you, our dear mothers, wives, daughters, and sisters, eternal youth, joy, and beauty.[11]

Failing to recognize such salutations for what they truly are—expressions that traditionalize gender ideology—many of the country's women are flattered by these public declarations of "esteem." They give no hint of understanding that in accepting this sort of patronizing "Hallmark" salutation as a tribute to them, they forego their own interests as women deserving of equality and respect. To look upon such a greeting as something more than a condescending "greeting card" message is to diminish all women.

Still, not every woman is of a like mind. Ethnologist, feminist scholar, and one of our contributors, Oksana Kis', was so incensed by the presidential message that she dispatched a scorching open letter to him, which several internet sites promptly posted.[12] Informed women from all parts of Ukraine joined her in a chorus of condemnation, confirming the fact that at least some women no longer welcome such debasing, saccharine expressions of affection; but the same gesture also had its dark side. Negative responses, perhaps stemming from a misunderstanding of the intent of this open letter, outnumbered the supporting comments, providing additional evidence of how much work still lies ahead.[13]

In Ukraine, the 1995 Beijing Conference had supplied the impetus for a coalescence of women's organizations. It also acted as an incentive for the passage of early legislation on equal rights and opportunities. Regrettably, although all such changes represent a hopeful beginning, these developments have yet to generate a widely accepted gender-neutral paradigm of a kind that discourages women from fantasizing about their alleged empowerment. The tendency on the part of many to believe in their own centrality is based upon a deeply rooted ancient matriarchal myth of women as guardians of the family hearth. In all likelihood, this position would have been the source of their empowerment in clan life, inasmuch as presiding over such a female domain also indicated the virtual inevitability of a women's presence at all deliberations. The matriarchal myth it engendered appears to have justified the titular esteem in which Ukraine's women have always been held.

Although this penchant for identifying with some legendary matriarchal ideal has begun to diminish somewhat, especially among younger women, significant numbers continue to embrace the symbol of some prehistoric female centrality to validate their sense of personal worth. For their part, sexist men persist in turning this cherished ideal to their own purposes by encouraging the atavistic belief.

Chapter Organization

Like their counterparts in many parts of the world, Ukrainian women have suffered from scholarly neglect throughout history. In an attempt to give them a richly-deserved voice, the present collection highlights the various strategies that women in Ukraine employ to claim subjectivity and exert agency, to carve out a measure of social, economic, and political space for themselves in an exceedingly difficult liminal space, constrained in large measure by their own essentialist prejudices.

The contributions to this volume are grouped into three parts—consisting of women's voices recovered from a variety of in-depth oral interviews, narrative accounts of various facets of women's choices and gender activity, as well as analytical interpretations from an array of disciplines devoting works to gender and feminism. The chapters were submitted in three languages—English, Ukrainian, and Russian; all appear here in English. Detailed case studies offer compelling evidence of the diversity of female responses to their altered circumstances in a transitional milieu, which resonate with those of women in other postcommunist countries. As such, they represent a noteworthy contribution to the overall body of women's transcultural narratives, as well as a long-overdue corrective to the history of Ukrainian women

Cinzia Solari draws us into a repartee of female migrant workers, mostly from western Ukraine, as they travel by bus from Italy for a brief visit to their homeland. Her chapter is based upon their experiences in the host country, which the women describe with genial wit and ready humor. Conversely, disparaging remarks about the homeland they are about to enter reveal the dark lens through which they view it. But one cannot escape the feeling that for all their jocular exchanges, these women harbor thoughts about their native land that are far more serious, more problematical, more nuanced than their public jibes suggest. The negative judgments of the present state of Ukrainian society betray a serious disenchantment with this beloved "imagined community," which has frustrated their idealized vision of it, yet the same individuals promptly come to its defense in response to outside criticism.

The transition from a totalitarian social order to an open democratic society brought in its wake economic turmoil, the rise of systemic privileges of men over women, and relegation of the latter to their "rightful" domestic space.[14] Such prejudicial attitudes have resulted in occupational segregation, and severely impede employment prospects for younger women, forcing many of them back into the narrow domestic space they had sought to escape. At the same time, economic hardship for families and a bleak outlook for their children's future have forced many of the older women into a labor force that, paradoxically, is closed to them. This hapless situation has generated an entire class of female migrant workers, and radically altered traditional family structures. Forced by a grim economic reality to seek their livelihood abroad, women migrants share a conflicted view of Ukraine. Their experiences in the Italian "home away from home" have brought into stark relief impressions of a homeland left behind in which nothing functions, dirt is everywhere, people are crude, and corruption endemic. For all of its perceived inadequacies, however, external criticism of that "dysfunctional" homeland still has the power to invoke rapturous expressions of pride in its beauty, its rich history, and its culture. There is a fine irony in the women's aching desire to return to such a "dirty, corrupt" homeland, which had relegated them to the realm of the unemployed, forced them to become migrant workers, and labeled them prostitutes for working in a foreign country.

Alexandra Hrycak draws on data accumulated during her ethnographic field research in Ukraine to expand the narrative on the female migration flow from east to west, and to reflect on the temporary migrant life of Ukraine's males as well. Gender-determined occupations, seasonality of employment opportunities, and different destination sites have resulted in dissimilar experiences for each sex. Men tend to gravitate to Russia (and occasionally to Poland), where they are employed in construction or agriculture—seasonal occupations that virtually preclude the possibility of forming a stable exilic community in a foreign country.

Subverting their former patriarchal reality, as Hrycak makes clear, the migrant women move from care giving at home to the status of primary breadwinners as caregivers abroad. Unlike their male counterparts, female migrant workers find access to employment in relatively stable occupations—mainly in the domestic sphere—occupations that do not depend upon any particular time of the year. The personal contacts that evolve from their close associations with employers, interaction with existing immigrant communities, and new friendships with local men for some, combine to help these women form deep personal connections in the host country. Freed from the patriarchal constraints that regulated their daily lives in Ukraine, the women become increasingly independent, with the result that many attach themselves to their new environment and its distinctive cultural experiences more or less permanently.

Complicating, and more often than not precluding, any potential return is the difficulty, even impossibility, of reintegration. Bad mothers, and failed performance as wives, are accusations that shadow female migrant workers, stigmatizing them as "loose women" in ways that men working abroad are never labeled. This often leaves those women who have already sacrificed so much for their families with little practical choice but to remain in the receiving country, where they can look forward to a life of low-status, menial work, as opposed to pursuing a career for which they had trained at home. In so doing, they form hybridized diasporas, consisting almost exclusively of women functioning in both binary roles: as primary breadwinner and as those who perform traditional women's work in order to earn this "bread." The transition from one culture to another, and associations with places of both departure and destination, creates a sense of belonging to two discrete worlds. The hybrid feminine space that they create institutionalizes their traditional feminine duties by transforming them into paid employment. From this perspective, the women can imagine new life possibilities. At the same time, emotionally and psychologically they are still tied to that homeland left behind, and many nourish a rosy dream of returning one day—when they finally hear those magical words: "Things are much better here, mom. Please come home."

A respondent named Faina had yet another story to tell. She related it to Sarah Phillips in the form of a biographical narrative. Contrary to the female migrants just discussed, this remarkable woman chose to live out her life in her native Ukraine without any expectation of improved circumstances. She made it her mission to help less-fortunate compatriots deal with the harshness of their post-Soviet reality.

The much-touted education, which had benefited millions of Soviet subjects, was the epicenter of discrimination in Faina's life as a Jew in Soviet-occupied Ukraine. She experienced anti-Semitism in school while growing up, and later in the workplace. Despite the detrimental setbacks, especially as a student, with low grades unfairly given for superior academic achievements and access barred to prestigious universities, Faina was determined to make the most of her severely restricted opportunities. With unswerving commitment to her native country, and the Soviet empire of which it became a part, she chose a life of active membership in the Communist Party, serving with dedication the system that diminished her in so many ways. After the fall of communism, however, she stepped back from this fidelity and declared: "Sometimes today I am embarrassed about my party activism—I read Soviet newspapers, and I carried the Soviet reality. It was a false reality, as I have learned." Faina refused to dwell on her misguided decision. A born activist with an unyielding determination to give her life meaning, she transferred her allegiance to the new Ukraine. When not at her regular employment, she threw herself into organizing and leading a self-help network for the indigent and the elderly, with the same dedication that she had brought to her work as a Communist Party activist in the previous life.

The next chapter, by Oksana Kis', takes us on a journey back to life under communism, as her respondents reflect on Soviet-era experiences accumulated during their long years under communist rule. Kis' has assembled a diverse set of oral testimonies on loyalty and belonging, from three regions of Ukraine—the east, west, and south. Three key factors left their imprints on the respondents' mental maps and accounted for their conflicting views of life in the Soviet system: geographical origins, social and ideological acculturation, and ages at the time of incorporation into the USSR. Not unexpectedly, they tell a more complex, more multifaceted, and more nuanced story than their words alone convey. Not infrequently, testimonies can be circumscribed by limits of language, trauma, and memory, by the suppression of cultural memory (Pratt 2009: 3–22), yet each offers a glimpse into the dynamics of loyalty creation, whether through acculturation, some inner sense of commitment, or a conversion.

Kis''s interviewees were all retired, and beneficiaries of the same Soviet social policies—free education, job security with generous paid vacation time, free housing, healthcare at no cost, and upward mobility, not to mention the sense of community and belonging that a collectivist life offers. The separate experiences of the women on opposite sides of the geographical and political divides created a bipolar world for them. Inasmuch as western Ukraine was not occupied by the Soviets until World War II, and women in the other regions under study here had been part of the USSR since they were children, their responses reflected the different ways in which the respective sides responded to the benefits and their cost in the Soviet system. Interviewees from the eastern and southern regions, living in Soviet-occupied Ukraine throughout their lives, never knew any other existence. They survived Stalin's reign of terror, witnessed the horrors of an artificially engineered famine that took the lives of millions, and scores of them saw loved ones either sent to prisons with little hope of survival or vanish into Stalin's infamous camps. Yet they manifested an astonishing capacity for suppressing the negative aspects of communist rule; some were even able to reminisce fondly about the entire Soviet system. We can only speculate on their unarticulated motives; what we do know is that somehow these women are able to subordinate the unspeakable suffering—their own and that of others—to the benefits of social policies that provided upward mobility through education and socially sanctioned opportunities for individual advancement. They could even justify the sacrifices of a few (including parents) as a fair price to pay for the blessings enjoyed by many. Moreover, there were those among them, particularly women from the southern region, who denied altogether the mass suffering imposed by the communist regime. Many of these women dismissed all criticism of Soviet rule, and explained away charges of mass persecutions with "not everyone who was punished was innocent" as a means of justifying their own fidelity to the system. In the opinion of the author, loyalty to one regime or another—"which helps to guide action and furnish identity"—was the single most important motivator of the women's responses, irrespective of their ideological convictions, the age at which they became part of the Soviet system, or even the geography that separated them, although such factors are not to be discounted.

For those individuals in the east and the south, the Soviet demise represented an overwhelming tragedy; it signaled the disintegration of the only culture, the only homeland, they had ever known. To repudiate that existence would have been tantamount to admitting that their lives had been a lie, as Faina eventually did in Sarah Phillips's chapter. Paradoxically, even as they mourned the loss of that overdetermined time and space, occasionally a note of condemnation slipped into the women's narratives. It conveyed subtle hints of perceived flaws in a treacherous system, lacking freedom of speech and religion, where regimented life suppressed all personal initiative, all creativity.

For their part, western Ukrainian women—whose pre-Soviet life experience differed so dramatically from that of women in the south and east—displayed an unqualified abhorrence of the communist system. Although they suffered persecution under Polish control, before being forcibly incorporated into the USSR in the 1940s, the use of their native language, freedom of worship, and free speech had not been proscribed—discouraged but not forbidden. And despite having escaped Stalin's Great Terror in the 1930s, which took countless millions of lives, they leveled much greater criticism at the Soviet regime than their compatriots to the east and south who had suffered under it. Even with their detestation of the communist system, however, their responses betrayed hints of a grudging acknowledgment that at least a small measure of good had come out of that regime. Yet, generally speaking, when they reflected upon their Soviet past, western Ukrainian respondents did not neglect to emphasize the intolerable burden of human suffering that had made the Soviet entitlements possible. In their eyes the loss of personal freedoms and coerced lifestyle that accompanied incorporation into the Soviet system represented an unsupportable price to pay for the benefits it offered. For them, independence signaled the end of a detested tyrannical system, a welcome relief from a half century of oppression, the absence of basic human rights, and imposition of a foreign (Russian) tongue. Above all, it meant the restoration of a cherished homeland, accompanied by a renewed affirmation of their Ukrainian national identity; no entitlements could compensate for the loss of such precious freedoms.

Multiplicities of Gender

Victoria Haydenko opens the second section in this volume by reminding us that gender typing begins at an early age in a child's life—formally at the preschool and primary school levels. She analyzes stereotyping patterns in primers and observances of children's holidays, and brings into relief some of the same obstacles that Oksamytna identifies in her responses to Taran's questions in the third section. Haydenko, especially, underscores the dearth of suitable teaching materials. Most of those authorized for use in preschool and primary school education reinforce the very gender stereotyping that they purportedly seek to refute. She offers a convincing illustration of the difficulties in circumventing such stereotypes, with her description of a New Year's Day fairy tale about an idealized fictional country called *Divmalia*. In it girls and boys study and play on so-called equal terms. This allegedly gender-neutral space is illustrated by "unisex" activities for children, even as their attire sends a conflicting message. Boys are pictured wearing shorts whereas girls appear in dainty dresses with bows in their hair. Contrary to the stated purpose of producing gender-neutral examples, this picture projects a gender-specific message. Haydenko presents an array of examples analogous to those mentioned elsewhere in this collection as evidence of traditional stereotyping: outdated teaching methods; inadequate resources; poorly trained, ill-compensated, and indifferent teachers; as well as the ideology-bound (male) administrators who remained in power after the demise of the Soviet system, refusing to make concessions to the changes that an ever-evolving educational system requires.

There is a strong link between language and one's access to social power and status, Laada Bilaniuk concludes in her study of genderlect and variations in its use. Its successful application entails more than just acquiring facts and proper speech patterns. The context in which words are used matters, as does the specific choice of words attached to that context. Language conveys encoded messages that resonate in their own special way with the particular environment in which they are found. This can be demonstrated by referring to an article apart from this collection titled "The Feminization of Culture," by Oksana Prykhod'ko, in which the author discusses the respective educational qualifications of women and men.[15] She refers us to a sample survey of 1,500 individuals. It demonstrates that 63 percent of the respondents with a higher education are women, a fact that should invest them with superior social status, although clearly it does not. Sadly, Prykhod'ko compromises her own gender-coded message somewhat by referring to all 1,500 individuals as "man" (*cholovik*)—a Russian calque. Such an application of the unmarked masculine paradigm to signify both sexes requires no imagination to apprehend in it a subliminal message that diminishes women.[16] Surprisingly, most Ukrainian women with whom I discussed this inclusive term had no idea what I was talking about. They seemed oblivious to its sexist nature, as was evidenced by their patient explanations, provided many times over, that the term is generic, that it is used for both sexes without any negative overtones. Try as I might, I was unable to persuade them that this is precisely what is wrong with it—using an inclusive masculine term that so diminishes women routinely, unthinkingly, to designate both sexes. Gendered language translates into gendered behavior, as Laada Bilaniuk herself emphasizes.

Choice of language is an important consideration in other respects as well. For instance, in a bilingual society such as Ukraine it can become a commanding site for negotiating an ethnic identity or enhancing one's own image. Insofar as power is less accessible to females than it is to males, the Ukrainian women's strategic (and seemingly natural) choice is to substitute the use of a "high-status" language, such as Russian, or more recently English, for Ukrainian as their medium of communication. Laada Bilaniuk's survey indicates that an overwhelming number of Ukrainian women do indeed prefer Russian, presumably to elevate their own standing (even if the choice is unconscious), although she also emphasizes that this does not suggest assimilation to Russian culture. An occasional reversal of this trend of resorting to a world-class language can be found as well. Yulia Tymoshenko is a case in point. Having grown up speaking Russian, in her adult years she made a conscious decision to switch to Ukrainian—a language with limitations as an avenue to social advancement. Admittedly, unlike women aspiring to upward mobility, she made this choice from a position of strength by embracing the liminal and moving it to the center of an already highly successful life. Paradoxically in her case, however, in this instance the less prestigious Ukrainian language was elevated to a higher status insofar as it helped to advance her political career.

Mariia Tytarenko presents us with evidence of other possibilities for raising the women's status. To illustrate, she takes us inside the media—to print journalism. In the west, this medium went through some powerful transformations during the 1960s and 1970s. Two disciplines—literary writing and journalism—were merged and morphed into what was called "new journalism." Tytarenko probes the implications of such a union when it reached Ukraine and concludes that it represented a sea change for its women. Not only did it offer unprecedented opportunities for female writers, whose numbers in journalism are increasing conspicuously, it also provided a relatively lucrative new income stream for them. In a rapidly changing society such as transitional Ukraine, which severely impedes female earning potential, journalism has become a rare exception to the women's lack of earning power in virtually every other area. Moreover, rising numbers of women are distinguishing themselves not only as journalists, but as media administrators as well.

Tytarenko's contribution to this volume also addresses another of the recent forms of media communication—the outgrowth of new journalism known as blogging, and its offspring, twittering. These latest genres are described on the web as "a free social messaging utility for staying connected in real-time." Both function as interactive web sites for ongoing chronicles of information posted by journal bloggers. In Ukraine where blogging still consists largely of paid contributors, males dominate the space. For the present, then, this facet of journalism does not offer the same lucrative income potential for women that they enjoy in other areas of this profession, but as the trend toward journalism with a women's face continues to mount, it is likely to be only a matter of time before women begin to dominate the blogosphere as well.

Premise and Practice

Invoking Johnson and Robinson once again, the "intersection between nationality and gender ... unveils the ways in which gender instability ... is shared by identity and ideology." They characterize this intersection as "a site of contestation which ... allows women to choose from among different gender constructions" (2007: 9).

The opening chapter of the third section introduces a dialogue on the interconnectedness between nationalism and gender. Maria Rewakowicz conducts her discussion around women's literary discourse, with an emphasis on female literary output as it is interpreted in two centers of gender studies—Kyiv and Kharkiv. An examination of writings by women connected to the Kyiv center leads Rewakowicz to conclude that nationalist concerns figure only rarely in its works. Feminist perspectives and excellent scholarship, marked by experimentation in methodology and theory, characterize its output.

Contrary to this assertion, adherents of the Kharkiv Center charge Kyiv's gender scholars with a national bias, and present their own orientation as "neutral and unmarked." Rewakowicz calls attention to the fact that in light of its pro-Russian course, it is the Kharkiv center that manifests a national bias. For her part, Tatiana Zhurzhenko, who expands the discourse to include gender centers other than Kyiv and Kharkiv, theorizes that the Kharkiv school conforms to an international profile of gender studies, which renders it an unmarked paradigm. Rewakowicz counters with her thought-provoking observation that in reality it is the Kyiv school, with its Ukrainian orientation, which is unmarked, that it "appears to have a national Ukrainian bias only because the Kharkiv center so completely lacks it." In the end, however, these reciprocal charges simply reinforce the binary opposition implicit in the respective viewpoints, irrespective of national orientation.

All such disputes serve to underscore a key question posed by Zhurzhenko in her contribution to this collection: is it possible to refer to every variety of feminism in Ukraine as Ukrainian? When one takes into account Kharkiv's allegedly international orientation, her answer can only be a resounding "no." Zhurzhenko scrutinizes the role that nationalism plays in constructing gender identities, and reaches the conclusion that a two-way process is at work in Ukraine, because in that country national boundaries are not congruent with national feminist discourse. Viewed in this light, as much as nationalism might manipulate feminist/gender interests, in its turn feminist theory can be said to contribute to the construction of the concept of Ukrainian nationhood and negotiation of its borders. What is more, because gender and nationalism were both victims of communist ideology and its totalitarian implementation, Zhurzhenko considers them natural allies. This contravenes the position adopted in Kharkiv; its gender studies exponents "portray nationalist and feminist discourses as inevitably conflicting and hostile," Zhurzhenko explains. The entire polemic leads the author to conclude that inasmuch as adherents of the Kharkiv center have positioned themselves outside the discourse of national feminism in Ukraine, they have simply set themselves apart from the national orientations of all gender centers elsewhere in the country. These differing viewpoints supply yet another framework for examining feminism and developing an understanding of the prospects for multiple gender constructions which Ukraine's independence has made possible.

In the final chapter of this collection, Liudmyla Taran ushers us into the world of prominent Ukrainian women who have forged successful careers for themselves in the face of seemingly overwhelming odds. She conducts conversations with three participants: Larysa Kobel'ian'ska and Svitlana Oksamytna—unambiguous, self-declared feminists—and Yulia Tymoshenko, who categorically rejects feminism as a self-descriptor. Taran begins the first of her exchanges with Larysa Kobel'ians'ka, coordinator of the UN-sponsored program "Gender Education in Ukraine," and indefatigable advocate of equal rights and opportunities for women. She and her like-minded female colleagues routinely lobby the Ukrainian government to adhere to the rules on equal rights established by the European Community, and to introduce amendments to Ukraine's constitution that reflect these values. At the same time, not happy with the protracted pace of legislation, Kobel'ians'ka has worked tirelessly for the speedy passage of two important gender-friendly laws enacted in 2001 and 2005 respectively.

She places a high premium on education, but goes beyond many of her peers, who value it principally as a path to professional success and monetary rewards. Kobel'ians'ka regards education an indispensable agent of acculturation to the values of gender parity, and a powerful tool to be used for grooming women for political office. She too is an intractable critic of the current educational system in Ukraine, for its outdated methods, official inertia, and perpetuation of gender stereotyping. Convinced that pedagogical reform and elimination of a gender bias can be achieved only through effective legislation, Kobel'ians'ka has arranged numerous consciousness-raising events—seminars, workshops, and retreats—for prominent officeholders and other members of the country's governing elite. These meetings are designed to stimulate transformative dialogues on feminist and gender issues, and to mobilize support for gender-friendly laws and practices.

The second of Taran's three respondents, Svitlana Oksamytna, is also a self-described feminist. She is a gender-studies scholar who uses her position as a professor of sociology to guide students in new approaches to thinking about the sexes.[17] Oksamytna assigns research topics calculated to raise student awareness of the diverse circumstances under which gender roles are created and diffused. Carefully channeled research on a host of gender issues has not been a standard practice among Ukrainian educators. Although it has become an effective socializing tool in Oksamytna's classroom, what the students learn through this technique has yet to seep into the consciousness of the general populace, or even move into the educational conduits. Most people, especially those who reside outside the major cities, remain largely ignorant of the true meaning of such terms as *gender*, let alone *feminism*.[18]

Taran's third respondent is the former Prime Minister of Ukraine Yulia Tymoshenko, heroine of Ukraine's Orange Revolution, in 2004, a politician with a spine of steel, and recipient of numerous prestigious awards for leadership. She exerts an unparalleled influence in the patriarchal world of Ukrainian politics. With her keen appreciation for the force of words, Tymoshenko attributes much of her success, both in business and in politics, to a good education, but does not join in the litany of praise of the Soviet educational system as its facilitator. Instead, Tymoshenko credits a woman, her single mother, with offering encouragement and making the indispensable sacrifices to advance her daughter's studies. As Tymoshenko has observed, "[my mother] did everything to ensure my education." Although the former prime minister eschews the label "feminist," she urges women to expand their political agency. She calls upon them to support all female candidates for political office, while avoiding exclusively women's political factions, which, she insists, invariably end up as adjuncts to male politics.

All three "conversations" were conducted in 2002, at a time when Kobel'ians'ka and Oksamytna were actively promoting gender education in Ukraine, and Herculean efforts were required to achieve even modest gains. The glacial pace of progress can be illustrated by an article, dated five years later (2007), in which Tatiana Tal'ko advances arguments against Ukraine's backward educational system, and bemoans the absence of viable gender studies programs. Her position is virtually identical to that of Kobel'ians'ka and Oksamytna (among others) more than half a decade earlier. Tal'ko reinforces their earlier assessments of a lack of progress by noting that one of the chief causes is entrenched Soviet-era inertia in the patriarchal structures governing higher education. Even though so-called gender-neutral programs have earned a place in Ukraine's institutions of higher education, a single unmarked male paradigm continues to dictate their norms. Generally speaking, men are portrayed as the quintessential educators—eternally objective and rational—whereas ambitious women aspiring to academic careers often are openly condemned as irrational and subjective female "deviants" (2007: 139–47).

Conclusion

To sum up, some of the most recent events, especially those highlighting a feminist consciousness, organized in 2008 and 2009, have indicated that a fresh wind is blowing in the direction of Ukraine, that some unaccustomed paradigms of public expression are beginning to replace the old models. The neoconservative, matriarchal culture, and its "poster child" Berehynia, are gradually giving way to postmodern expressions of identity among some of the younger citizens. No longer encumbered by the deeply rooted matriarchal legacy, the new generation of women has appropriated the post-Soviet space for its own site of negotiation, thus opening up a host of possibilities for additional gender renegotiation. Young women are beginning to respond to the new challenges by recoding older images of quintessential womanhood, and mounting increasingly serious protests against abuses of women.

A comparative study of two journals—*Piata Pora* (Kyiv, 1993), and *Ia* (Kharkiv, inaugurated in 2003)—portals to a recoding of conventional female stereotypes—sheds light on the difficult terrain traversed by gender-justice enthusiasts over the past two decades. As suggested earlier, the first publication was ahead of its time in Ukraine. Although constricted by much conventional thinking, causing it to mix feminist writings and essentialist pieces about women, it did provide an important key to rethinking gender relations in Ukraine. For its part, *Ia* devotes itself exclusively to articles on gender and feminism. Unlike *Piata Pora,* it makes no concession to conventional pieces about women, but the ten year spread required to reach this level of revisionist publication reveals the difficulties inherent in reforming a traditional culture. The aftermath of the Soviet demise produced an environment that enabled Ukraine to pursue a liberalizing market economy and witness a sexual revolution of a kind never before seen in Ukraine. Each offers a host of possibilities for gender (re)definition. In the present collection, a dialogue with women from various walks of life on the impact of the postcommunist system in their lives has engaged scholars from both sides of the world—Ukraine and the west. This initial impulse has been expanded to embrace a wide ranging set of gender definitions; their diverse applications to real-life situations in today's Ukraine; the variability within women's circumstances; and the disparate stratagems employed for coping with the asymmetrical status of women.

The most recent visible opponents of this present state of affairs is a radical group of young people—mostly female university students--intensely committed to the concept of gender parity, seeking an end to the stereotyping and prejudice that so frequently lead to violent abuses of women. Although passionately dedicated to the cause of eradicating social ills, their immediate target is the rapidly escalating sex industry and trafficking of women. New and startling forms of demonstrations and bizarre street theater, featuring female protesters in trashy outfits that exaggerate the typical attire of a street prostitute, are calculated to make the sex trade an object of ridicule and disgust (see Figure 1.1). Long-term objectives of the organizers, who call their organization FEMEN, include helping to inculcate a strong social consciousness among its members, and building leadership skills of a kind that can successfully combat the current appalling abuses against women in Ukraine. FEMEN uses scandalous street theater to highlight the evils and ugliness of these abuses, especially prostitution, and their deleterious effect on the process of stereotyping Ukrainian women.[19] Shocking onlookers into thinking about the problem is the most effective way to mobilize support for change, according to its leader Anna Hutsol (see Figure 1.2). Today, as they reinvent themselves, these young women in their late teens and early twenties (many of them students and young professionals) are finally making that transition as they embark on radical, often outrageous, demonstrations of opposition.

Figure 1.1 Demonstration: 22 May 2008, on main thoroughfare Khreshchatyk, in Kyiv, launching FEMEN's "Ukraine is Not a Brothel" crusade. Image courtesy of FEMEN.

Figure 1.2 Street Theater on Freedom Square (Maidan). Portrays Ukraine's women conveying FEMEN's opposition to pimps and traffickers who contribute to the country's reputation as an affordable sex playground. Image courtesy of FEMEN.

Becoming an influential women's political party is also on their agenda—its founders have an eye toward making it the strongest women's political force in Europe. Compare this to the position adopted (not altogether unjustifiably) by Yulia Tymoshenko, who cautioned against female exclusivity, lest the women's organization be reduced to an auxiliary of some male-dominated party and its program. The founder of this organization is a remarkable woman with well established leadership skills, named Anna Hutsol—a rare individual of a kind that seldom comes along.

Although literature on women in Ukraine is on the rise, this, to my knowledge, is the first English-language collection of articles on women in Ukraine to combine such a compilation of in-depth interviews with accounts of the various spheres of communication in which women play key roles, reports on female activity in diverse sectors of Ukrainian life, and theoretical analyses of gender and feminist issues by scholars from various disciplines. It is hoped that our readers will be motivated to pursue further discrete studies, not only of Ukrainian women, but of those in other postcommunist spaces as well, thereby contributing fresh insights into the existing narratives on cross-cultural female experiences in transitional societies. The images here illustrate how far women have come since freedom of expression was banned in the former Soviet Union, and the pioneering post-Soviet generation of women began raising their first cautious voices in the female cause. Like today's women themselves, both gender and feminism in Ukraine have revealed many of their faces.

Notes

The title of this chapter, and its accompanying proverb, were inspired by Pulitzer Prize winners: Nicholas D. Khristof and Sheryl WuDunn, who wrote *Half the Sky: Turning Oppression into Opportunity for Women Worldwide*. New York: Alfred A. Knopf, 2009.

1. The book is on Russia, but much of its content applies with equal validity to the post-Soviet Ukrainian space.

2. Her origins remain shrouded in mystery, but—somewhat akin to the classical Greek "triple goddess"—in her role as the presiding "hearth mother," the preliterate Ukrainian matriarch is said to embody the mystery of life as guardian of the past (women and children frequently were interred beneath the hearth over which the senior female member of the clan presided), custodian of the present (by virtue of her central role in clan proceedings, all of which transpired around the hearth), and symbol of eternal rebirth, its life source. At some point in the nineteenth century, this matriarchal topos began to manifest signs of waning. The symbol was reanimated and ultimately morphed in the twentieth century into the now widely recognized sign of Berehynia.

3. The article first appeared in *Slovo i Chas* (Word and Time) no. 6, in 1991. It was reprinted in *Pavlychko* (2002): 19–28.

4. The work was published by Osnova Publishing, founded by one of Ukraine's early and most dedicated feminists, Solomea Pavlychko, who also translated it.

5. http://www.ukraineobserver.com/articles/217/816.

6. In a separate reference during her presentation, she concluded that women's essential-ist attributes destined them for second-rate status.

7. We must, of course, not discount the possibility that increased reporting of the crime accounts for some the dramatic increase.

8. It came into effect in January of 2006.

9. Telephone interview with Tamara Melnyk (former adviser to the Ministry of Justice in Ukraine) on 14 April 2008.

10. The president's Press Service, accessed 7 March 2008: http://www.president.gov.ua/news/9119.html

11. Quoted in Tamara Zlobina 2009.

12. http://zgroup.com.ua/article.php?articleid=260. Also http://politikan.com.ua/1.php?rej=1&idm=60201&idr1-1&idr2=0&idr3=0&kv_m2=0&kreg=&aleng=1. See also: http://community.livejournal.com/feminism_ua/345930.html#cutid1. This last site also featured a spirited discussion. The author e-mailed me news of the responses to her letter on 19 March 2008.

13. For a discussion of this affair see Kis's interview in Hrabovs'ka 2009: 32–35.

14. On a more hopeful note, a recent article (9 July 2009), by *Kyiv Post* editor Tetiana Stad-nyk, on women in business, indicates rising evidence of Ukrainian women benefiting from a growing market for female employment as more international companies come on line and hire local professional women.

15. It appeared in *Dzerkalo Tyzhnia* 8 (587), 10 March 2006.

16. Whenever I raised the issue, Ukrainian women were quick to remind me, not without justification, that we in the west also use an inclusive term routinely—"mankind." This too should be changed, I agreed, but my response was that its application is much less pervasive, much less frequent, much more abstract than the daily references to women as "*cholovik,*" which is not only offensive but confusing.

17. Professor Oksamytna was recently appointed Dean of Arts and Sciences, and chair of the Sociology Department at Kyiv Mohyla University. This is still a rare privilege for a woman.

18. In a campaign to promote an understanding of feminism, on the eve of International Women's Day in 2008, a book-signing event took place in the Smoloskyp Publishing House and book store, launching a forty-four-page book titled *Feminizm I* ... (Femi-nism and ...). Illustrations of comic-book-like caricatures of feminists on popular bubble gum wrappers were accompanied by brief comments designed to raise the con-sciousness of rank-and-file women. Its target audience is fifteen- to forty-year-olds. This is the first such effort in Ukraine. Its creator was Tamara Zlobina, a Kharkiv-based feminist.

19. The dissonance between text and image is portrayed against the background of Ukraine's idealized symbol of womanhood "Berehynia"—protectress of tradition, cul-ture, nation, and motherhood—atop her pillar on Maidan. The undifferentiated pro-files of Ukrainian women behind their Kabuki masks signify their dehumanization in a culture that sees women as instruments of male gratification. FEMEN uses this con-cept in street theater to illustrate the country's reputation as a "cheap" sex playground for foreign visitors ($99.00 signs).

Bibliography

Bohachevsky-Chomiak, Martha. 1988. *Feminists despite Themselves: Women in Ukrainian Community Life. 1884–1939*. Edmonton: Canadian Institute of Ukrainian Studies, University of Alberta.

Hrabovs'ka, Iryna. 2009. "Genderne parytetne suspil'stvo v Ukraini. Sotsial'na utopia chy real'na perspektyva"? *Ia* 2 (22): 36.

Johnson, Janet Elise, and Jean C. R. Robinson, eds. 2007. "Living Gender." In *Living Gender after Communism*. Bloomington: Indiana University Press.

Pavlychko, Solomea. 2002. *Feminizm*. Kyiv: Osnova, 19–28.

Pratt, Geraldine. 2009. "Gender, Place and Culture." *A Journal of Feminist Geography* 16, no. 1 (February): 3–22.

Tal'ko, Tatiana. 2009. "Genderne partnerstvo iak vykhovnyi ideal Ukrain's'koi vyshchoi shkoly siohodni." *Ia* 2 (22): 139–47.

Vydrin, Dmytro. 2007. "Zhinka, Glamur I Polityka." *Dzerkalo Tyzhnia*, 8–16.

Zhurzhenko, Tatiana. 2004. "Strong Women, Weak State: Family Politics and Nation Building in Post-Soviet Ukraine." In *Post-Soviet Women Encountering Transition: Nation Building, Economic Survival, and Civic Activism,* edited by Kathleen Kuenast and Carol Nechemias, 23–43. Baltimore: Johns Hopkins University Press.

Zlobina, Tamara. 2009. "Buty feministkoiu/buty zhinkoiu." *Ia* 2 (22).

CHAPTER 2

Between "Europe" and "Africa"

Building the New Ukraine on the Shoulders of Migrant Women

Cinzia Solari

No one knows how many Ukrainians are working in Italy.[1] *Forum,* a Rome-based newspaper published in Ukrainian and Russian argues for two million. The bishop of the Ukrainian Greek Catholic church in Rome proposes that 500,000 is a more realistic number based on attendance at church events. The head of the Italo-Ukrainian Christian Association suggests over one million. What is certain is that every Sunday between 8 AM and noon, five thousand Ukrainians pass through a large parking lot behind Rome's Garbatella metro station. The metro's main exit brings you out to a neighborhood with small shops and apartment buildings.

In observing this regular movement through the subway station, I notice that the few Italians on board exit through the main doors. One weekend, I follow a group of women out the back exit chatting in Ukrainian rather energetically for 8:30 on a Sunday morning. Here, the subway station narrows into a hallway that leads us outside onto a square cement platform. It overlooks a large parking lot known as "the Garbatella," packed with mostly middle-aged women whose winter coats cover straight, solid-colored skirts and button-down blouses with busy prints. Despite the cement staircase descending into the throng of people, the platform gives the impression of being suspended in midair. I lean up against the retaining wall to take in the scene.

Fifty white courier vans, most at least a decade old, line the perimeter of the rectangular lot. Some vans carry workers with valid documents between Rome and what seems like most cities and even villages in Ukraine, but drivers make the bulk of their money carrying goods back and forth.[2] Many of the people below come every Sunday to send packages and money back to their families in Ukraine, building relationships of trust with specific drivers who they know will personally hand the money or package to their loved ones. Loved ones in Ukraine may then send with this same driver letters, photos, mayonnaise, or *kovbasa* (sausage) to their family member working in Rome, nostalgic for anything from home. All the vans have their double back doors thrown wide open in front of mountains of plastic bags stuffed to capacity. Women stand in small groups fussing over whether the breakables are well packed, sharing the latest pictures of their grandchildren, and comparing notes on their jobs as domestic workers, mostly live-in caregivers to the elderly. In the center of the rectangular space, lined with courier vans on all sides, is a row of tented booths selling newspapers, magazines, and books in Ukrainian and Russian. Thousands of people are browsing the books, chatting with long-lost friends, or hurrying to find their courier van, arms weighted down with bulky plastic bags.

Surveying Rome's Ukrainian community from above, I am struck by the fact that the crowd of thousands below is almost all women. Even more striking is the age of these women. Unlike most migrant communities that are made up of young people in their twenties and thirties, the women bustling below are in their forties, fifties, and sixties. Teresa, a Filipina woman in her midthirties and my contact in one of the domestic worker unions with a mostly Filipina and South American clientele, commented last week, "I just don't understand. Lots of the Ukrainian women who come here to care for the elderly look like *they* could use a caregiver! What is wrong with their daughters that they send their elderly mothers abroad to work instead of going themselves?"

Why Babushka Works in Rome

Nearly all of the Ukrainian workers I speak with in Rome are university educated with professional work histories and most assert that they never imagined they would go abroad to work. Rather, they expected to finish careers, retire, and raise their grandchildren—so the decision to leave home was a profoundly painful one. In Soviet Ukraine, women with young children were expected to work while their mothers as grandmothers or *babushky* cared for the children, did the housework, and stood in bread lines, freeing their daughters and daughters-in-law for the labor market (Verdery 1994). Roxalana expected to do for her daughter what her mother had done for her.[3] She says: "I am a *babushka* and I thought I would be with my grandson during the day and take care of the house while my daughter worked." Yet the coming of market capitalism to postsocialist Ukraine has meant the expulsion of women from the workforce and Roxalana's daughter, like many others, is now a career housewife by default (Bonnell 1996; Zdravomyslova 1996; Zhurzhenko 2000).

Roxalana explains, "I felt useless at home. All I was doing was fighting with my daughter over, you know, what to feed my grandson, how to dress him, and how to discipline him. And with just my son-in-law working and my small pension, there was not enough money. So I came here [Rome]."

It is precisely older women who have been doubly displaced from their jobs and their expected roles within extended families. Marginalized in Ukraine, many have left to work in Italy. It is no surprise then that looking out over the Garbatella I should see a sea of middle-aged women rather than young women or men of any age. I remembered the last time I stood on that cement platform. I was with Tania, a vibrant woman in her fifties who taught Ukrainian history to high school students in L'viv before leaving for Rome to, as she put it, "clean toilets." She said bitterly, "Do you see all those women down there? They carry Ukraine on their shoulders and don't think they don't know it … and don't think they are happy about it either."

Not only is the Garbatella a site where goods and people are shuttled between Italy and Ukraine, but it is also where many come in the hope of finding work. Or, in Tania's words, this is where "*babushka,* who has worked all her life and should be retired, comes to ask for more work." I descend from the cement platform into the crowd. At the bottom of the staircase women are lined up on both sides making a human corridor through which we are all forced to walk in order to enter the Garbatella. Some women hold signs that say: "Looking for work" while other women murmur discreetly to those entering the Garbatella that they are "selling work." Selling work is considered morally reprehensible. It means that a woman has been working for an Italian family for several years but now, having learned the ropes, has found a higher-paying job in some other family. She tells her first family she is leaving but not to worry, she will recommend a competent replacement. She goes to the Garbatella where the newly arrived and the most desperate go to find work and offers, sometimes for several hundred Euros, to sell the telephone number and address of her former employer with the promise that she will *most likely* hire her.

Women who have a friend or a relative in Rome have someone to help them find a place to sleep and hopefully a job. The friend or relative will ask her employer, always referred to as "my *Signora,*" if she knows of anyone who is looking for a woman to care for her mother or children. Sometimes women are lucky. One informant, Oksana, tells me that she met a Ukrainian woman, Olga, on the bus. Chatting she told Olga that she was looking for work. Olga quickly took her number saying that her *Signora*'s sister was looking for a woman and all her friends had work right now. Oksana explains, "Olga told her *Signora* that we went to university together and that I was a very reliable worker. I got the job! I never saw Olga before that ride on the bus! We're not even from the same city!" The women holding the "Looking for work" signs have not been so lucky. I used to look at their faces as I entered the Garbatella, but today I stare at my feet to protect myself from the pain I know I will see there and push through the corridor to the other side.

Looking over my shoulder back at the platform at the top of the stairs, my eye catches lettering on the side of the retaining wall on which I had just been leaning. Someone has spray-painted in large, orange, stenciled block letters: "*YUSHCHENKO NASH PRESIDENT*" (Yushchenko our President). However, it is October 2004 and Leonid Kuchma is Ukraine's president. It would not be until a month later that I would come to recognize the full significance of that sign, when people would fill the streets of Ukraine in protest, in defense of fair elections, and in support of the pro-western presidential candidate Viktor Yushchenko; and when I would see the mass demonstrations in solidarity with the Ukrainian protesters in Rome and witness the long lines of people waiting to vote at the Ukrainian embassy, many of them holding "*Tak Yushchenko!*" (Yes Yushchenko!) banners. They were dressed in the same bold orange color as the spray-painted letters above us.

There are many competing visions of the Ukrainian nation struggling for ascendancy (Wilson 2002). The majority of Ukrainians working in Rome come from western Ukraine (Shehda and Horodetskyy 2004). L'viv, western Ukraine's cultural center, is home to a particular vision of Ukrainian nationhood sometimes referred to as *Galician nationalism*. While eastern and southern Ukraine were absorbed by Russia in the seventeenth century, resulting in a weak sense of Ukrainian national identity in those regions, western Ukraine's contentious relationship with Poland has led the former Habsburg territory of Galicia to see itself as "the potential agent of national unity and the keeper of the true faith on behalf of the rest of Ukraine" (Wilson 2002: 43). In this nationalist vision, the Ukrainian ethnic nation has been around since the dawn of time, but its linear progression was interrupted by Russian imperialism that severed Ukraine from its European roots (Wilson 2000; Wolczuk 2000). The nation-building project associated with this variant of nationalism, a minority view but one with disproportionate influence, is to follow a European model of nation building where the Ukrainian nation is based on Ukrainian (not Russian) ethnicity, Ukrainian (not Russian) language, the Ukrainian Greek Catholic church or Ukrainian (not Russian) variants of Orthodoxy, and a reconstructed historical memory of an authentic, pre-Soviet Ukrainian culture (Wilson 2000; Wolczuk 2000). This is expressed by many of my informants: as Ukraine should be unified like Italy—a nation made up of Italians, who speak Italian, share a Catholic religion, and have an Italian culture. Migrants in Rome are well versed in this nation-building project (Solari 2006b). While I do encounter dissenting opinions, the majority of migrants I speak with equate the election of Yushchenko with joining "Europe" and a resulting economic prosperity that will enable them and all those working abroad to finally go home. "Europe" is a state both of being (abundant consumer goods, unfettered economic opportunities, political freedom), and a destination, the goal toward which they are all working.

Is Ukraine "Europe" or "Africa"?

I make my way to the #8 courier van to meet Valia. When I find her, the driver, a young man, is weighing her many plastic bags on a bathroom scale and charging her €1,80 (US$2.35) per kilo. Valia hugs me and introduces me to the driver, saying that his sister is a wonderful pianist, one of Valia's former students. She then eagerly shows me what is in the bags. Her *Signora* gave her some used clothes in good condition and Valia pulls on the tags reading, "Prada, Prada, Valentino, Promodo." Valia's eyes beam. They are her daughter-in-law's size. "She is young," Valia says, "and she should dress nicely." Another bag has foodstuffs in it—Baci chocolates, Parmigiano-Reggiano cheese, Lavazza espresso coffee, and Mulino Bianco cookies. She would never buy these name brands for herself, she says with a wink; they are gifts. She has also found a good deal on a set of pots and pans and is sending the whole set over. I see that there are two other women in line who have found the same deal and are also sending the pots and pans back to Ukraine. Valia takes an envelope from the driver containing photos her son sent her from L'viv. There is no place to sit at the Garbatella, so we find a spot on the periphery of the lot out of the flow of foot traffic and Valia tears open the envelope. She scans all the photos quickly, smiles to herself, and then goes through the pictures again slowly. They are all of what to my eyes is a beat-up car with various people standing in front of it. Valia explains that her son bought the car with the money she has been sending home. "It is a nice car! And see how pretty my daughter-in-law is?" I look down at a petite blond woman draped over the hood of the car laughing for the camera. "No, no, Ukraine is not Africa!" Valia exclaims as if in response to an unarticulated question we all knew was hanging in the air.

The question "Is Ukraine 'Europe' or 'Africa'" does seem to be always hanging in the air at the Garbatella. Italians, whose limited understanding of Ukraine is simply that it is "in the East" or "part of Russia," often presume that Ukraine is a Third World country in the same category as African countries. Until recently, Africans made up the largest percentage of migrants in Italy. In the last decade, Africans have been surpassed by migrants from eastern Europe. Many Italians assume that Ukrainians and all migrants *del'Est* (from the east) come from a place that is undeveloped, lacking running water, electricity, proper housing, and an education system—a place that in their popular imagination is like "Africa." Why else would all these women come to Italy for work? My informants bristle at the comparison.[4] Valia is not alone in saying indignantly, "Italians think we live in mud huts like in Africa!" Just as "Europe" refers to an ideal of plentiful consumer goods and democratic freedom, for Italians and Ukrainians alike, "Africa" symbolizes a condition of abject poverty, starving children, and stunted human potential.

In Italian spaces, I often hear migrants from Ukraine tell a consistent and coherent narrative of Ukrainian nationhood in which not only is Europe the inspiration or the destination for a particular kind of nation-building project, but Ukraine *is* Europe. Yet the Garbatella—one of the few meeting places for a population that is otherwise atomized, each worker isolated in the private home of an Italian family—is a space of collective imaginings and possibilities. Here Ukraine has a much more precarious status. At the Garbatella, "Europe" and Ukraine's impending glorious entrance into the global middle class exist simultaneously with the fear that Ukraine could go the way of "Africa" and descend into the abyss of poor countries, the forgotten underbelly of globalization.

The Garbatella is made up of something more than the people, the buses, and the plastic bags. Hope and desperation, difficult pasts and possible futures wax and wane with the crowd. Roxalana peers over Valia's shoulder as she shows me another photograph, this time of her cousin smiling and standing by the driver's door of her son's new used car. "Next week, my daughter is sending me new pictures of my grandson," Roxalana announces. Looking at the courier vans, Roxalana asks, "Will you go home this summer, Valia?" Valia nods yes without taking her eyes off the pictures. Roxalana does not have documents and has not been home in five years because of the difficulty of reentering Italy.[5] "It is nice to think that if I really had to, I *could* go home. Maybe my daughter's letter will say: 'Things are much better here mom. Please come home.'" Valia casts a doubtful look in my direction but says nothing. In this Ukrainian space on the outskirts of Rome, the possibility of the journey home and the possibility of Ukraine's bright future are tangible and ephemeral, certain and precarious, clear and contradictory.

The Contradictions of Living Between

The position these women inhabit is one of contradictions that often bubble to the surface. But at the Garbatella, the women have room to navigate these tensions and smooth over the rough spots. Here one can hold contradictory tastes and beliefs. Speaking with your *Signora*, for example, requires a consistent narrative about what Ukraine is and why you are in Rome. But at the Garbatella, you can run into an old friend and ask: "Olia, after all these years we meet in Rome?! Why are you here"? "Same reason you are here: Bread! Money!" At the same time she asserts that Ukraine is not poor, is not Africa. You pay to send Baci chocolates back home while maintaining Ukrainian chocolate is far superior. You send Prada clothing to your daughter-in-law, while your own clothing marks you as "eastern," *una donna del'est.* You meet university friends who graduated with you from the engineering program, and exchange stories of how to best deal with your elderly Italian ward's prickly personality. You explain how in Italy you "feel like a human being" and in the next breath explain that doing live-in work is "like being in prison." Once I make it through the corridor of desperate women looking for work, I can almost feel the complex mix of east and west, Soviet and European, sometimes coexisting peacefully and sometimes in conflict, but always with a hint of possibility, brush up against me. What news will the courier van bring? When can I return home to visit? Perhaps things in Ukraine are getting better and I can go home for good? Soaring above it all is the promise of joining Europe in bold orange lettering against the gray concrete: "*YUSHCHENKO NASH PRESIDENT.*"

If the promise of Europe in the form of consumer capitalism and self-determination soars above it all, the changing gender regime underlies it all. In fact, gender is constitutive of both this migration pattern and the nation-building project. The coming of the market to Ukraine has displaced older women, many *babushky,* from the workforce and made them redundant in their families as their daughters become housewives fulfilling, in the current post-Soviet discourse, their "true" biological calling as women.[6] *Babushky* become a pool of workers who migrate abroad, satisfying a demand for capital back home and domestic workers doing "women's work" in Italy. Gender constitutes migration. This migration in turn supports the Ukrainian nation-building project, and becoming "Europe" (a move toward the capitalist market and prosperity) rather than "Africa" (no market and poverty).[7] The nation-building project requires a reconfiguration of Ukraine's gender order.[8] In contrast to the Soviet extended family now criticized for distorting the "natural" personality of men and women by producing "masculine" working mothers, "weak" men, "abandoned" children, and strong *babushky,* the post-Soviet Ukrainian family is based on a mother-housewife and husband-breadwinner model (Ashwin 2000; Wanner 1998). Yet, this nuclear family, upon which the economic and social structures of the "new" Ukraine are being built, is not economically feasible in today's Ukraine. In order to make it possible for daughters to become housewives, and their husbands to be "restored" to their status as "breadwinners," *babushky* must go abroad to work and send back their wages. Here gender constitutes the nation.[9]

If the contradictions of the position these women inhabit bubble to the surface and are smoothed over or negotiated at the Garbatella, these tensions reassert themselves more forcefully and explode into view as workers return to L'viv by bus to visit their families. The bus ride from Rome to L'viv is not a site of open possibility like the Garbatella, where one has not yet embarked on the journey and likely will not leave at all. This allows them to imagine many possibilities for the future. At the Garbatella, there is enough room for the many contradictions to exist side by side. This becomes impossible on the bus. Moving between—the journey itself—is a site of "maybe," of more limited imaginings where the material reality of things imposes itself more forcefully, as the bus moves one closer to the object of one's imaginings (Ukraine, home, family). At no other point in my research is the tension between these many contradictions so pronounced, so palpable, and ultimately unsustainable as on the bus leaving Europe and approaching Ukraine.[10] Here the painful sacrifices these women make and the ironies created by the way gender constitutes migration in one direction, and the nation-building project of the new Ukraine in the other, become inescapable.

Getting on Board

Several months after my visit with Valia at the Garbatella, I ask Natalia how to get a seat on one of the vans. Natalia, a strong and fiery personality, is in her early thirties; she works for a Ukrainian-and-Russian-language newspaper in Rome. Natalia says that I am crazy for even thinking about taking a courier van to L'viv. She says she did it once, was miserable, and now she flies even though flying is three times as expensive. Besides being uncomfortable, Natalia says the guards at the border tried to make her pay a bribe. She showed her employee card identifying herself as a journalist and threatened to write about it in the paper. They let her go, but she knows of drivers leaving passengers not willing to pay the bribe at the border. Natalia's brother walks in shaking his head at our conversation. He says his computer was confiscated at the border because he did not have a receipt of purchase, and suggests I create a fake receipt for my laptop and get someone to put a stamp on it. "If they want it they'll take it, but it is worth trying." The horror stories of the courier vans continue. One informant, Sasha, tells me he rode back to L'viv, a three-day trip, and they never stopped, not even once for a bathroom, because the driver said if they stopped bandits would rob them. Even Ukrainian priests had stories to share of vans full of women returning to Ukraine with their "pockets stuffed with money" being robbed and losing all they had worked for. I am not planning on "stuffing my pockets with money," but as a researcher, losing my laptop would be tragic and being left at the border, perhaps precisely because I do not have my pockets stuffed with money, does not sound appealing either. Yet it seems to me that more recently the van rides have become rationalized in the Weberian sense. A complicated system of bribes, included in one's ticket, appears to keep the bandits at bay and the border guards happy without the passengers ever knowing who is getting paid what.

Much of Italy goes on vacation in August and, according to the national labor contract for domestic workers, domestics are also entitled to a month of paid vacation. Many women cannot go home because they do not have documents that will allow them to return to Italy. Others choose to stay in Rome and cover for women who are going home, earning double wages for the month. Oksana is going back to a village outside of L'viv. While I do not have a reservation on the bus she is taking, she suggests I try to ride with her. Oksana has many bags, and her friend Sofiya comes with us to help carry them all. Sofiya, fifty-eight, has white hair, watery eyes, and a quiet sadness about her. The second Sunday that the Ukrainian meeting place has been moved from the Garbatella to Rebibbia, a site even further outside Rome's city center, is 7 August 2005. Everyone is complaining about how uncomfortable Rebibbia is and I heartily agree. Whereas the Garbatella is a paved parking lot and a well-delineated space flanked by fencing and the metro station, Rebibbia is a vast expanse of cracked red earth. Oksana's reservation is not on a courier van, but on one of the much larger buses that seats forty people as opposed to the vans' eight or ten passengers. As the moment of the journey approaches, I begin to realize how helpful having a travel companion is and will be. I anxiously attempt to wish myself onto the bus with Oksana. Meanwhile, it is only 9 AM, but the sun is already hot and beating down on us. Every time a car drives by or the wind picks up, we are covered in Rebibbia's thick, red dust, which sticks to our sweaty bodies. While I nonchalantly announce that I will just take a courier van if there is no room for me on the bus, Sofiya senses my increasing concern and says, "Don't worry. This is a small thing compared to the bad that can happen." I smile weakly and answer, "Of course, everything will work out." I am embarrassed. I have not one but two passports in my pocket (both a US and an Italian passport and am worried about what risks I am willing to take to keep to my research schedule. Sofiya has been working in Italy for three years and because she does not have documents has not been home in all that time. She watches with longing as people pay their fare, €90 (US$115), and board the bus for home.

While I chat with Sofiya, Bohdan, a man I have met a few times through an informant, recognizes me. He is also in line for the bus and when he pays for his seat he goes to see if he can find me a place in one of the vans. He announces that van #25 is going to L'viv and the driver is a friend of his so "my safety is guaranteed." Oksana becomes visibly upset, repeating that the vans are not safe, while Bohdan continues to insist his friend will look after me. "Why don't you go with your friend and give your seat to Cinzia. You are a man," suggests Oksana. Bohdan shrugs his shoulders and walks away. "You see? Even he doesn't want to take the van. They are not safe and will only cause you problems Cinzia. Trust me. I would never take one of those vans. If you

don't get on this bus, make a reservation and get on this bus next Sunday. ...
You see what weak men we have?" At noon, covered in dirt and exhausted
from standing for hours in the sun, the last of us, including me, finally board
the bus and begin our three-day journey to Ukraine.

The Bus Ride—Mounting Contradictions

Passengers on the bus are, of course, mostly middle-aged women, but there are
a few exceptions. There are three young Ukrainian women with their Italian
partners, visibly working-class men. One couple is bringing their three-year-
old daughter to Ukraine to see her grandparents for the first time. There are
also a few Ukrainian men, including Bohdan, and a twenty-something Ukrainian boy who speaks Italian with a Roman accent and wants to talk about cars:
how much they cost in the United States new and used and whether I know
anything about how much it costs to rig the suspension so that they bounce
like in rap videos. Unfortunately, I am of little help. Then there are two older
Italian men with their middle-aged Ukrainian girlfriends sitting up front. The
older Italian men are loud and even though they are at the front of the bus,
the whole bus can hear their conversation. They keep complaining and joke
condescendingly about the "rustic" situation in which they have found themselves. After several crude comments about the lack of a toilet on the bus, a
Ukrainian man from the back of the bus shouts at them in Italian to be quiet,
then goes on to say that they are unable to handle the bus ride because "Italians fall apart at the first whiff of bad coffee." The Italians quiet down but their
hand gestures make clear that they continue complaining to each other and
their girlfriends. Oksana is more sympathetic, saying that the trip is harder for
Italians than Ukrainians because Ukrainians are "used to it." "Used to what?" I
ask. "Hardship," Oksana replies.

The sentiment that Italian bodies are "soft" and so experience the bus ride
as more difficult than do their Ukrainian counterparts reflects an understanding that the differing histories of the two countries are borne on the physical bodies of its citizens. Some scholars think of Ukraine as "postcolonial,"
recently emancipated from Russian imperialism (Rubchak 1996; Wilson
2002). A complex dislike of Russian domination permeates the stories of these
women. On the one hand, many women have stories of relatives who were sent
to the gulags[11] for wearing Ukrainian peasant garb, speaking Ukrainian, or accused of being a Ukrainian "nationalist."[12] On the other hand, migrant women
bemoan the loss of economic stability under the Soviet Union and the security
of knowing your social place in the world. Even as many of these women celebrate Ukraine's freedom from Russia, there is a recognition that not only is this
freedom from Russia precarious, but the push towards Europe may simply be

exchanging one master for another. There is concern that Ukraine may enter this new world of global capital as a slave to the national interests of others.[13] This relationship of inequality between countries is writ small in Rome, in the relationships these women have with their European *Signoras*.

Liuba and Giuglio: Weak/Young Italian Bodies vs. Strong/Old Soviet Ones

Liuba, age thirty-two, has been working in Italy for four years as a live-in, caring for two children ages seven and four. She is stocky with straight, chestnut brown hair, a round face, and large brown eyes. Liuba is an economist by training and worked in a bank in Kyiv until her pay was cut repeatedly and she was forced to quit. "So," she says, "I decided to embrace capitalism and start a small business." She traveled to Russia to buy shoes and sold them at a profit in Ukraine. Liuba explains that she was doing quite well for herself and even managed to buy an apartment. "But then," she goes on, looking out the bus window, "things got worse economically and standing in the bazaar all day, even when it was 25 degrees Celsius below zero, was no longer worth it." She nods when I suggest that it is more common for older women to come to work in Italy. "Yes, but when you are twenty-eight and unmarried, life is difficult for you in Ukraine. If you are not married by twenty-five, you are already an old maid! My parents have only small pensions and I have no husband to help me. My mother's friend was returning to Italy. She invited me and I came." Economic philosopher Tatiana Zhurzhenko (2001) observes that women's identities in postsocialist Ukraine are mediated by a free-market ideology and while the possibilities might at first glance seem endless there are in fact only two acceptable identities for women: housewife (in support of a male breadwinner) and businesswoman (who should nurture the Ukrainian state by bringing morals and values to the market). For Liuba, a woman considered too old to marry and lacking the capital to make entrepreneurship economically viable, both identities are out of reach. Liuba has much in common with the middle-aged women that make up most of the passengers on the bus: she too was doubly marginalized in Ukraine before migrating to Italy.

Liuba sends money back to her parents who keep what they need and put most of it away for her. However, glancing at Giuglio, Liuba says she no longer knows where she will live. In his early thirties, Giuglio has a factory job as a welder. They have been dating for five months and are on their way to visit the hot springs in the Carpathian Mountains for a week of vacation. Giuglio looks classically Roman, with jet black hair and dark eyes, and is gentle, almost bashful. His face is pale despite his olive skin; he is holding his stomach, trying not to move. The bus we are riding is not Greyhound. It spends so much time swaying side-to-side that I wonder if we are moving forward at all. The bus stops at a gas station so we can use the restroom. Back on the bus, one of the men tells Liuba, loudly enough for others to hear, that Giuglio vomited. Oksana calls out, "Does anyone have anything for this boy to take?" Almost instantaneously, over a dozen surrogate Ukrainian mothers are hovering over Giuglio, offering all kinds of home remedies. I am grateful that I have not let on how queasy I am feeling. "Italians are just not used to hardship," Oksana announces. Several women pipe up in agreement. "They cannot take this ride! When I tell my *Signora* how I go home she just says '*Mamma mia, oooo mamma!*'" (Laughter) "The smell of bleach alone gives my *Signora* a headache. Can you imagine if she actually had to use it to clean?" scoffs another. A third woman chimes in on a serious note, "I think our bodies are just made differently." "Don't be silly, we are hard because Soviet times made us hard. My *Signora* is eighty-two and she looks like our women do at fifty-five! She never had to *work*; she never had to *worry*. These things make you old." "Oooo," exclaims the woman whose *Signora* could not handle bleach, "When we join Europe we will all look younger!" (Laughter). "Actually, I think I am getting more wrinkles the closer we get to Ukraine!" (More laughter.) For the rest of the trip, Oksana would call out periodically, "So how do you like the ride, Giuglio? Next time you'll fly, right?"

Italians and Ukrainians have had different pasts, and that is reflected in these women's understanding of weak Italian bodies and strong Soviet ones. While we usually assign a negative connotation to the adjective "weak" and a positive one to "strong," it was not consistently so in this context. On the one hand, weak Italian bodies were disparaged—the Romans who would "fall apart" at the "first whiff of bad coffee," or the *Signora* who "never had to work." And yet, these women hope their children will be spared the harsh circumstances of their life and have the "weak" bodies that result from an abundance of consumer goods and never needing to stand in a bread line. The discussion of bodies moves from being about the past to being about possible futures. Their "strong" Soviet bodies are also "old"—prematurely aged—but the economic prosperity represented by joining the European Union might erase somewhat the physical marks of Soviet-era hardships. Just as one woman imagined her face gaining in age as she moved towards Ukraine, one might also imagine a woman looking younger as she moves towards Italy. In L'viv I would interview the children of women working in Rome, several of whom would note that their mother did in fact look "ten years younger" since migrating to Italy. Ironically, these "old" Soviet bodies that to Western eyes need the aid of a care provider are in fact providing care to Italians whose "bodies at eighty-two look like a Ukrainian's at fifty-five." The caring labor that Ukrainian bodies perform for Italian bodies, such as bathing, dressing, cooking, and cleaning, preserves the "youth" of Italian bodies while aging their own. Perhaps it is this relationship between bodies—Italian/Ukrainian, master/servant, Europe/Africa—that gives the dichotomy between "Europe" and "Africa" and concern over Ukraine's future such power in the collective imaginations of these women. These tensions are inscribed not only on the bodies of migrant women but on their psyches, as the following discussion of Polina and *la Depressione* or "the Depression" attests.

Polina: *La Depressione*

Polina, forty-six, is going home for the first time in five years. On a bus of matronly Ukrainian women, Polina stands out. She has a stylish haircut with deep red highlights. She is slender, dressed attractively in Italian garments, and oozes what I can only call "attitude." She often sits on her heels with her knees on the seat so that she can face backwards and chat with Liuba and Giuglio, who are in the seat in front of me and Oksana. Polina eyes my wedding band. "Your husband lets you ride a bus into a foreign country where you will stay for months by yourself? He isn't jealous? Are you sure your husband is Italian?" she inquires in Russian loud enough for others to laugh and nod their heads. "Ahh, but you do not know where I will sleep in L'viv. I am staying at a Catholic convent once I get there," I quip back with a smile. Polina laughs, leans her belly up against the back of the seat and settles in for a chat.

Polina cares for an elderly Italian woman with Parkinson's disease. Live-ins have only Thursday afternoons and Sundays off and, like most women doing this work, she describes it as "being in prison." Polina speaks Italian well and has an Italian boyfriend. She says, "I go from being in prison all week to being in prison with him on the weekend. Even if I just raise my eyes to look at someone he says, 'Oop, there she goes! Who did you find?!'" Polina jokes that she is not used to jealousy because Ukrainian men are "not so jealous." "Plus, my ex-husband was such a drunk that he never knew where I was or with whom most of the time."

Before leaving for Rome, Polina worked as an accountant in a state-run store on the periphery of L'viv. She explains that she never expected to go abroad to work, but now she likes Italy and does not want to live in Ukraine again, where she says it is "dirty" and the people are "uncivilized" and "rude."[14] The only way to stay in Italy is to marry, but she is not convinced this is her best option. Her boyfriend is much older than she and jealous; marriage, she says, would be like "living in a golden cage." While Polina asserts that she does not miss anything about Ukraine, she does miss her children and is visibly excited to see them. Polina has a twenty-year-old son, Yuriy, and a twenty-six-year-old daughter, Anna, who has three children of her own, a large and expensive family by Ukrainian standards. In the five years Polina has been away,

Anna had twin girls and Polina has yet to meet them. Yuriy, a fifteen-year-old boy when she left, is now a university student studying business. In the Soviet Union, making profits from the market was not only considered immoral but was illegal for the most part (Humphrey 2002). Now, many of the children of my informants are majoring in "international business." Polina explains that she is working in Italy to pay for her son's university education and to earn money to help her daughter and three grandchildren. She says, "The world has been turned upside-down." Not only is her son's chosen career alien to Polina, but so is her daughter's. Anna, despite having a university education, is a housewife. Her husband does not want her to work and Anna does not see herself returning to the workplace. For women of Polina's generation, reared in Soviet Ukraine where housework was considered unproductive labor and being supported by one's husband an embarrassment, it is difficult to imagine a housewife as a chosen identity (Zdravomyslova 1996). Polina believes her daughter's university education is going to waste. Shaking her head in disbelief, she describes what a good student Anna was, declaring forcefully, "She is a chemist, not a housewife!"

Polina's daughter illustrates that not only have the structural opportunities for women and men in the labor market been altered by the coming of the market and the retreat of the socialist state, but the ideological terrain has shifted as well. The icon of the Soviet superwoman, a celebrated and capable woman worker building socialism alongside men, is now seen as an enemy of nature responsible for the weak families that are said to be the cause for much of what is wrong with postsocialist society (Rubchak 2001; Verdery 1994). In fact, returning women to the home and their "natural" roles as mothers and wives is understood in nationalist discourse as a "way of getting back to the essence of what it means to be Ukrainian" (Rubchak 1996: 318). The new icon of Ukrainian womanhood is Berehynia, a modern incarnation of an ancient pagan goddess imbued with the contemporary meanings of protectress of Ukraine's "true" culture and language as well as guardian of the domestic hearth (Rubchak 1996). Yet Polina and many other women like her working in Rome are weary of this new image of ideal womanhood. They experience a range of emotions from ambivalence to disappointment and even outrage that their daughters, after all the sacrifices they have made for their education, do not work in their fields of expertise but "sit at home."

The process through which gender is mobilized as a constitutive element of both migration and nation adds other layers of irony and contradictions to the reality of Ukraine's nation-building project. Women like Polina migrate to make being a career housewife—an identity they often wish their daughters would reject as economically possible—by doing paid housework abroad. Most of the women I spoke with in Rome noted painfully that Ukrainian president Kuchma publicly called "all our women abroad" "prostitutes." One informant exclaimed sarcastically, "Well then, I must be an old prostitute so my daughter can be Berehynia at home." These women find that the patriarchal nature of the European family model subjects them to living in golden cages if they should marry in Italy. And yet their labor reproduces the same model in Ukraine, rendering their sons patriarchs and their daughters dependents.

As the bus moves closer to Ukraine, the space these women have to negotiate these contradictions is compressed until, unlike at the Garbatella, they can no longer coexist. Since the contradictions cannot be resolved, they are displaced and take on a life of their own in the women's collective understanding as "*la Depressione*" or "the Depression." My conversation with Polina is interrupted by people at the front of the bus singing a Ukrainian folk song. Polina props herself up on her knees, and begins belting out the tune waving her arms in the air as if directing a choir. Oksana raises her eyebrows and turns to me, "I am very surprised that someone with her character can do live-in work." Another woman, Sveta, leans over and says sympathetically, "Let her enjoy herself *la Depressione* will soon take over" Oksana nods knowingly.

While our conversation is in Russian, "the Depression" is always said in Italian, *la Depressione*. When I ask Sveta what she means, she says, "When she [Polina] gets home and realizes her son has been paying his teachers to pass his classes rather than studying, and her daughter tells her she has no right to tell her how to raise her children or handle her husband because she has been doing just fine without her, *la Depressione* will appear. I was as happy as she when I went home the first time. I had been in Italy four years and I went home for my son's wedding. I paid for that wedding—every kopeck—but I was just a guest! I was a *guest* at my son's wedding, understand?" Another woman whose name I never learn smiles widely, revealing a mouth full of gold teeth, "It's true! When you are here the first time you think *la Depressione* only exists in Italy because you are alone and far away from your family. And then you go home and see that no matter how much money you make, you will always need more, that all the same problems are still there and your children grow up even without you." She shakes her head and retreats back to her seat. Others chime in speaking of *la Depressione* as if "it" (or rather "she," since it is feminine in Italian) is a fellow passenger on the bus, one who keeps to herself and then shows up, unexpected, on your doorstep in Ukraine, an unwanted houseguest at a time when you thought you would be happiest. "You realize that in Italy you are a *straniera* (a foreigner) and you have been dreaming about going home, crying because you miss your family, your friends, being in charge of your own house; then when you get there you think, 'How did I ever stand these dirty streets, this small kitchen, these rude, unintelligent people?' And so *la Depressione* arrives." "Well," interjects Sveta, "right now we are going home to our Ukraine!" She leads them into another folk song about *nasha Ukraina* (our Ukraine).

It is through changes in the gender order that both this migration pattern and "*nasha Ukraina*" are achieved. This mutual constitution forces these migrant women to inhabit a contradictory space. They are school teachers, economists, and engineers doing paid domestic work abroad, a job category considered so lowly it did not even exist in the Soviet Union in which they grew up.[15] Through remittances, such migrant women are making economically possible a nuclear, European family that has no place for them as Soviet *babushky*. They are external agents in building the "new" Ukraine, one that scorns the "old" Soviet Ukraine and the moral system that shaped their way of understanding the world. These Soviet women are building a *European* Ukraine. Whereas the nation-building work older women do through migration is either unrecognized in public discourse or denigrated by the label "prostitute," the women themselves are painfully cognizant of their sacrifices. Indeed, as Tania said standing on the cement platform and looking down at the expanse of women at the Garbatella, "They carry Ukraine on their shoulders, and don't think they don't know it." Yet, these women believe Ukraine's European future is not guaranteed. Despite all their efforts, they fear their children might end up living in "Africa"—an economically depressed space populated by "broken" families and "weak" men and racked with corruption. When we arrive at Ukraine's border, events that suggest to them that Ukraine might indeed go the way of "Africa" cause these irresolvable tensions of gender's mutual constitution of migration and nation to explode.

Oksana: Exploding Contradictions on the Ukrainian Border

Oksana, fifty-one, has been working in Italy for almost four years. She is from a town an hour outside of L'viv, but as a young student she won a competition to enter a five-year university program in literature and writing at an institute in Moscow. Oksana hoped to get what she called a "literary position" in film, theater, radio, or newspaper, but her religious leanings had always kept her out of the Komsomol or the Young Communist League. Without membership she was denied access to those jobs. Instead, she taught courses at a local university. After the collapse of the Soviet Union, Oksana landed a job at a publishing house where she translated religious texts from Russian, Polish, and Church Slavonic into Ukrainian. Her economic problems increased as her parents became ill and their pension barely paid for one trip to the pharmacy a month. A neighbor suggested she go to Italy with her for the Year 2000 Catholic Jubilee, and she did, overstaying her visa to work as a live-in.

Now, riding through northern Italy on Sunday afternoon, Oksana speaks a lot about "our Ukraine." When she is not teasing Giuglio by repeating—"So how do you like the bus ride? Will you fly next time"?—she asks him jealously about his vacation plans in the Carpathian Mountains. "Yes," she says to Giuglio in Italian, "Italians think that Ukraine is Africa, but when they see our rolling hills and green fields they too say Ukraine is beautiful. Wait until you bathe in the springs! I am a patriot! I love Ukraine and you will too! Really, it is just like Europe."

We ride through Austria all night and stop at the Hungarian border for passport control early Monday morning, where we are held for four hours. When we finally make it past the check point, we get off the bus for a bathroom break. Bohdan had spent considerable time at the last rest stop trying to convince me (he just assumed I needed convincing) that L'viv was "just like Rome": "just as beautiful," "just as cultural," "just like Europe." During this stop, he goes to buy his morning coffee. Back on the bus he announces solemnly, like a melodic tolling of a bell: "Europe ends here: €2 for bad coffee."

Our passports are checked again on the way out of Hungary, and we wait three hours at passport control to enter Ukraine. While the bus is stopped, we walk across the border to the bathroom. Oksana is horrified by what we find. The bathroom is filthy, and there is an elderly Ukrainian woman who wants to be paid for the use of a toilet and the right to one square of toilet paper. Oksana says to the woman, "If you are asking people to pay then the bathroom should at least be clean." This quickly escalates into a screaming match that leaves Oksana furious. As we wait for others to exit and walk back to the bus, we hear Bohdan also giving this old woman a piece of his mind, screaming, "Europe! You people want to be Europe?" Oksana is fuming, and a general frustration and anger is bubbling under the surface that in reality has little to do with the old woman and the dirty bathroom. "You see?" Polina shouts, "The bureaucracy does not work here! Nothing works here! How could I ever live here again? NOTHING WORKS!" I note that we had waited just as long at the Hungarian border, but the comment is lost in an eruption of laughter. I look out the window to see a man running alongside his car with the front door open and one hand on the steering wheel and the other on the open door, literally pushing his car across the border. "See, Cinzia"? Oksana yells, "This is Ukraine! Get your camera ready, you will see a lot more things like that!" She shakes her head, "This is Ukraine."

Our passports are finally returned, and, as we start to pull across the border, we are stopped again by a border guard who tells us he wants to inspect our bags. I silently will him not to find my laptop. Polina screeches, "I don't even want to go home anymore! This crap is our life!" To my surprise, the whole bus rises in spontaneous protest. The many tensions of these women, caught between "Europe" and "Africa," "old" and "new" Ukraine, explode out of the bus. People stream out onto the asphalt and everyone is yelling. The border guard is absolutely taken aback. Oksana begins organizing sending some people to stay in the bus and watch peoples' belongings there and asking others to stand beside the bus in front of its main luggage compartment. In the meantime she rips a sheet of paper from my notebook and starts to collect signatures, yelling that she is immediately going to fax a petition to the Ukrainian embassy in Rome. "Cinzia, are you writing all this down?! Make sure it all goes in your book!" She turns to the border guard and says, "We have a foreign journalist writing a book about Ukraine with us. She'd like your name for her book and I'd like your name for my fax to the embassy in Rome!" Polina stomps over, looks the guard in the face and yells, "We're in AFRICA!" pulling at her stylish red hair. The Italian men are yelling and gesticulating as only Romans can, egged on by their Ukrainian girlfriends who figure angry Italian men cannot hurt the cause. The border guard decides that this is more trouble than it is worth and, after opening one bag and waving his flashlight around, he sends us on our way.

It is quiet on the bus as we ride into Ukraine. Looking at the faces of my fellow travelers, Soviet people, I try to make sense of the revolt I had just witnessed and wonder what gave them the courage to stand up to the border guards. Was it a sense of indignation that Ukraine was not behaving like Europe in front of migrant workers who have made such painful sacrifices to build a European Ukraine? Did they feel they had a lesson to teach about behaving like Europeans? Perhaps having lived in Italy where corruption is not part of everyday interactions, they simply had less tolerance for the bribes the border guard was sure to ask for? Or maybe the courage came not from their experiences abroad but from the stories of their children and those who stood up in Independence Square in Kyiv a few months earlier for the values of the Orange Revolution: honest elections, transparency, eradication of corruption, social and economic justice, and full membership in the European Union?

We do not reach our final destination of L'viv until early the following morning. As we ride through the western Ukrainian countryside, Oksana explains the themes of various folk songs that speak of rolling hills, beautiful women, the family hearth, and the plight of partisan soldiers. "You see, they are all about the beauty of Ukraine and the beauty of its people." It has been a bumpy ride since we crossed the border and the side-to-side swaying of the bus is now joined by a sometimes violent bouncing up and down. Giuglio grows ever paler. We hit a patch of particularly bad potholes and Oksana's face sours, "How do you like our roads? That's Ukraine!"

Epilogue

After three months in L'viv, I board a bus headed back to Rome. This time I am without a travel companion. The bus is still empty and I slip into a window seat. Three women get on the bus chatting and laughing, swapping stories about how many times their *Signora* had called them in Ukraine begging them to come back soon, what a mess the houses they had been cleaning would be, and even whether their elderly wards would still be alive when they got there. Two of the women slide into the seat across from me, so one woman sits next to me still chatting across the aisle. I am thrilled. I imagine the three of them taking me under their wings much like Oksana did on the trip here. At a pause in the conversation, my seat mate turns and looks at me. Before I can say a word, she grabs her bag and switches seats. As the bus begins to fill, another woman boards, begins to sit down next to me but, before she actually hits the seat, she realizes that I am not of this context and, in a move I can only describe as an impressive showing of abdominal strength, stops herself mid-air and moves to another seat. As we depart, trying not to melt into the side of the bus, I brainstorm how to make this a meaningful ethnographic experience. The bus stops in small villages outside L'viv, picking up people at each stop. At one of the more remote villages, a woman wearing a kerchief on her head, her arms weighted down with plastic bags that I later learn are filled with enough fried fish to feed a small army for much more than three days, boards the bus and sits down heavily next to me. Slava has a round face, brown and creased from the sun. I notice that her hands show that she does farm work. She smiles at me as she removes her kerchief. Several hours pass before Slava realizes I am not Ukrainian. My foreignness seems indistinguishable to her from the city-dwellers who boarded the bus in L'viv.

As the bus moves us closer to Ukraine's border, Slava begins sobbing as she kisses a wallet-sized picture of her eleven-year-old son. Slava's husband left for Poland two years ago. He has been working off and on and sends back what money he can, but it is not enough to send their son to university one day. Slava has a sister already in Italy and Slava is on her way to join her in the hope of finding work as a live-in. Slava's sister gave her half of the €2,200 (US$2,860) it cost to buy a ten-day tourist visa and she borrowed the rest with an interest rate of 12 percent. The plan was that her husband would come home and take care of their son while Slava is in Italy. But one never knows when the visa will come through and Slava had to leave today, the day before her husband is supposed to return. Slava shakes her head: "Already I have not seen him for two years and now I don't know when I will see him again. When will I be able to go home?" Her question hangs answerless between us.

They take our passports at the Austrian border, the border with the European Union, the border that matters most. I am terrified for Slava. Nothing about her looks like a tourist and I am afraid they might not let her through. Slava is too preoccupied by the photo of her son—wondering if she will find work right away, if her husband will really make it home from Poland, and if her aging mother can keep up with an active eleven-year-old boy—to worry about crossing the border. I sigh with relief as the bus pulls into Austria. Slava's tear-filled eyes meet mine as she offers me a piece of fried fish "You see, when my son is grown he will either say to me, 'We have nothing. Why didn't you go abroad like everyone else?' Or 'Why did you abandon me?'" She did not like her "choices." If Slava stays, she risks that her son will live in "Africa." In order to ensure that he will live in a "European" Ukraine, Slava must migrate to Europe, leaving Ukraine and her son behind. The mutual constitution of migration and nation, achieved through the manipulation of gendered relations, has forced Slava to join the other migrant women in this space of impossible contradictions—sometimes negotiable, sometimes exploding to the surface, but always experienced as a deep ache by the individual women and the loved ones they leave behind.

Notes

I thank Michael Burawoy for his thoughtful comments and encouraging me to let the ethnographic data lead not only my analysis but my writing. I also thank Laleh Behbehanian, Emily Brisset, Xiuying Cheng, Marcel Paret, Ofer Sharone, and Edward Walker. A special thanks to Marian Rubchak for her careful reading of this piece.

1. This paper draws on material I gathered in August 2005 riding the migration circuit from Rome to L'viv and back, as well as six months of field work in Rome's Ukrainian community, where I conducted ethnographic research, sixty-one formal, in-depth interviews with domestic workers from Ukraine, and over twenty interviews with community leaders. It is also informed by data gathered in 2004–2006 as part of a larger project. These data include interviews and ethnographic material collected during my time in the field in L'viv interviewing thirty-eight children with one or both parents abroad and fifty-three domestic workers from Ukraine in San Francisco and Los Angeles. I am a United States-born native speaker of English. As the daughter of Italian immigrants, a care provider, and a gardener, I grew up speaking Italian at home. While fluency in Italian proved to be invaluable in many ways, my language of communication, even with Ukrainophone informants, was Russian. At the Garbatella and on the migration bus informants spoke Ukrainian, Russian, and Italian depending on the context, and also Ukrainianized and Russified many Italian phrases for which direct translations do not exist.

2. Ukrainian workers usually enter Italy on a tourist visa bought at Ukrainian "travel agencies," then overstay the visa to work. In 2004, a tourist visa to Italy cost up to €2,500 ($3,300). In order to work in Italy legally, foreign workers must have a work visa or *permesso di soggiorno*. The majority of foreign workers in Italy are without legal papers. Those who have been legalized usually obtained legal status during an amnesty period. Italy's 1998, 2000, and 2002 amnesty laws contained special provisions that favored the legalization of domestic workers. The Italian state recognizes that its increasingly elderly population is facing a "care crisis." Because migration to Italy from Ukraine began in the second half of the 1990s, with the largest influx occurring from 1998 to 1999, many Ukrainians were legalized during the 2002 Bossi-Fill Bill. This required employers to fill out paperwork and agree to pay social security (*contributi*)

to the government on behalf of their employee. Foreign workers who obtained a *permesso* must renew it every year, or every other year, and show proof of employment.

3. A relatively young retirement age supported the extended family so that grandparents were still physically able to provide childcare and other reproductive labor. The official retirement age is fifty-five for women and sixty for men. Those who performed jobs considered "dangerous" retired at even younger ages. Many of the migrant women I met in Rome were high-school teachers like Roxalana, who were able to retire even in their early forties after twenty years of service.

4. One informant, Klara, says that working with Italians is difficult because: "We are of different nationalities, and they do not think highly of us. They say we are people from the Third World! Yes, this is how they interpret us—Third World women—and it isn't true at all!" Yet Klara is often asked by Italian employers to explain why she is doing live-in work in Italy and she finds this task frustrating: "Even their [Italian] mentality is different. They cannot understand how you can work your whole life and have nothing. ... We come here to earn money so we can send our kids to school, buy an apartment, and also to buy meat." Another informant, Olena, expressed this frustration in another way "How can I explain to Italians that I have a higher education and I remember the respected person I was in my country; *and* with the first money I made in Italy I put in a water line to my house because before there was only a well"? These women are caught between global discourses of the First World (Europe) and the Third World (Africa), neither of which they felt captured the complexity of Ukraine in transition. Without access to a global discursive script that encapsulates their experience of Ukraine in terms of an everyday understanding of "development," migrant women in Italy grappled with the gap between Ukraine and First- and Third-World discourses signified by Europe and Africa.

5. All names are pseudonyms.

6. Anthropologist Katherine Verdery (1994) notes that socialist states pushed labor-intensive industrialization plans that required women's labor power. This economic fact produced socialism's emphasis on gender equality and the policies that facilitated it, such as generous maternity leaves and state-sponsored child care. According to Verdery, this altered gender relations within families. Women's participation in the labor force gave them increased power relative to men in the household unit. At the same time, the state usurped certain patriarchal functions and undercut the familial authority of men. The state's socialization of some household tasks made women dependent on the state rather than their husbands. In fact, in what Verdery calls the "gender regime of socialism," both men and women were dependent wards of a paternalist state that made decisions in the whole family's interest. With the coming of market capitalism, the socialist welfare state that had once taken on some of women's nurturing and caregiving roles is now considered too costly in a free-market economy and it is devolving these responsibilities back onto the shoulders of women. Indeed, the gender organization of capitalist households cheapens the cost of labor for capital by assigning reproductive labor to women and calling it "housework," which is unpaid. This cheapening—calling reproductive labor "housework"—makes postsocialist economies more viable. Verdery writes, "The chief alternative Eastern Europe's women might anticipate is what has happened in more-advanced economies: the commodification of household tasks into services (day care, cleaning, meal provision, and so

forth) for which a working couple pays something closer to their real cost than is paid when these are 'housework.' Until the commodity economy becomes as pervasive in Eastern Europe as it is in the developed world, however, postsocialist Eastern Europe will be returning to the housewife-based domestic economy, superseded at least in part by both socialism and advanced capitalism" (254).

7. Wilson (2000) argues that whether Ukraine follows a path of integration with Europe or a return to the Russian sphere is far from determined. Which way Ukraine orients itself is of great geopolitical interest and will have an important effect on the balance of power in the whole Eurasian region. Here I argue that not only are migrant women engaged in a particular nation-building project, but through migration they actually push Ukraine, and the (re)construction of its institutions (social, economic, political), perhaps unwittingly, down the path towards Europe.

8. Zhurzhenko (2004) notes that in Ukraine the shift to this nuclear family model, what she calls the rise of "neofamilialism," is "indispensible to the process of constructing national identity as European," (27).

9. The theoretical orientation of this paper was inspired by Hondagneu-Sotelo (2003). In her introductory essay, Hondagneu-Sotelo argues that the gender and migration literature can be grouped into three stages. The first stage emerged in the 1970s and early 1980s. Feminist scholars simply studied women, long neglected in migration studies, and added them to existing paradigms. This was superseded by an interest in gender as a set of relations, but the studies, according to Hondagneu-Sotelo, focused primarily on changing gender relations in families and local immigrant communities, as if institutions such as labor markets or welfare agencies are devoid of gender. She argues that there is a third stage of gender and migration research emerging, and suggests that we think of "gender as a key constitutive element of immigration." In this paper I have taken Hondagneu-Sotelo's suggestion seriously and wrestled with what it might mean for gender to be "constitutive" of migration. I might have explained this migration of women from Ukraine the way female migration is usually explained, following Anderson (2000), Chang (2000), or Hochschild (2002): Poverty in Third-World countries "push(es)" women who desperately need to provide for their children to migrate to First-World countries, where there is the simultaneous "pull" of higher wages. While I am not suggesting this framework is inaccurate, I am proposing that thinking about gender as constitutive allows us to see a much more complicated story in the case of Ukraine, one that thrusts our thinking outward to economic systems, moral orders, and nationhood.

10. See Solari 2006b for a time during the Orange Revolution when the claim to Europe by Rome's Ukrainian community was made with great consistency.

11. *Gulag"* refers to a system of forced labor camps in the Soviet Union.

12. Soviet nationality policy sought to root out "bourgeois nationalism," while fostering "internationalist values" in the hope of creating a single "Soviet people." I found that my respondents reclaimed the term *nationalist* and gave it a positive connotation. They proudly declared, "I am a nationalist!" with the same if not greater frequency as the more acceptable phrase by Soviet standards, "I am a patriot!"

13. These sentiments point to a possible tension between this type of nation-building project (emphasizing a shared ethnicity, language, religion, and historical past) with a simultaneous claim to a supranational European identity. See Taras et al. (2004) for an interesting discussion about the appeal of "transnational identities" in Ukraine.

14. During the course of my research, many women voiced sentiments similar to Polina's, while also expressing pride in their country—citing great literary figures, the richness of their history and culture, and the hardworking nature of Ukrainian people. This ambivalence, like many of the contradictions tied to the social space these women inhabit, was particularly salient during the bus ride. For most, this ambivalence existed alongside a deep yearning to return to their families and their former lives in Ukraine.

15. For a look at how Ukrainian and Russian domestic workers in San Francisco negotiate this change in work status, see Solari 2006a.

Bibliography

Anderson, Bridget. 2000. *Doing the Dirty Work? The Global Politics of Domestic Labor.* New York: Zed Books.

Ashwin, Sarah, ed. 2000. *Gender, State, and Society in Soviet and Post-Soviet Russia.* New York: Routledge.

Bonnell, Victoria. 1996. "Winners and Losers in Russia's Economic Transition." In *Identities in Transition: Eastern Europe and Russia after the Collapse of Communism,* edited by V. Bonnell, 13–25. Berkeley: Center for Slavic and East European Studies, University of California.

Chang, Grace. 2000. *Disposable Domestics: Immigrant Women Workers in the Global Economy.* Cambridge, MA: South End Press.

Hochschild, Arlie Russell. 2002. "Love and Gold." In *Global Women: Nannies, Maids, and Sex Workers in the New Economy,* edited by Barbara Ehrenreich and Arlie Russell Hochschild, 15–30. New York: Metropolitan Books.

Hondagneu-Sotelo, Pierrette. 2003. "Gender and Immigration: A Retrospective and Introduction." In *Gender and U.S. Immigration: Contemporary Trends,* edited by Pierrette Hondagneu-Sotelo, 3–19. Berkeley: University of California Press.

Humphrey, Caroline, and Ruth Mandel. 2002. "The Market in Everyday Life: Ethnographies of Postsocialism." In *Markets & Moralities Ethnographies of Postsocialism,* edited by Ruth Mandel and Caroline Humphrey, 1–16. New York: Berg.

Rubchak, Marian J. 1996. "Christian Virgin or Pagan Goddess: Feminism Versus the Eternally Feminine in Ukraine." In *Women in Russia and Ukraine,* edited by Rosalind Marsh, 315–30. Cambridge: Cambridge University Press.

———. 2001. "In Search of a Model: Evolution of a Feminist Consciousness in Ukraine and Russia." *European Journal of Women's Studies* 8 (2): 149–60.

Shehda, Natalia, and Oleksandr Horodetskyy. 2004. "Ucraini in Italia: Una Realtà Sempre Più Presente." In *Europa Allargamento a Est e Immigrazione,* edited by Oliviero Forti, Franco Pittau, and Antonio Ricci, 299–307. Rome: Carita Italiana.

Solari, Cinzia. 2006a. "Professionals and Saints: How Immigrant Careworkers Negotiate Gendered Identities at Work." *Gender & Society* 20 (3): 301–31.

———. 2006b. "Transnational Politics and Settlement Practices: Post-Soviet Immigrant Churches in Rome." *American Behavioral Scientist* 49 (11): 1528–53.

Taras, Ray, Olga Filippova, and Nelly Pobeda. 2004. "Ukraine's Transnationals, Far-away Locals and Xenophobes: The Prospects for Europeanness." *Europe-Asia Studies* 56 (8): 35–56.

Verdery, Katherine. 1994. "From Parent-State to Family Patriarchs: Gender and Nation in Contemporary Eastern Europe." *East European Politics and Societies* 8 (2): 225–55.

Wanner, Catherine. 1998. *Burden of Dreams: History and Identity in Post-Soviet Ukraine.* University Park: Pennsylvania State University Press.

Wilson, Andrew. 2000. *The Ukrainians: Unexpected Nation.* New Haven, CT: Yale University Press.

———. 2002. "Elements of a Theory of Ukrainian Ethno-National Identities." *Nations and Nationalism* 8 (1): 31–54.

Wolczuk, Kataryna. 2000. "History, Europe and the 'National Idea': The 'Official' Narrative of National Identity in Ukraine." *Nationalities Papers* 28 (4): 671–94.

Zdravomyslova, Elena. 1996. "Problems of Becoming a Housewife." In *Women's Voices in Russia Today,* edited by Anna Rotkirch and Elina Haavio-Mannila, 33–48. Brookfield, VT: Dartmouth Publishing Company.

Zhurzhenko, Tatiana. 2001. "Free Market Ideology and New Women's Identities in Post-Socialist Ukraine." *European Journal of Women's Studies* 8 (1): 29–49.

———. 2004. "Strong Women, Weak State: Family Politics and Nation Building in Post-Soviet Ukraine." In *Post-Soviet Women Encountering Transition: Nation Building, Economic Survival, and Civic Activism,* edited by Kathleen Kuehnast and Carol Nechemias, 23–43. Baltimore: Johns Hopkins University Press.

CHAPTER 3

Women as Migrants
on the Margins of
the European Union

Alexandra Hrycak

The breakup of the Soviet Union was followed by dramatic waves of migration (Shamshur and Malinovska 1994).[1] One of the waves has brought hundreds of thousands of women from Ukraine to work in the European Union, most of whom find themselves doubly marginalized as workers. First, they are illegal, unauthorized or undocumented workers—that is, they do not have permission from the state to work. Typically, they arrive on tourist visas and overstay. They are consequently subject to arrest and deportation if state authorities discover them. Second, nearly all labor migrants are employed in the informal economy. As informal workers, migrants are not entitled to legal protection. They are vulnerable to abuse by unscrupulous employers and intermediaries such as recruiters, have little or no access to healthcare, and are often expected to work around the clock, with no rest periods or days off. They have no protection against these and other common abuses, such as nonpayment or underpayment of wages.

In the west as well as in Ukraine, the media views women migrants primarily as sex slaves, forced to work involuntarily as prostitutes in brothels or on the street. States and NGOs at both ends of this migration chain see these migrants mainly as victims of human trafficking. Drawing on a review of the literature, and on research I conducted with migrants and women's rights activists during ethnographic fieldwork, this chapter argues that such depictions have misrepresented women migrants. Most of those who leave Ukraine for the European Union find employment in private homes as careworkers for the elderly, the young, or the ill. Typically, they migrate abroad to support their family, in particular children. But their illegal status, and the nature of their work, tend to preclude a visit home. They might remain absent for long periods, often more than a year. Because of their extensive period of living abroad, they contribute to the development of the receiving country, in this case Italy, and the formation of a new women's diaspora.

This chapter is part of a larger project that examines the programs and projects that have emerged to address women's issues since the Soviet Union collapsed and Ukraine achieved independence (Hrycak 2005: 69–81; 2006: 69–100; 2007c: 75–94; 2007b: 208–25). Women's organizations in Ukraine have received considerable assistance from Western sources, with the largest sums devoted to the prevention of trafficking in women. My findings on this form of aid help to explore how and why extensive Western involvement fails to address the needs of these migrants, and more broadly, other Ukrainian women. As I argue below, antitrafficking initiatives intended to rescue women from sex slavery and return migrants to their home communities have provided aid to some. They are believed to have led to changes that protect potential migrants from abuse at the hands of human traffickers. Unfortunately, thus far initiatives to fight their trafficking problem have been unable to stem the tide of illegal immigration or assist in reintegrating returning migrants. Instead of working to protect the rights of most women migrants, antitrafficking crusades continue to direct resources toward protecting victims of coerced sex by unscrupulous criminals. By continuing to code women who cross borders as prostitutes, they might unintentionally be reaffirming the damaging stereotypes that lead to labeling migrants fallen women.

Western Ukrainian Migrant Women

In 2001, while conducting research on women's activism in Ukraine, I met Marta, a local entrepreneur in her early forties who was living in a small town in western Ukraine.[2] During the Soviet era, Marta was employed as a manager in a textile factory on the outskirts of the city of L'viv. After Ukraine's independence, Marta's salary stopped and eventually she lost her job. Marta and her husband struggled to make ends meet, but found it nearly impossible to provide for their two young children on his income alone. Initially, she relied on the survival strategies she developed in response to the chronic shortages of the 1980s. Marta began to grow more of the family's food and became more dependent on her informal network of kin and friends for other goods, such as winter clothing for her children. As time when on, she and some of her friends began to earn money as shuttle traders, selling small quantities of Ukrainian goods in open-air markets in neighboring Poland, then returning with Polish goods for local sale. Marta also began growing flowers to sell in downtown L'viv during the winter.

Eventually, Marta became one of a handful of women whom Western donors, and their local Ukrainian partners, considered their success stories. In the late 1990s, she learned of a new project funded by the US government to assist unemployed women in starting their own business. Marta wrote a passionate application describing her dream of opening a flower shop, and was thrilled when the program accepted her. She received training in writing a business plan, approaching creditors and investors, and other related skills. At the conclusion of the program, Marta was given a small loan enabling her to rent space in her township to open a flower shop. She also was designated president of a business club established to provide ongoing support to other women entrepreneurs who finished the same program.

Marta was eager to tell me more about her shop as well as her business club. However, when I called several weeks later to pay her a visit, I was told that she had gone abroad to Italy to look for work. Surprised by her unexpected disappearance, I inquired among other members of her organization as to why a successful entrepreneur like Marta would leave two children, a husband, and a business behind, risking so much to look for what was certain to be a menial job. I was told that she felt that she had no choice. Her older son had been accepted as a tuition-paying student at a local university, but because he did not win a scholarship, Marta and her husband had to borrow several thousand dollars to pay for his admission and tuition. Mired in debt, she was certain that the relatively meager earnings of her flower business would never enable her to repay this money, let alone the loan for her flower shop.

Marta's case provides a dramatic example of the shifting nature of employment opportunities for women in western Ukraine, as well as the contradictory nature of postcommunist programs designed to address women's needs. She also exemplifies a growing trend that has received little acknowledgement or discussion, either in Ukrainian studies or in postcommunist scholarship on gender, of post-Soviet women who leave behind their family as a temporary measure in their quest for enhanced opportunities for their children.

Most Western examinations of women's migration from Ukraine focus upon sex trafficking or, more broadly, on human trafficking. During my research representatives of women's NGOs and young women desiring to work abroad repeatedly told me that trafficking of women for forced prostitution remained a problem, but had declined significantly. Antitrafficking campaigns had successfully raised awareness among teenagers and young adults of the risks of going abroad. This led to changes in state visa policies and it is now virtually impossible for teenagers or young adults to obtain a visa for travel to Western countries. What has grown far more common is circular labor migration by middle-aged women. I encountered numerous instances of women who left Ukraine on tourist visas for work abroad, mainly as undocumented domestic workers. Studies have found that the need to pay for their children's education constitutes a leading cause of women's temporary labor migration.[3] I learned that, typically, once they find work these women overstay their visa and remain in the receiving country for years at a time.

While Marta's story of migration shared common features with many others I heard, I found her case noteworthy for a second reason. Her case bore no resemblance to the focus of so many Western and domestic women's rights initiatives in Ukraine, the stereotypical "trafficked woman." Marta was in the small minority of women who were given opportunities for staying in the country through an antitrafficking initiative that provides the necessary means for launching a small business. Yet, despite her training in business administration and access to start up capital, even as a new entrepreneur offering a product that has a steady local demand, she remained unable to earn enough to provide for her family's shifting needs.

Millions of dollars of Western aid has been directed toward antitrafficking initiatives, whose aim has been to persuade women in Ukraine that their local opportunities for employment are superior to conditions they will face in some foreign country. Yet Marta, and many other women in their thirties and forties, have continued to travel abroad, knowing that the flower shops and other small businesses they start in western Ukraine with Western support will never generate the kind of income that they can earn in Italy, where migrants report that on average they make ten times over their typical earnings in Ukraine.[4] The logic behind the economic empowerment discourse promoted by Western donors is that local women are irrationally blind to economic opportunities until they are trained through Western projects. But in truth, Western economic empowerment projects practice selective rationality—often praising women for starting small businesses that might remain marginal and unable to generate sufficient income to meet their actual needs, and condemning them for going abroad. The bitter truth is that women like Marta, who go abroad to work as nannies and act as caregivers to the elderly, earn far more than they would at home. And, perhaps because their earnings exceed those of most men, such women have become the focus of much resentment and blame for social problems in the home country, ranging from contributing to promiscuity among teens to alcoholism among men.

Temporary Labor Migration

Numerous studies conducted in the early 1990s found widespread dissatisfaction with local living conditions in Ukraine, and considerable interest in temporary labor migration. Roughly half of Ukraine's population has expressed a desire to work abroad temporarily. A tenth seek to emigrate permanently (Shamshur and Malinovska 1994). These studies have led to predictions of an imminent collapse of the Soviet Union, followed by a "brain drain," a wave of professionals migrating out of Ukraine. It was initially predicted that this migration would be composed mainly of unmarried men in their twenties and early thirties.[5] Since these predictions were made, a sizeable population of temporary labor migrants, *zarobitchany*, has in fact departed Ukraine.[6] Because much of this movement is undocumented, it is difficult to establish how many individuals are involved. The most reliable estimates indicate that from two to five million Ukrainians have left the country to seek employment outside the country. The main destinations are Russia, Poland, the Czech Republic, Italy, Portugal, and Spain.[7] Labor migration has increased considerably during the past decade, and contrary to initial expectations women constitute a significant share of this labor drain; this has generated considerable concern both at home and abroad.

The subject of labor migrants is frequently raised in Ukraine, particularly in western Ukraine, where it is common to hear that there are virtually no able-bodied adults of working age left in small towns and villages. Particular attention is lavished upon social problems caused by the disappearance of "mothers" and "wives," working mainly in the European Union.[8] I encountered many Ukrainians who lament the fact that this migration has devastated the family members and communities that women leave behind. In discussions of public policy, women labor migrants are charged with having caused a rise in the number of "social orphans," tens of thousands of children abandoned by their parents and now living in state children's homes, shelters, or on the street. Labor migration is also widely viewed as contributing to other social problems, such as drug addiction among teenagers and alcoholism and promiscuity among adult men.

Meanwhile, women migrants typically remain in contact with family members, and regularly send home remittances, letters, or, increasingly, e-mails. By the standards of their home communities, they send back substantial sums,[9] but that money is frequently regarded as polluting its recipients, as well as the women migrants themselves. It is not uncommon for their high earnings and prolonged absences to fuel speculation that they are "selling themselves" or "being kept" by men abroad.

Disproportionate attention has been paid to the disappearance of adult women from western Ukraine, yet overall this particular segment of labor migration is gender balanced, with women and men equally likely to migrate in search of temporary work.[10] However, researchers have found significant gender differences in their destinations.[11] Women tend to go west, to the southern tier of the European Union, where they take informal jobs as caretakers for the elderly, sick, and young--in Italy or Spain.[12] By contrast, men migrate from western Ukraine to work either in construction in Russia or else in construction or agriculture in Poland and the Czech Republic. Somewhat less frequently, they might also migrate to the southern tier of the European Union, Portugal in particular.

Women's labor migration is much more common in western Ukraine than in the rest of the country. Generally speaking, labor migration elsewhere in Ukraine remains predominantly a male phenomenon. Men who migrate from eastern Ukraine overwhelmingly seek work in Moscow or other urban centers in Russia. Most lack educational credentials,[13] whereas women from eastern Ukraine are much less likely to engage in temporary labor migration.[14] Those who do leave tend to be well educated.

Among the main reasons driving transnational labor migration is the push caused by poor economic opportunities in migrants' countries of origin, and the pull caused by labor needs in destination countries. Both push and pull factors vary greatly by gender. There is a consensus in the recent studies on the impact of gender in the workforce that women were more likely than men to lose their jobs in response to the post-Soviet closure of state enterprises. During the first decade of Ukraine's independence, the proportion of women among the registered unemployed reached a peak of over 80 percent by 1992, decreasing slowly over the next six years. Since 1998, it has remained stable at just over 60 percent (Hrycak 2001: 135–58). Once women lose their jobs, they are more likely to remain unemployed, or to be offered insecure and poorly paid positions, with their monthly compensation averaging 30 percent less than that of men.[15] While all women face gender discrimination in the Ukrainian labor market, educated women encounter the greatest disparity between their credentials and local employment opportunities. This disparity, as well as a desire for a university degree for their children, might place even greater pressure on professional women to seek work abroad (Hrycak 2007a).

The demand for "cheap" migrant labor is the main factor that pulls migrants to seek employment abroad. An examination of this demand in the European Union helps to explain further why women appear more likely than men to find a need for their services. They are drawn to work in the European Union to address what scholars often call a growing "care deficit," caused by increasing numbers of women in wealthier countries moving into the labor force. This leaves them unable to meet their traditional obligations as caregivers at home, duties that are also mounting in Ukraine as the local population ages.[16]

According to sociologist Laura Agustin, there is a strong demand in the European Union for migrant women in three main areas: cooking, cleaning, and housekeeping in private homes; caring for the sick, the elderly, or the young; and providing sexual services in various locales (Agustin 2007). There is also a demand there for migrant men to work in such areas as construction and agriculture. But unskilled male workers from Poland, and other new members of the European Union, have also migrated west to work in construction and agriculture, and they already dominate this niche (Coyle, 2007:

37–50), leaving men from Ukraine at a disadvantage in competing for these jobs.

Clearly, push and pull factors that motivate migration vary by gender. Consequently, women and men are channeled into different kinds of work, and tend to migrate to different geographic locations. Men continue to find seasonal work in locales that have been longstanding destinations of labor migration from Ukraine. According to 2007 estimates, roughly one to two million Ukrainians, nearly all men, are employed as seasonal laborers in Russia (Haiduts'kyi 2007). They also migrate to work in Poland and the Czech Republic, where there are 100,000 to 200,000 temporary workers from Ukraine. By contrast, other migration streams consist almost exclusively of women, who migrate to Italy and Spain.

New Women's Diasporas

Today as the result of emigration, approximately one quarter of all Ukrainians in the world live outside their homeland. Sizeable Ukrainian diasporas are located in the United States and Canada. Initially, these communities were formed by the arrival of adult males at the end of the nineteenth and beginning of the twentieth centuries. Some settled permanently and arranged for their families to join them.[17] These communities were later expanded by a new wave of transnational migration, consisting of displaced persons and refugees fleeing western Ukraine when it was annexed to the Soviet Union during World War II. Typically, these postwar migrants were families that settled in the older, established communities.

At present, women have taken the lead in founding new Ukrainian diasporas in Italy and Spain, where previously there were relatively few Ukrainians living. A closer look at the new community in Italy illustrates the degree to which this diaspora differs in its sociodemographic makeup from the North American diasporas formed in the past. According to anthropologist Olena Fedyuk, who is conducting a study of labor migrants traveling from Ukraine to Italy: "90 percent of this migration consists of women, with an average age of around forty-five. Of all the migrants, 64.3 percent are married, 90.4 percent have children, and only 5.5 percent have their children with them in. Women who are unable or unwilling to take their children along leave them at home with their fathers, grandparents, relatives, or elder siblings" (2007).

The size of this new "women's diaspora" in Italy is difficult to estimate. The Italian Ministry of Internal Affairs reports that, as of 2006, there were some 117,000 Ukrainians registered in the country. But Fedyuk cites research estimating that there might be as many as 600,000 or 700,000 Ukrainians living there.[18] Most are women from western Ukraine who are working informally as caregivers.

Many labor migrants were employed in skilled positions in their home countries. After the Soviet Union's collapse, numerous state enterprises with a predominantly women's labor force, were closed or privatized in western Ukraine. Consequently, women became more likely than men to lose their jobs, not to mention access to childcare, as well as other benefits. This absence of local employment opportunities for women channeled many of them into petty trade in open-air markets, or into a shuttle trade between their home-towns and nearby countries. Initially, Poland became a popular destination for shuttle traders from western Ukraine. At this time, it required no visa. Numerous western Ukrainians had relatives in Poland whom they had long wished to visit, and because many of them spoke rudimentary Polish there was virtually no language barrier. At first, these women made a relatively good living in cross-border petty trading. In the late 1990s they began to be displaced by larger-scale local trading networks that provided new channels for transporting and selling goods across borders more cheaply. Increasingly, with the rising cost of education, housing, and other basic needs, women petty traders began looking for work abroad, in countries where they had no ties. Many started to migrate to Italy, owing to the ease of legally obtaining a tourist visa through local travel agencies.

These workers are gradually creating a new diaspora, formed largely around their identity as Ukrainian labor migrants. The community's main foundation at present is the Ukrainian Catholic church. Around ninety communities are currently served by Ukrainian Catholic priests, as well as by the services and support provided by Roman Catholic organizations such as Caritas. The community has started to develop regional and local associations as well. These include the Christian Association of Ukrainians in Italy, the Association of Ukrainians in Italy, Ukraine Plus, the Association of Ukrainian Women, and the Association of Ukrainian Women Workers. Community leaders working through these organizations have established newsletters and internet-based communications networks that allow members of the diaspora to keep in touch with each other. They have also started to build ties with municipal authorities, trade unions, and international organizations such as the Red Cross. Indeed, they have even started to work with the International Organization for Migration on the issue of human trafficking.

Labor migrants who settled in Italy appear to have engaged in more extensive community organizing as a distinct "transnational community" or diaspora than those in other common destinations, such as Russia.[19] There could be several reasons for this. Perhaps the most important might be that the migrants in Italy experience a more prolonged, more complex period of displacement. Temporary labor migration might at first glance appear to have similar effects on both men and women, sorting both into low-skilled, menial jobs that are highly stratified by gender. But migration experiences also vary considerably by gender. Men typically stay abroad for short periods, returning home during off seasons. Overall, male migrants also experience greater status consistency at every stage of the migration process. They travel with relative ease to work in locales such as Russia, which have a visa-free regime and are familiar to many in Ukraine. Moreover, they tend to be employed there in jobs that are relatively consistent with their past occupational status. And, most importantly, they have greater opportunities to maintain frequent contact with their families. Male migrants also tend to be viewed as conforming to men's gender roles as breadwinners and those with children are often praised for being good fathers, willing to sacrifice for their offspring.

Women migrants, by contrast, are viewed as deviant. In important respects, the circumstances of their migration cause them to behave in a manner that does not conform to societal expectations of roles that women are meant to play in the family. Most women who migrate from Ukraine to work in Italy have children, and, as already noted, they go abroad to provide for them. Because irregular labor migrants who have overstayed a previous tourist visa can experience difficulty returning to the European Union they remain absent for a year or more at a time. Moreover, in their capacity of caregivers, occupations which know no season, women can no longer act as their family's primary caregivers. They become the family's breadwinner by default, filling a role coded as masculine.

A final and related status discrepancy is the fact that women's migration from Ukraine to destinations in Europe was long taboo. Throughout the Soviet era, Communist Party leaders represented western countries in moralistic terms, as capitalist dens of iniquity where women were routinely forced by poverty to sell themselves.[20] Similar associations have been made in the media. This public discourse has encouraged much speculation about the dissolute life women migrants lead when they seemingly abandon their local domestic roles in order to earn money in foreign households.

Western Government Debates and the Ukrainian Response

What sorts of policies should Western governments, international organizations, the European Union, and the government in Ukraine, promote in order to address the needs of this growing number of undocumented workers? Generally speaking, the governmental response in the European Union toward recent transnational labor migration has been negative. It has generated harsh and punitive laws to restrict labor immigration from the former Soviet Union. According to Marko Bojcun, the European Union has adopted "a policy of exclusion at its borders, and the repatriation of all unregistered migrants apprehended by the authorities inside the member states" (Bojcun 2005).

Although policymakers in the European Union promote policies intended to protect women's rights, they have ignored the problems confronting the majority of women migrants working informally in the European Union. The policies and programs they developed to handle irregular migration have also contributed to reinforcing public perceptions that most women migrants from countries in transition from communism are sex workers.[21] Generally, European Union programs and campaigns have focused exclusively on protecting such "victims" of "transnational trafficking gangs."[22] Campaigns to combat trafficking in women first were launched in the late 1990s. In 1997, Western donors and international agencies identified trafficking in women as a critical area of concern for post-Soviet countries (Johnson 2001: 153–69). At that time, the US government, which was then the largest donor in Ukraine, began programs to encourage domestic NGOs and the Ukrainian government to address conditions that lead to trafficking through legal measures, policy reforms, media campaigns, and pilot programs, or projects to help prevent trafficking and to assist trafficking victims.[23] The European Union, which has now outspent the United States to become the largest donor in Ukraine, has continued this campaign. Today, the European Union considers stemming illegal migration and trafficking top priorities. Like the United States, it also funds antitrafficking programs to implement policies of exclusion and repatriation.

Trafficking prevention programs typically assume that women are leaving Ukraine to work illegally in the European Union mainly because they are unaware of local economic opportunities. The donors contend that the fate of most undocumented labor migrants is trafficking, with many unwittingly falling into the hands of transnational prostitution rings. According to this logic, illegal women's transnational labor migration is best handled by raising public awareness of this state of affairs in both sending and receiving countries, and assisting trafficking victims in a successful return to their countries of origin.

The government of Ukraine has incorporated trafficking prevention into a broad range of state programs for improving the status of women. It has also adopted legislation and special programs on eliminating trafficking. From 25 November to 10 December, annually, beginning in 2001, women's organizations in all regions of the country participate in a global campaign, "Sixteen Days against Gender Violence," during which measures for preventing trafficking are implemented. Public information efforts are carried out, featuring local pop music stars, such as Ruslana, on billboards and in television clips that draw attention to telephone hotlines, and other services aimed at helping to prevent trafficking of women. Stories about the horrors of sex slavery appear in the newspapers, on the radio, and on television. Women's organizations hold public seminars on trafficking. They organize training sessions for representatives of law enforcement, education, and medicine that provide them with strategies for addressing the needs of trafficked victims. These programs do provide potential migrants with basic information, and they also appear to have helped some of the survivors. Simultaneously, however, the problems that ordinary labor migrants face are rarely considered. As a result, the hundreds of thousands of women who go abroad are seen largely through the prism of antitrafficking campaigns (Keryk 2004).

There are numerous women's organizations and women's advocates seeking to raise women's status and protect their rights in Ukraine. However, they lack the funds needed for institutionalizing programs addressing the needs and interests of migrant workers. Western donors now expect women's NGOs in the European Union and Ukraine to enforce the policy of exclusion and repatriation of undocumented workers. Among Western donors, the US government provided most of the early funding devoted to women's issues in Ukraine.[24] For instance, in 1999, Winrock International, a USAID contractor, received roughly $10 million in funding from the US government for projects that focused on trafficking prevention in Ukraine.[25] These projects established several nationwide networks, including Women for Women crisis centers, local women's credit unions, women's business incubators, battered-women's shelters, women's health providers, and hotlines for victims of violence or abuse. Initially, the European Union's Technical Aid to the Commonwealth of Independent States (TACIS) Program played a small role, but its activities have increased now that Ukraine borders the European Union and is being considered for candidacy. TACIS has provided grants to several women's programs that other Western donors initiated to fight trafficking. Through Western funding, a nationwide network of antitrafficking centers has come into existence to provide psychological and job counseling, as well as legal, medical, and other services to help women cope with the collapse of the local economy and related problems such as domestic abuse. These activities might have provided a base for raising public awareness of the issues migrant workers confront, but, except for continued backing of sex trafficking issues, most donor projects were discontinued due to a lack of funding well before they were institutionalized.

The public response in Ukraine toward women involved in transnational labor migration has been complex and contradictory, but largely negative. In important respects it has mirrored the European discourse and the depiction of sex workers promoted among Western governments and Western aid providers. At its core, the discourses through which women migrant workers are discussed continue to draw upon Soviet propaganda about "social parasites," the term the Communist Party used for those individuals, it argued, who chose to reject the Soviet way of life and become involved in prostitution, smuggling, and other illegal black-market activities (Waters 1989).

Generally speaking, discussions of women who go abroad as undocumented laborers make two arguments in Ukraine. According to one prominent version, Ukrainian women who migrate are assumed to go abroad voluntarily to engage in sex work because this is the easiest and quickest way for them to get rich (Hughes 2005). Leonid Kuchma, when he was still president, adopted this same perspective when he referred to Ukrainian women working in Italy as prostitutes "who did not want to work in Ukraine."[26] According to a second version, women who migrate in search of work are said to be going abroad to "sell themselves" because they have been made so desperate by poverty and have no other way to feed their children. In this second variant, it is acknowledged that economic desperation brought about by capitalism is itself a primary motivating factor, rather than an unwillingness to work hard. But again, there is an underlying assumption that many migrant workers are sexual deviants, in other words "bad mothers and loose women." Indeed, the current leader of the Communist Party in Ukraine, Petro Symonenko, blames the government for encouraging women to migrate abroad. He argues that such women are damaging Ukrainian society both by facilitating the spread of alcoholism, drug abuse, and AIDS, and also by abandoning their true role—that of bearing and raising healthy children. Both versions scapegoat migrant woman, blaming them for triggering a collapse of morality that brings with it a host of social ills, formerly associated with capitalism in the Soviet Union.

It is undeniable that some migrants who cross borders illegally, with the assistance of smugglers, fall into the hands of sex trafficking rings and are coerced into prostitution.[27] However, Western antitrafficking projects greatly exaggerate the magnitude of the problem in Ukraine.[28] They have fueled sensationalist claims in the Western press, and later, among human rights groups, that trafficking is responsible for the disappearance of 400,000 women. Were this estimate accurate, then *all* of the women from Ukraine who migrated abroad to look for work in the 1990s must have been trapped into involuntary sex work.

In response to concerns raised about the fate of Ukrainian migrant workers, the parliamentary ombudsman for human rights conducted an investigation on this issue. It concluded that Ukrainian workers in Italy, and elsewhere in the European Union, labor as caregivers, cleaners, or domestics.[29] Similarly, studies of temporary labor migration find that most Ukrainian labor migrants in the European Union are middle-aged women who go abroad voluntarily because they lack economic opportunities at home and can find better-paid work as caregivers abroad (west Ukrainian 2002). But the representations that dominate government, mass media, and public responses tend to brand them as "fallen women," a misrepresentation that creates major problems for migrant women when they attempt to return to their communities.

Conclusion

Women frame their decision to leave their children for work abroad mainly through a discourse of maternal suffering and self-sacrifice.[30] Unable to provide the children with educational opportunities on their meager salaries, women, many of whom are educated, seek temporary work as caregivers in more affluent countries in the European Union. By performing care work in foreign households, migrant women not only contribute to their host country's economy, they also add considerably to their home country's economy.

Since independence, these migrant workers have formed significant communities outside Ukraine's national borders. Those within the European Union have grown considerably, mainly in response to migration from western Ukraine. These new diasporas are likely to continue growing, as the trends that lead to a care deficit in European Union countries continue. As long as employment opportunities abroad remain superior to those in Ukraine, it is likely that women will continue to seek work in the wealthier EU countries. I have suggested that the sex trafficking frame through which these women have been perceived is shared both by Western policymakers and the Ukrainian state. The effect of this is a further marginalization of the women working abroad. Furthermore, this same framing tends to make their return home difficult. The misrepresentation of these women as sex workers is likely to continue having unfortunate resonance at home, as it plays on anxieties regarding "normal" as opposed to "deviant" gender roles. Programs to protect women's rights should develop frames that do not threaten to stigmatize them. The women's projects, funded mainly to fight trafficking, also need to be encouraged to broaden their scope by addressing the needs of the hundreds of thousands of migrating women in search of work, to view them as disenfranchised by an increasingly globalized economy and in need of public advocates.

Notes

This essay is based on nine months of ethnographic fieldwork and interviews conducted 2001–2008 with advocates of women's rights in Kyiv, L'viv, and Kharkiv through the financial support of the International Research and Exchanges Board and Reed College. I thank the many people who generously helped me to conduct my research. In particular, I wish to thank the representatives of the state agencies and women's organizations in Ukraine that agreed to be interviewed for this study.

1. For additional information on migration to and from Ukraine, see Dietz, 2007.
2. Marta is a real individual. To protect her identity, I have altered a few details in her story and adopted a pseudonym.

3. West Ukrainian Center "Women's Perspectives" and Winrock International. *Ukrainian Women Labor Migrants* (L'viv: 2002).

4. Ibid.

5. Ibid.

6. Many labor migrants who originate in Russia and other former Soviet republics, as well as in Africa, the Middle East, and Asia, have also passed through Ukraine on their way to Western destinations. The International Organization of Migration estimated that there were 1.6 million such transit migrants in Ukraine in 2000. They are beyond the scope of this paper. For a discussion of transit immigrants, see Paweł Kaczmarczyk and Marek Okólski, *International Migration in Central and Eastern Europe—Current and Future Trends* (New York: United Nations Expert Group Meeting on International Migration and Development Population Division, Department of Economic and Social Affairs, United Nations Secretariat, 2005).

7. For an overview of debates on the number of temporary migrants, see Kerstin Zimmer, *Time of the Migrants,* in Transitions Online 18 January 2007. http://search.ebscohost .com/login.aspx?direct=true&db=aph&AN=23798729&site=ehost-live. For a discussion of migration from Ukraine to the European Union, see Dietz, *Migration Policy Challenges at the New Eastern Borders of the Enlarged European Union: The Ukrainian Case.*

8. For a discussion of the reasons why western Ukrainian women are more likely to go abroad than women from other regions of the country, see p. 58 in Nora Dudwick, Radhika Srinivasan, and Jeanine Braithwaite, *Ukraine Gender Review* (Washington, DC: World Bank Social Development Unit, Europe and Central Asia Region, 2002). Throughout my research, I was frequently made aware of depopulated villages in western Ukraine, the working-age residents of which had gone abroad, leaving behind the aged and very young.

9. It is difficult to verify such reports, but one such migrant informed me in 1998 that, in one year, she earned $36,000 working as an in-home caregiver to an elderly woman. By contrast, at her job in a Ukrainian theater as an actress, she earned roughly $50 per month.

10. On the gender composition of western and central Ukrainian migration streams, see Zimmer, *Time of the Migrants.* An anthropologist who studied migration from a southwestern town in Ukraine observed no significant gender differences: "The collapse of the Soviet system has triggered the disintegration of the political, economic, and physical infrastructure, as well as the concomitant departure of almost all those able to obtain visas to emigrate." See Blank 2004: 349.

11. For a discussion of the backgrounds and migration histories of Ukrainian female migrant workers in Italy see: West Ukrainian Center, "Women's Perspectives." For a general discussion of their backgrounds and migration trajectories, see also Helma Lutz, *Landscapes of Care Drain: Care Provisions and Care Chains from the Ukraine to Poland, from Poland to Germany* (Cork, Ireland: University College, 2005). Accessed 7 July 2007. http://www.ucc.ie/en/DepartmentsCentresandUnits/Sociology/ DepartmentResearchProjects/DocumentFile,33211,en.doc.

12. For an overview of the destinations of women labor migrants, see Ukrainian Parliament Commissioner for Human Rights, *Special Report of the Ukrainian Parliament Commissioner for Human Rights on the Status of Observance and Protection of the*

Rights of Ukrainian Citizens Abroad (Ombudsman, n.d.) Accessed 5 July 2007. http://www.ombudsman.kiev.ua/S_Report1/zm.htm.

13. For an overview of Ukrainian migrant workers in Russia, see Hormel and Southworth 2006: 603–23. See also "Russia," Ukrainian Parliament Commissioner for Human Rights, *Special Report of the Ukrainian Parliament Commissioner for Human Rights on the Status of Observance and Protection of the Rights of Ukrainian Citizens Abroad.*

14. I base my description of transnational labor migration from eastern Ukraine upon a study of a medium-sized eastern Ukrainian town. This sociological study, conducted in 2002, found that the majority of temporary labor migrants were men who travel to Russia or other parts of the former Soviet Union. For further details, see Hormel and Southworth 2006.

15. For an analysis of the gender dynamics of the labor market in Ukraine, see United Nations Development Program, *Gender Issues in Ukraine: Challenges and Opportunities* (Kyiv: UNDP, 2003).

16. For a discussion of the migration of women from poor countries to address the care deficit caused by higher employment rates among women in wealthy countries, see Ehrenreich and Hochschild 2003.

17. There have been four major waves of migration from eastern Europe to the west. For an overview of the sociodemographic profile of these four waves, and a discussion of the shifting role Ukrainian women played in migrant communities outside their homeland, see Hrycak 2004.

18. Other sources suggest that there are only around 200,000 labor migrants from Ukraine in Italy. See Dietz, *Migration Policy Challenges at the New Eastern Borders of the Enlarged European Union: The Ukrainian Case.*

19. I base this statement not only upon my research, but also upon my experience with transnational networks of Ukrainian studies scholars, with whom I have regularly been in contact as vice president, and then president of the American Association for Ukrainian Studies, which is affiliated with similar organizations in Russia, Poland, Italy, and other countries with a sizeable Ukrainian population.

20. My characterization of communist propaganda regarding women "selling themselves" in the west derives from the frequent references to this phrase that I heard throughout the course of my fieldwork. For a further discussion of the official Soviet representation of sexuality, gender, and prostitution, see Waters 1989: 3–19.

21. On the case of stereotypes of Ukrainian women in Italy, see Keryk 2004.

22. For an analysis of the tendency to focus exclusively on sex workers, see Agustin 2003: 377–96.

23. For an overview of US policy toward trafficking of women from countries in transition from communism, see IREX (International Research and Exchanges Board), *Putting an End to the Trafficking of Women in the NIS and CEE.* 1 December 2000. http://www.irex.org/publications-resources/policypapers/trafficking_women.pdf.

24. I base this statement on my research and on the results of a 2001 survey of all registered women's organizations. See Sydorenko n.d., table 8.

25. In 1999 the US government awarded "Community Responses to Domestic Violence and Trafficking," the first of three grants that would total over US$3 million. The project trained several local NGOs in Ukraine (as well as Moldova, Armenia, and Uzbekistan) to conduct lobbying, advocacy, and public awareness campaigns. Local women's NGOs

formed an advisory board, comprised of community representatives, to strengthen the coordination of local efforts for the prevention of domestic violence and trafficking. These local women's NGOs also conducted advocacy initiatives to increase the level of awareness of policymakers in local and national government about domestic violence and trafficking in humans through public hearings in city councils and national parliaments on human rights, gender-based violence, and government response to crimes against women. In addition, USAID awarded Winrock $4.3 million between 1998 and 2004 to operate a project called the Anti-Trafficking Program. This project created trafficking prevention centers in seven Ukrainian cities (L'viv, Dnipropetrovs'k, and Donetsk in 1998; Zhytomyr, Kherson, Chernivtsy, and Rivne in 2001). These centers provided services to assist women who were experiencing domestic violence or lacked economic alternatives, and, as a result, were viewed as vulnerable to trafficking. Each of these centers was based in a partnership between Winrock and a local NGO. See Winrock International, http://www.winrock.org/.

26. For a survey of the furor Kuchma's comment evoked in Ukraine, see Keryk 2004. Agustin (2003) argues that the general phenomenon of sex trafficking can be seen as a moral panic that draws attention away from real issues involving female labor migrants.

27. For an analysis and review of trafficking of Ukrainian women, see Hughes and Denisova 2001: 43–67.

28. It appears that the figure claiming that 400,000 Ukrainian women have been trafficked into prostitution can be traced back to an article written by Irina Sandul: "East European Women Trapped in Sex Slavery," *Washington Times* (11 March 2001), where the author appeared to have mistaken state statistics on the overall number of women who have migrated abroad for the official Ukrainian figure on how many women were trafficked. This figure later came to be seen as a fact. For a report on trafficking that cites this sensationalistic article as if it were fact, see: *A Human Rights Report on Trafficking in Persons, Especially Women and Children: Ukraine.* The Protection Project. Accessed 10 July 2007. http://sos.vrm.lt:81/files/Ukraine.pdf. Similarly, see the National Organization for Women, Northern Virginia chapter's statement on sexual slavery: http://www.dullesnow.org/slavery.html.

29. Greece was the one destination in the European Union where Ukrainian women were found by the parliamentary study to be at the greatest risk of being trafficked into commercial sex work. The other destinations are countries that are not members of the European Union—Croatia, Bosnia and Herzegovina, Turkey, and Japan, but their overall numbers were small, making it inconceivable that hundreds of thousands of Ukrainian women could be involved. In 2002, at the time of the study, there were an estimated three thousand illegal migrants from Ukraine in Greece, while in Turkey, the overall number of Ukrainians was two thousand; most were believed to be working illegally. Ukrainian Parliament Commissioner for Human Rights, *Special Report of the Ukrainian Parliament Commissioner for Human Rights on the Status of Observance and Protection of the Rights of Ukrainian Citizens Abroad.*

30. For an illustration of one such narrative see Fedyuk n.d.

Bibliography

A Human Rights Report on Trafficking in Persons, Especially Women and Children: Ukraine. The Protection Project, March 2002. http://sos.vrm.lt:81/files/Ukraine.pdf. Accessed 10 July 2007.

Agustin, Laura. 2003. "A Migrant World of Services." *Social Politics* 10 (3): 377–96.

Agustin, Laura Maria. 2007. *Sex at the Margins: Migration, Labour Markets and the Rescue Industry.* London: Zed Books.

Blank, Diana R. 2004. "Fairytale Cynicism in the 'Kingdom of Plastic Bags': The Powerlessness of Place in a Ukrainian Border Town." *Ethnography* 9 (5): 349–78.

Bojcun, Marko. 2005. "The European Union's Perspectives on the Ukrainian-Russian Border." *Eurozine.* http://www.eurozine.com/articles/2005–01–12-bojcun-en.html. Accessed 5 July 2007.

Coyle, Angela. 2007. "Resistance, Regulation and Rights: The Changing Status of Polish Women's Migration and Work in the "New" Europe." *European Journal of Women's Studies* 14 (1): 37–50.

Dietz, Barbara. 2007. *Migration Policy Challenges at the New Eastern Borders of the Enlarged European Union: The Ukrainian Case.* Munich: Osteuropa-Institut.

Dudwick, Nora, Radhika Srinivasan, and Jeanine Braithwaite. 2002. *Ukraine Gender Review.* Washington, DC: World Bank Social Development Unit, Europe and Central Asia Region.

Ehrenreich, Barbara, and Arlie Russell Hochschild, eds. 2003. *Global Woman: Nannies, Maids, and Sex Workers in the New Economy.* New York: Metropolitan Books.

Fedyuk, Olena. n.d. "Halyna, A Ukrainian Mother Abroad, Work is Elsewhere." http://www.plotki.net/wie/cms/article/23/portrait-15. Accessed 5 July 2007.

Haiduts'kyi, Andrii. "Mihratsiinyi kapital v Ukraini: Prykhovana real'nist'." *Dzerkalo Tyzhnia.* http://www.dt.ua/2000/2020/56473/. Accessed 10 July 2007.

Hormel, Leontina, and Caleb Southworth. 2006. "Eastward Bound: A Case Study of Post-Soviet Labour Migration from a Rural Ukrainian Town." *Europe-Asia Studies* 58 (4): 603–23.

Hrycak, Alexandra. 2001. "The Dilemmas of Civic Revival: Ukrainian Women since Independence." *Journal of Ukrainian Studies* 26 (1–2): 135–58.

———. 2004. "Keynote Address: Changing Forms of Community: Eastern European Women at Home and Abroad." *Symposium on Canadian Society's Integration of Women from Eastern European Cultures.* Edmonton, AB.

———. 2005. "Coping with Chaos: Gender and Politics in a Fragmented State." *Problems of Post-Communism* 52 (5): 69–81.

———. 2006. "Foundation Feminism and the Articulation of Hybrid Feminisms in Post-Socialist Ukraine." *East European Politics and Societies* 20 (1): 69–100.

———. 2007a. "Gender and the Orange Revolution." *Journal of Communist Studies & Transition Politics* 23 (1): 152–79.

———. 2007b. "Seeing Orange: Women's Activism and Ukraine's Orange Revolution." *Women's Studies Quarterly* 35 (3/4): 208–25.

———. 2007c. "From Global to Local Feminisms: Transnationalism, Foreign Aid and the Women's Movement in Ukraine." *Advances in Gender Research* 11: 75–94.

Hughes, Donna M. 2005. "Combating Sex Trafficking: Advancing Freedom for Women and Girls, Keynote Address." Paper presented at the Northeast Women's Studies Association Annual Conference, University of Massachusetts, Dartmouth. (5 March).

Hughes, Donna M., and Tatyana A. Denisova. 2001. "The Transnational Political Criminal Nexus of Trafficking in Women from Ukraine." *Trends in Organized Crime* 6 (3/4): 43–67.

IREX (International Research and Exchanges Board). 2000. "Putting an End to the Trafficking of Women in the NIS and CEE." http://www.irex.org/publications-resources/policy-papers/trafficking_women.pdf. Accessed 1 December 2000.

Johnson, Janet Elise. 2001. "Privatizing Pain: The Problem of Woman Battery in Russia." *NWSA Journal* 13 (3): 153–69.

Kaczmarczyk, Paweł, and Marek Okólski. 2005. *International Migration in Central and Eastern Europe—Current and Future Trends.* New York: United Nations Expert Group Meeting on International Migration and Development Population Division, Department of Economic and Social Affairs, United Nations Secretariat.

Keryk, Myroslava. 2004. "Labour Migrant: Our Savior or Betrayer? Ukrainian Discussions Concerning Labour Migration." *Migration Online.* http://www.migrationonline.cz. Accessed 13 July 2007.

Lutz, Helma. 2005. "Landscapes of Care Drain: Care Provisions and Care Chains from the Ukraine to Poland, from Poland to Germany." University College Cork, Ireland. http://www.ucc.ie/en/DepartmentsCentresandUnits/Sociology/Department ResearchProjects/DocumentFile,33211.en.doc. Accessed 7 July 2007.

Shamshur, Oleg, and Olena Malinovska. 1994. "Ukrainian Migration in Transition." *Innovation: The European Journal of Social Sciences* 7 (2): 165–75.

Sydorenko, Oleksandr. "Zhinochi orhanizatsii Ukrainy: Tendentsii stanovlennia." Kyiv: Center for Innovation and Development, n.d. Available at http://portal.uwf.kiev.ua/.

United Nations Development Program. 2003. *Gender Issues in Ukraine: Challenges and Opportunities.* Kyiv: UNDP.

Waters, Elizabeth. 1989. "Restructuring the 'Woman Question': Perestroika and Prostitution." *Feminist Review* 33: 3–19.

Zimmer, Kerstin. 2007. "Time of the Migrants." *Transitions Online.* 23 January.

CHAPTER 4

Prove It to Me

The Life of a Jewish Social Activist in Ukraine

Sarah D. Phillips

I first met Faina Iakivna Neiman in September 1999, when I was conducting research in Kyiv for my dissertation in cultural anthropology on women leaders of nongovernmental organizations in post-Soviet Ukraine.[1] Over the next six years, I developed a deep friendship with Faina, a role model for whom I feel a great deal of affection and respect. I conducted a series of life history interviews with her between 1999 and 2005, always in the office of her organization, "For Survival." Without fail, I came away from our conversations inspired

Figure 4.1 Faina Neiman, Kyiv, 2005.

by Faina's work ethic, boundless energy, sense of humor, self-confidence, openness, and commitment to serving others. She switched effortlessly between Russian and Ukrainian in her narratives, but here I have rendered all spellings in Ukrainian, for the sake of consistency. What follows is Faina's account (a word she used frequently) of her own life, in her own words, a fitting tribute to a woman who enriched the lives of so many, and leaves behind a lovely legacy. Her life story speaks to the Jewish experience in Ukraine, the role of women in Ukrainian politics and civil society, and the problems of old age in a transitional society. Of course, every life story is different, and no one person's experience is representative of an entire generation, gender, class, religious, or ethnic group. Faina's rendering of her life story reveals how her evaluations of self and society have been shaped by a range of dynamic interactions and positionings, including interpersonal relationships and the institutional structures that have governed her life.

Early Life History

I was not born in Kyiv—I was born in Zhytomyrs'ka oblast', in a village called Dzerzhyns'k, in Dzerzhyns'kyi *raion*. Now the village is called by its prerevolutionary name, Romanov. It's in what used to be the Pale of Settlement. All my relatives on my mother's side died during the war. Once I gave a lecture and I passed around a photograph of my grandparents. Grandpa was wearing a peaked cap, and he had a big beard. Grandma had a scarf on her head—not in a triangle like they wear now, but a big square one like they had back then, tied on her head and hanging down her back. I asked the audience, "How old would you guess they are?" They answered, "Sixty, seventy." I passed around another photograph of a handsome young man with dark, curly hair, and a woman—she had the same sort of dark, curly hair, very pretty. In the picture with them were the two old folks. I told them, "The young couple went first to register their marriage, and then to the parents' house." The audience figured out that the old couple must be only about forty-five or forty-seven years old. Then I told them the story—the young couple was my parents, who got married and visited my mother's parents for their blessing.

This all happened in 1937, the same year I was born. My mother was twenty-three going on twenty-four, and shortly after she got pregnant, my father was taken. Mother was left alone with me. My father never came back. He was very large, with a *chèvelúre* of big curls. They say that in the camps, the strong ones died first. But we never found anything out, never learned how father died. For a long time my mother walked around, holding her pregnant belly, asking, "Where's my husband?" Once a woman from India asked me, "Faina, when have you felt most protected in your life?" "Probably when my mother walked around with her hand on her belly—since then I don't remember feeling protected." My mother was a teacher, but she was investigated immediately as the wife of an enemy of the people. He was imprisoned, after all.

My grandpa was pious, a very religious person. They had four children at home—my mother was the only girl. And when the war broke out, everyone started escaping. In our town there was no railroad, so people escaped however they could—in a cart, on foot. Of course not everyone escaped right away. My mother and I left—well, if you can call it leaving, since we "left" for three whole years, walking, and my mother had to carry me a lot. I was three years old when the war started. My grandpa and grandma came to see us off. Grandpa said he wasn't going anywhere, so of course grandma didn't either. He was religious, everyone in the town knew him, he had never offended anyone—so why would he leave? He said he had nothing to fear, so he and grandma stayed behind.

You've heard about Babyn Yar, and there were many such histories in Ukraine—I could tell you a lot more.[2] My grandparents were shot, along with eight hundred other Jews in the village, and buried in a pit they had been forced to dig themselves. I sometimes call it a grave, but it wasn't a proper grave—just a big hole in the ground where eight hundred people lay. Later the director of the school in Dzerzhyns'k wrote a book about the village during the war. He said that before the war, 82 percent of the village was Jewish, but after the war Jews made up less than 1 percent of the village.

One of my mother's three brothers had died before the war. Another was in the military before the war started, and he was sent to the front. Mother's other brother, the eldest, was born in 1906—at the beginning of the war, he was thirty-five years old. You can imagine what it meant to be the eldest. He worked in Moscow in a factory where they made machines for agriculture. When the Germans started moving closer to Moscow, the machines were moved to Siberia, and the workers, including my uncle, were sent and left there in the steppe to build a new factory. Now that place is in Oms'k, but back then it was on the outskirts of Oms'k. When mama and I left Ukraine, we ended up across the Volga, in the Urals. We found mother's eldest brother outside Oms'k, and decided to stay there, too. There were seven years' difference between mother and my uncle, and he helped support her a bit, because she was with me and without a husband. So we stayed there during the war, and when the war ended, we returned here to Ukraine. But my uncle wasn't allowed to return to Moscow. He was obliged either to give up his apartment there or to relinquish his party membership, which would have meant he'd be jailed and killed.

After the war, mother and I got an invitation to return to our village, and we gladly did so. I started school a year late. I remember how we kids went hungry after the war, and we scrounged around for food to eat. We didn't get enough nutrients and sometimes ended up eating the whitewash off the walls. I recall walking through the forest with mother, and stumbling upon the bones of the Jews who had been shot. Foxes had dug holes in the big pit and eaten the remains, and they left the bones strewn throughout the woods. We walked through the forest, and my mother would point them out: There's a leg, there's a finger. I couldn't help but wonder whether the scattered bones of my grand-parents were right there under our feet.

But there were some people in the village that helped the Jews, and we always remembered them fondly. Once on television I talked about a woman who took care of a small, dark, Jewish baby whose mother was shot. The woman was Polish, and she told the Germans that her fifteen-year-old daughter had gotten herself into trouble and it was her baby. Thanks to that program, those people were reunited—the Polish woman was already dead, but they found her daughter, and the "dark little baby," a grown woman who now lives in Israel.

My mother knew a lot of discrimination as a Jew. She had two children—I was in school when we came back to Ukraine, and my little sister was eleven years younger. I was born before the war, and she came after. When I was in fourth grade, we moved from the village to Kyiv, but they sent mama to a vil-lage outside of Kyiv to work. She didn't know what to do, with two little daugh-ters in the city. And they wouldn't give her work in Kyiv: "There is work there in the village, so that's where you'll go." Mama didn't have money to travel every day, so she stayed in the village the whole week, in order to come back here to Kyiv with at least some earnings.

I finished a Ukrainian-language school here in Ukraine. Then after the tenth grade, I tried to get into Polytechnical University, but I wasn't admitted because of my nationality.[3] They gave me a low grade, but refused to show me my work with an explanation of the grading. They had a quota—8 percent Jews could be admitted to the Polytechnic, and no more. So in order to make the quota, some paid for a spot, or got in through their connections. As for the rest of us, they couldn't stop us from taking the entrance exam, but we weren't going to make it no matter how well we did on it. So you take the exam, turn it in. He is thinking to himself, "Why are you trying? You won't get it." You answer the questions very well, and get everything right, but he just gives you a "2" [a "D"] and says, "You answered it poorly." There have been many such instances in my life.

So when I didn't get into the Polytechnic, I left for Oms'k again, to live with my uncle and enter the technical school, with a specialty in textile manu-facturing. It was a hard life, and my uncle helped mama at least a little bit by taking one extra mouth away from home so things would be easier for her. He and all his family are buried in Oms'k, may they rest in peace. I wanted to be a sewing engineer. So I became a seamstress, and first I was sent to the Urals to work, where there was a lot of radiation, although it was not publicized. Back then they didn't say out loud what radiation was, but all of the rocket factories and uranium mines are in the Urals, and all the secret, underground factories. There were accidents there, but they were always covered up.[4] And when they said they would close the Urals for exit because of the radiation, I left for Ukraine and returned home. Since then I have stayed here. I always felt that, as far as my work assignments went, I was given second-rate ones because of my being Jewish.

During that lecture, after I showed the photographs, I told everyone that now (pauses, begins to weep) I am older than my grandpa and grandma were when they were shot. I'm the eldest in my family now. I never married; I never had my own family. After my father died, my mother married again, and they had another daughter. No one else is left, just my sister and I. I think this has a lot to do with my becoming a leader. My whole life I was helping people; for some reason it has come naturally to me.

Earlier I worked in a kiosk outside the "Bolshevik" factory here in Kyiv. I was the trade union representative. Some items went missing, and they tried to arrest one of my colleagues, but I knew she hadn't done it. I didn't go along with it. I suffered for that, because the higher-ups reprimanded me: "You have to get your workers together, and declare her guilt so she can be arrested." But I couldn't do that. After that incident, I decided to continue my education so I could gracefully leave that position and stop doing that "social work." When I entered the university, I just told them, "I can't study and be the trade union representative, because I have evening classes."

I also worked in Irpin' as a floor manager in a textile factory.[5] We worked until 12 o'clock at night, actually until 12:30. Then I had to run to catch the commuter train (*elektrychka*) in Irpin' to travel back home to Kyiv, and I got home at 1:30 in the morning. We had only one day off, not two like they have now. I had just turned thirty. I was in charge of young workers, girls of seventeen or eighteen, and oftentimes I had to talk with their parents, to help keep the girls in line. Nobody taught me how to do it, but all the same there were many cases when I had to intervene in the workers' personal lives, and help them when they got into trouble. Maybe being in the Komsomol [the Communist Youth League] prepared me for it, or maybe it was just intuition. Later I went to work in the metro [the subway system], where I was director of the planning department connected with labor and salary. I had a lot of responsibility.

You know, I have not been dependent on anyone all my life, so maybe that's how I got where I am today. But I have seen both good and bad. When the border was closed, for example, I practically didn't travel abroad. I think I was denied exit because I am Jewish. Those who had connections, or had more money, were allowed to travel, but Jews were forbidden to travel in any case. It wasn't just that we were forbidden to leave—to emigrate—we were forbidden to travel. I wasn't planning to emigrate. I was born here. My parents were here, and my grandfather. I was born here, I retired here. So I'm entitled to complain if I think something is not right. But what if I leave for another country—will I say that something is not right there? I didn't put anything into that country that would entitle me to say something negative. Here I know the language—Russian—and I know the national, Ukrainian, language irreproachably well. I can speak some Yiddish, too. If I went somewhere else, I wouldn't know the language. Where would I start? It would be nice to go for a visit, to look around, for example, but anything more—no. But I wasn't allowed to travel like others did; they were able to learn about different places and see things; I couldn't.

If we look at the positive side—people in the Soviet Union were more learned, all the same. They wore us out—we read a lot—we were assigned entire reading lists. There were stronger professionals during Soviet times. But a person who was discriminated against for belonging to a different nationality had to really work themselves to the bone in order to keep up and survive. I'm the sort of person who tries not to get offended, but don't doubt that I've had many unpleasant experiences because of my background. There was one incident—maybe there was more to it, but I always associated it with my being Jewish. After I began working at the metro, I decided to continue my education, in the economics department at Shevchenko University. I had already worked for years, and everyone knew that I worked as a norm setter (*nomirovshchik*). And norm setting was one of the subjects we were studying. Everyone else in the class came to me for help, because of my work experience and my knowledge of the subject. We went to an "Olympiad" [competition] in Moscow, and then we took our exams in Kharkiv. Regardless of our age, we were all trembling and worried. Finally the instructor came out to give us our grades. I was first, but I wasn't nervous—no matter what grade I received, I knew that I knew the material. He gave me a "3" [a "C"]. What was I supposed to say? I didn't say anything. A few of those who had asked me for help were given "5s" ["As"]. As I left the room, I told the others my score, but didn't say anything else. And later they went to that instructor; they spoke with him, and he changed my score to a "4" [a "B"]. What do you think, why did that happen? Because I'm a woman? Or because I'm Jewish? Those who had studied with me were uncomfortable in front of me, because they received a better score than I did. And my knowledge was higher than theirs. I'm sure that incident was "nationalistic." There were others. But I found less of that, less nationalism, in Siberia. Maybe here the population is bigger and discrimination is more developed, ever since the tsar's times. When the government wants to hold on to power, what does it do? It poisons one nation, then another, forcing people to sit there and take it, peacefully. There have been many injustices here based on nationality. Sarah, don't touch my sore spot. There's a lot.

Early Years of Social Activism: Founding a Jewish Organization

Starting in 1988, when they allowed us to found civic organizations as the collapse of the Soviet Union was getting close, I got in on it. I wrote a letter saying I wanted to take part. At that time several Jewish leaders jumped at the chance and got together to establish a Jewish organization. I wanted to be involved there and in the Jewish choir, and I had already started my activities helping the elderly. When I joined the choir, I didn't know the Jewish language well enough, and my mother and father were both dead by then.[6] There was no one to ask, and when my parents were still around, they didn't teach me much. My mother always said, "Don't speak it. You might slip up and speak it and you'll get kicked out of school. Don't speak it." And later, when I wanted to learn more, there was no one to ask. Our plan was to travel to small towns and villages and collect songs. In those places, elderly people have preserved the old traditions and songs better. People there were always poorer, but they were merrier. When you read Sholom Aleichem, you see how merry they were. So I joined the choir and became a leader there, too. And it wasn't too long before we organized a holiday. That was probably the first time that Jews got together to celebrate. But soon problems began, and I could see that things were getting off track.

First, they began to send rabbis here from America. American rabbis. And with the help of some misguided local Jews, our local rabbi was ousted. Our rabbi had a higher education; he studied in Budapest, which was very unique. But everyone around him wanted to get in on the action, and he was ousted. At first I got along okay with the new rabbi, but it bothered me how he began to distinguish very sharply between what was "Jewish" and what was "not Jewish." And you have to understand our elderly Jews, they have lived in houses, in basements, and communal apartments, mixed together with people of all nationalities. If you bring a Jewish woman something, but don't give it to her Ukrainian neighbor as well, the Ukrainian will "peck" at her. They've lived together all their lives—how can you offer something to one and not the other? Often I would stop by the rabbi's to show him food baskets we were preparing to give out, and he'd say, "Faina, that isn't kosher." I'd say, "No problem. Let's leave that out, and you give me something kosher and I'll replace the nonkosher one." I did that to get on his nerves. The Austrians sent us food baskets that you wouldn't believe. But I brought them to show the rabbi first. There were sausages of the highest quality, and coffee and candies. They thought of everything. But the rabbi was unhappy because the sausage was not kosher. If he couldn't help someone, he'd send them to me: "Go to Faina." He counted on my goodwill.

Second, I didn't like how women were treated. You know how for Muslims, only a man can be the master, and women are always second. It's the same with Jews: the men pray downstairs, and the women pray separately, in the balcony or in the back rows. And many of them also looked askance at the elderly. At one of our celebrations, I designated a couple of tables for the elderly people. I was fifty by then, and that's already aged. Our space was very small, which meant that concerts came off well. Everyone wanted to invite their friends, but we had no extra seats. "Why did you invite these 'outsiders,' these old people?" they asked me. Those Jews were referring to the elderly Jews, the ones who had fought in the war. I got tired of the bad will they had towards the elderly Jews. I was also criticized for some of the things I did, and they pushed me aside pretty quickly. So I left that organization completely, and focused my work on the problems of the elderly.

In the beginning, I was focused on elderly Jews, but I quickly realized that I shouldn't limit my scope, because Jews and other groups have always worked together here, side by side. In 1990, for example, we conducted an evening where we had Muslims, Germans, Ukrainians, and Jews.[7] The Germans had mostly married other Germans, and they told us how their mothers had taught them: "Don't stick your necks out," because they were under suspicion after the war. And the Muslims told stories, too—they were exiled as traitors after the war. So we all had something in common, as peoples who had been victimized. And I began to think about how we've always worked together, vacationed together, and lived as neighbors. I realized that something should change, and since those celebrations went so well, we quickly shifted to a more international profile. So the theme of old age remained, but we didn't work any longer on a strictly national basis.

Remembering this makes me laugh: once I received a letter, from someone in power. Actually, I can't remember, maybe it was from someone like Mariia Orlyk, or Mariia Drach, or Atena Pashko, Chornovil's wife.[8] The letter was addressed to the "Jewish organization." I told them, "Show me where it's written in my charter that we are a 'Jewish organization.'" I am a Jew, but the organization isn't registered as "Jewish." Sometimes people assume that; their prejudices show through. We don't have those sorts of conflicts now, but they were common in the beginning.

The Organization "For Survival," and Problems of Old Age

I founded the organization For Survival in a kind of roundabout way. There's a saying, "I started making soup, but I ended up with something else." Everyone has moments like that. All my life, I took an active position—in school and in my work life. It feels like I have been a leader all my life, beginning with kindergarten and continuing from there. I am indefatigable. And I don't often give into others' opinions, if they contradict my personal position. It has always been difficult for me to "swim over" to someone else's side. I always say, "Prove it to me, and I'll go your way. Otherwise, I'm sticking to my own convictions." That leads me to remember my student days, here at Shevchenko University, where I was continuing my education. This was my second higher degree, and I was over forty years old. I remember one teacher of mathematics. You know what evening courses are like—people come there already tired, they all listen and everyone's thinking, "Oh, the faster the better, so I can get out of here early." But I wasn't like that; I always wanted to understand the material completely. The teacher would write and write on the board, and then turn around, "Are there any questions? No? Then on to the next one. …" He went through the material quickly and everyone was thinking, "I want to get home quickly, I want to sleep. …" I remember one incident when the teacher wanted to erase something and continue writing, and I said, "No! Wait a minute." He gave me a surprised look. I said, "Leave it, please, I don't understand." The others began to grumble; they were all middle-aged like me. I turned around: "Who understands? Go up there and explain it to me. Who understands?" I've never been afraid to speak out in a crowd. The teacher was unhappy, too. He was tired, and he also needed to get home. But he explained the problem further. I need a lot of proof. Prove it, and I will accept it.

You also have to consider the fact that I was active in the Pioneers, the Komsomol, and the Communist Party. Social organizations as such didn't exist—social organizations included the Komsomol, the Pioneers, and the Party. I was a member of an organization called the Book Lovers' Club, though. We would read books in common, and then meet at somebody's home, to discuss the works and the writers, and trade books with other members. But it wasn't even close to being a real social organization. Clubs like this were usually under the control of the party. The government didn't recognize any other social organizations. They didn't exist. And there was only one party. How could there be another party? They would throw you in jail. One Pioneer organization; one Komsomol; one party. That's it, nothing more. And I was in all of them. Recently I have been recalling things people have said to me over the years. "If you had been more accommodating, you would have gone very high." But that didn't work for me, bending to the will of others. I always had my own opinion. Because of that and the fact that I'm Jewish—my data—I didn't rise high in the party ranks.

While I was working, I was a member of the party, and therefore it was my burden, you could say, to conduct political propaganda work (*politinformatsiyi*) and political circles. Sometimes today I am embarrassed about my party activism—I read Soviet newspapers, and I carried the Soviet reality. It was a false reality, as I have learned. The Soviet regime arrested so many in 1937, and then put all my age mates in jail in the 1960s. They tried to convince us that these people were traitors, enemies of the people. But they weren't traitors. They just disagreed with what those in power were saying.

Today, as a person, I am interested in politics. I read the newspapers from cover to cover, and I conduct my own analysis. This wasn't true earlier. I don't read between the lines, exactly, but I compare different points of view and draw my own conclusions. Earlier all of us were forced to subscribe to three or four newspapers. "You are a Communist! You have to read *Pravda*! And *Pravda Ukrainy,* and this other one, too; and for your soul take *Komsomolka* as well!" Now no one forces us and many people can't afford to subscribe to newspapers anyway. Our organization subscribes to several newspapers, and we archive them, so our members can read them.

As I began to get older, it really bothered me how our society treats the elderly, both the government and the population at large. And I told myself, "You are going to be old one day too. So if you don't like how the elderly are treated now, change it! Then when you are elderly, you'll be treated as you wish to be treated." This was back in 1988, when I was fifty-one years old. I got tired of the state telling us, "You are obligated. ... You have the responsibility. ... You are required. ..." What about my rights? I have rights, too, not only obligations—I have lived my entire life in this country. So I began, informally, to help individual elderly people—first one, then another.

In the fall of 1988, we had a celebration for the Jewish New Year. There was a small boy who gave out flowers, honey, and apples, according to tradition, and we sang songs. The next day I got more than one hundred phone calls. If one person talks, you will immediately have a hundred people calling you. News gets around. I couldn't sleep at night, I couldn't sleep in my own home. Nothing but the telephone. A cultured person will not call after 10 PM. But I got calls at all hours. "But your line was busy," she'd say at 11 PM. And another would call at 1 AM! "Your line was busy." Elderly people, especially those trained by the Soviet regime, they are so demanding. As if I am obligated. I work too! And it doesn't interest her that I don't receive a salary for helping her, that I do a good thing because I care for her, and still go to work the next day. I was still working at the metro, in a fairly high position. Everything I was able to do was after work, thanks to the kindness of my heart and my own hands, my own legs. All my free time was spent on social work—my evenings after work and the entire weekend.

In this regard, not much has changed for me. Today I scheduled a meeting with another NGO director, a veteran of the Afghanistan war. He asked me, "Faina, when do you have your lunch?" I told him, "You know, I don't even know." As soon as I arrive at the office, there are endless phone calls, and I have to make all the decisions. I only eat at night. Others have their dachas ready, but my garden plot is not ready, my home is not cleaned, and my laundry isn't done, because I don't have time. Sometimes I sit my members down and tell them, "You must understand that I am a human being just like you. You clean your apartment, you read books—all while I run around. I run and search for new sponsors and new partners, so our organization can develop. And who is going to clean my home? I don't even have time to sleep."

The economic crisis continues to hit the elderly especially hard, which is one reason our organization is necessary. I calculated that before the economic crash, I put away 3,500 rubles—it doesn't seem like much, but it was for me. That money would have allowed me to get by little by little until the end of my days. By the exchange rate back then, after retirement I would have received a pension of 120 rubles a month; that pension would have allowed me to visit a sanitarium, go to the movies and the theater, and buy ice cream and cookies. Now I can't do any of that. On my current pension, which is seventy-five rubles, I can't allow myself those things.[9] So I search for a theater that will let us in for free on a certain day to listen and watch. I can't even think about the movies. Did you read the newspaper article where the journalist wrote about inviting me to a restaurant, but I refused? Earlier, with my salary, I knew all the restaurants in Kyiv. And not only in Kyiv; every year I vacationed at the sea. Maybe it was a small salary, but it allowed me to travel to the sea, if I saved in other areas. And now I can't travel, and I don't know where the restaurants are, because my pension is too small.

One of my members reminded me, "Faina, it's time to go water your garden at the dacha—everything is growing now." And I replied, "What must I do first? In my shower the water leaks. In my apartment, I don't know what to do first—I need to do repairs, put up new wallpaper. My kitchen sink doesn't work at all—it hasn't worked for three or four years. I don't use the kitchen because I don't have money to repair my sink. I draw my water for cooking from the bathtub. You are the only person I have told about this; I haven't told anyone. (Begins to cry.) What must I do first? What must I spend my pension on first? I must pay my apartment rent, because I refuse to be negligent before the state. Where must I spend my money? I didn't have a television for the longest time. It went on the blink and I couldn't find a replacement lamp for a long time. One friend scolded me, "Faina, buy a television for heaven's sake." I said, "Vasia, it is either put up a fence at the dacha, install water at the dacha because I can't carry it any more, fix the ceiling there, or buy wallpaper and put it up—I won't even mention sanding down the floors. Or fixing the sink and all those pipes in my kitchen. What should I tackle first? I need to do all of it." Therefore, what can I tell you? I calculated that on the pension I would have received earlier, I could have done all that, gradually. Plus I would have had that money that I saved up, all of which disappeared in the economic crash.[10]

At first, in the early days of the organization, I tried to help protect elderly persons who were single and lonely. They have it even harder, after all. Their homes are falling down and there is no one to help them. They have no one to talk to. But over time, we decided to modify our work. At one point we had a membership of 1,500, and that was just too many. We decided to scale down our membership to 150 people, and focus on those who strive to live an active life. At that time, I had about fifteen or twenty activists working with me, and they were all in charge of looking after ten or twelve elderly people in their district of the city. They were like social workers, checking in on those needy people, giving them a bit of company, and making sure they had enough to eat. They would do minor repairs in people's homes, cook for them sometimes, do their laundry, and take little walks with them. Then the activists would bring me documentation to show how much time they'd spent with their clients, and I was able to pay them a bit for their trouble. I got that money from sponsors.

Today we have a core group of twenty-five or thirty women; that's all our small premises can hold. Most of them have been through volunteer training, and they are our most active members. Earlier we held our volunteer trainings on Wednesdays, and after that, Wednesday became our workday, when we gather for our weekly meetings. We discuss the status of different projects, inform one another about things in the news that affect us and other pensioners, and give out work assignments for the week. We also read the letters we received. There are lots of other activities for members, too. On Tuesdays we have craft circles—several of our members are artists, and they teach the other women how to make different crafts. We have also had a lecture series, and other special activities, such as musical evenings, for our members. We've invited some very interesting speakers to talk about issues such as health, religion, literature, and music. Once a month we have a big party to celebrate the birthdays of those born during that month. We have a spread on the table, sing songs, and greet the birthday girls with cards and little things we've made for them.

All of our active members try to contribute something to the organization, and to one another. One woman always brings beautiful flowers, which puts smiles on all our faces. Another member is good at giving haircuts, so she brings her comb and scissors, and cuts people's hair after the Wednesday meeting. They share advice on where to buy the best products at the best price, and which pharmacies in town have particular medicines and good discounts for the elderly. It has been hard, but I've convinced the women to talk about the positive things in their lives. Earlier they were used to getting together and complaining about their poor health, their aches and pains. Now they have a more positive attitude. When one of our members ends up in hospital, we organize a watch and take turns visiting her, and bringing her meals, because the hospital food is just awful here. Each fall, we try to give out a big "ration" to all our 150 members. I don't like that term, *ration*, it sounds miserly—I'm talking about a very nice food basket. We include foodstuffs to get elderly people through the winter, things like macaroni, potatoes, apples, cabbages, carrots, onions, garlic, flour, oil, and different kinds of kasha. We've gotten support for this from different sources, including the UN, which gave us a grant for 1999, the year that was designated as the International Year of the Elderly. They also supported the purchase of some office equipment, and other things like medicines and eyeglasses for our members. There are also some young Americans living in Kyiv who have been very kind to us. They have helped us with food rations, and brought us donations of clothing.

The Soviets taught people to be dependent, and to wait for handouts. We teach people to live differently. Some of our elderly people go the Salvation Army, to eat in the cafeteria. I am against it. I would rather take food products to someone's house, so she can cook for herself. She will know that I am coming, and she must get up and make the bed. She must take off her robe and put on something presentable. I will bring her some *hrechka,* and she will remember, "Ah, buckwheat groats, I haven't made them in so long. Now how did my mother fix them?" She must use her brains, her memory. People still want to cook. If she can't think clearly, she will call her neighbor, "Won't you tell me what I should do?" She has to use her mind. She will go wash the pot. She will wash a bowl. She will put those products away in the cupboard, and arrange them. Some like thick soup and some like thin soup—she must make a decision. How much salt should she use? If she goes to a cafeteria, she eats whatever they give her. And when she is at home, she will think, "Ah! I won't make kasha from this; I'll make two servings of soup instead." So a person thinks about what she wants. What her tastes are set for—thicker, thinner, more salt, less. A person must live. You must never feed her.

For some reason elderly persons here are not adequately prepared for retirement. They get their "pension book" and are sent on their way. The first day she'll rejoice: "This is great! I don't have to run to work anymore." She cooks something today, cooks again tomorrow, and does her laundry the next day. Her apartment is all clean, but no one calls and she has no one to talk to. Then the horror starts—her pension is small, and there's no one to talk to, to commiserate with. So I think that people should start preparing for retirement early—they should think about how they'll live. I consulted with medical professionals about this, and I have my own opinions, too. It drives me crazy when people say, "We weren't ready for old age." What do you mean, you weren't ready? How did you get to age sixty or seventy without thinking about it? I understand if someone is run over by a car at the age of twenty and wasn't ready for it. But you've worked in a mine every day of your life and didn't ever think about becoming old?

We have a few men among our members, even though officially we are a women's organization. After I formalized it, we ran into a lot of competition. I was searching for ways to free us from that competition, and the term *women's organization* cropped up. That was something new. When donors carried out programs for women's organizations, they would tell us, "Your organization is not a women's organization." So we were left out of a lot of trainings, and grants. What do you mean not a women's group? Our membership was 90 percent women. So in the title I inserted the word *women's*, before *humanitarian*. But in the charter I wrote that men can join, too. So now everyone is satisfied.

Unfortunately, now that the Year of the Elderly is over, it seems that no one wants to work with elderly people any more. I have learned to talk about the healthy nation and a healthy population, but no matter how I put it, I can't make it work. When they say a healthy nation, they mean the reproductive nation, that is, those who are still in their reproductive years. And we are too old. When they say a healthy nation, they have children in mind. But children could never be healthy if we hadn't nurtured them.

Next month we will hold a celebration called "My Years, My Wealth." The name comes from a song by Kikabidze that we like to sing.[11] I've designed the celebration as a way to get our members to think about the positive legacies they will leave behind them. I told them, "Think about it, what have you left behind that is good?" I'm not talking about their careers, or their "official" achievements, but their talents, their hobbies. Now we are learning that people abroad often say, "I am proud of myself. ..." because of something. It was in poor taste among us, to say "I am proud." "Why are you bragging?" But I think the moment has come when we must say, "I am proud of that which I have left, or am leaving, on this earth." We usually say that old age begins when people start remembering the past. But I think it also begins when you begin accounting for yourself—what have I done, and what will carry on and remain? Each generation must leave something behind. You have to be able to find value in yourself. One of the women said to me, "Faina, I don't know how. I haven't done anything special, I just really love flowers. I have flowers that no one else does. I give everyone flowers." Another member replied, "Just imagine, when you walk in your garden—those are all your flowers. Imagine what a happiness that is for the earth, that you have all sorts of flowers, and you give everyone pleasure with them. You share them—that is happiness for the earth."

I am one of the youngest women in our organization. Some took part in the war, and others were like me, children of the war. At the beginning of the war, I was three years old. What do we leave behind us? I gave them this example: people always associate wars with the generals. But generals don't fight the war; soldiers do. There are very few generals. Mostly the battles are on the backs of the soldiers. We are privates. We are not heroes of the Soviet Union. But we carried that life, during the war, and today, too. I see this celebration as a way to prove to the government and the public that we do not eat bread in vain. We have earned ours. I don't want the evening to be only about accounting for ourselves; we will convince the government that they must look at us differently. They must bow to each elderly person who walks by. He has something good in him. And all the murders that go on today, there were not as many in our times. There were Stalin's camps, but hatred among people—no.

So I told each of the women, "In preparation for the celebration, remember." They began to talk among themselves, and remember how, after the war, when they were about fourteen, seventeen, eighteen years old, after school they helped clear the bricks and debris from Khreshchatyk,[12] which was bombed out. And what would Khreshchatyk look like if they hadn't helped restore it? I also gave them the example of the Chokolovka district where I lived in Kyiv—earlier it was a completely naked place. Before 1964 it wasn't even part of Kyiv proper. And now there are such big trees there. But they weren't planted by foresters—it was we, the Saturday workers. After work, on the weekends, we planted those trees. And now everyone is saying, "Ecology, ecology, we must save the environment!" Take a shovel and start digging. We planted something. Why are you complaining about ecology—tell us what you have planted. Another example: from Koziatyn to Popil'nia was a naked railroad.[13] And after the war there were very snowy winters. Our houses were covered with snow and we couldn't open the doors. We climbed through the chimney, and made a little path so the door could be opened! And when there was snow, the railroad was covered. Alongside the railroad we used poles and reeds to braid a snow fence, so that when the wind and snow blew, the snowdrift was held back and wouldn't cover the railroad.

My members and I decided that maybe next year we will make a contract with the city and find a little corner where we will plant a number of trees in the name of our organization. It is hard for us to dig at our age, but we've gotten excited by the idea. We are planning some activities to involve children, as sort of "meeting of the generations," and we want to include schoolchildren in the tree-planting project. A rift has happened between children and the elderly, and we want to work with schoolchildren and see what we can find in common.

We had another celebration where we taught each other about the traditions of different peoples. Our membership is very diverse—we have Jews, Russians, Ukrainians, women from the Baltics, Crimean Tatars, and so on. The women prepared traditional foods and crafts and were in charge of explaining what was on their respective tables. But when the time came for the Ukrainian table, I couldn't find anyone who could talk about it coherently! We have educated women, who brag about themselves, but when it gets down to it they aren't articulate, they can't do a presentation. More than that, they didn't even know the traditions. They brought the requisite traditional foods, but it turned out they didn't even know what they were bringing. I said, "You live in Ukraine! You've read the *Eneida*!" That's considered a classic of Ukrainian literature. It explains everything, what one should prepare on New Year's, including *shulyky*. They didn't even know what *shulyky* were—honey cakes with poppy seeds cut or torn into squares. I told them, "Listen, it will be a real shame if I, a Jew, end up having to take charge of your Ukrainian table, and explain your Ukrainian traditions and dishes to everyone." I said, "Go home and re-read *Eneida,* and we'll discuss it next time. Kotliarevs'kyi describes everything about holiday cooking."[14] So you see, the older generation is losing this knowl-edge, and they aren't reading the Ukrainian classics, which have fallen out of fashion, and this knowledge will be lost with the generations. We were glad we held that celebration, because the women remembered many traditions they had almost forgotten. It was much better than parties you see nowadays, where people simply open a can of red caviar.

There are other projects we've been working on. We have tried to build bridges between the elderly generation and schoolchildren, because we feel there's a lack of communication between the generations. Some of our mem-bers have grandchildren, but others don't and are lonely, so they enjoy spend-ing time with schoolchildren. We have adopted a local school, and we carry out activities with the children, and we also had a celebration called "Grand-mothers for Children" where we congratulated them with the holidays. We also worked on a program for rehabilitating homeless women, something we're well suited for because of our experience with marginalized populations. We invited those women to attend our art circles, and our lectures, and to work their way back into society.

· · ·

The organization that Faina founded and directed, For Survival, served three primary functions for members. It was a forum for socializing with other re-tirees that allowed elderly women to continue to contribute to society after retirement, and also an important source of mutual aid and support in the form of tangible material assistance (occasional cash payments, humanitarian aid, and food baskets), practical advice, and emotional and moral encourage-ment. It is important that over the years the organization moved into lobbying. Led by Faina, the women engaged in lobbying campaigns, fought for hard-to-arrange meetings with parliamentarians and other representatives of the state, and formed coalitions with other civic organizations. In 2005 the group was focusing especially on challenging proposed pension reforms, reforms that are likely to put women at a disadvantage because of their normally shorter work histories and lower wages. This aspect of For Survival's work was devalued by some bureaucrats and NGO representatives—Faina said that when she spoke up at public forums she often heard people muttering, "Now Faina will talk about her old people again." Because the group sought to retain Soviet-era blanket entitlements for groups such as the elderly—free public transport, sub-sidies for rent and utilities, discounts on medicines, and others—their work was interpreted by some as outdated and reflecting a Soviet mindset. Although Faina was well networked, and participated in a range of NGO coalitions, espe-cially those focusing on women's issues, her primary loyalty was to the elderly, and elderly women especially. She actively sought to help "seed" new advocacy groups for women pensioners in other parts of Ukraine.

Women in Politics

I was one of the founding members of the "Women's Parliament" in Ukraine. Throughout the whole world, women are raising their voices, and in other countries there are more and more women in positions of political power. But here, with every election, the number of women falls, in both the executive and legislative branches.[15] So the political women decided to consolidate their power in the Women's Parliament.[16] It's also a way to teach cadres how to work with the government, and to prepare themselves and others for political office, in parliament and in lower offices. Earlier we had two women ministers—today there aren't any. We had Siuzanna Stainyk in the Ministry of Justice, and the Minister of Family and Youth was also a woman. Now they've downgraded the Ministry of Family and Youth to a Committee, and a man took Siuzanna's place. [17] There are practically no women in the Cabinet of Ministers; they all occupy low posts.And very few mayors are women.

A big battle is taking place, and men understand that they have more power—more physical power, that is, not intellectual. It's my opinion that women are more reasonable, softer, and are more flexible. If women had more power, I think there would be more order. Women are more adaptable and savvier negotiators. Men are afraid of women, and women suffer because of that—they don't get promoted. A woman is like a horse—she does all the work, pulling the load, while a man above her supervises. That is very convenient for men. In other countries, where the government is more developed, you see more women leaders. They have already reached that level of equality, it seems. But not here. And I'm afraid it won't happen anytime soon.

To my chagrin, women don't support one another; rather, they are jealous of one another. If a woman really wants something, she goes right after it, and men don't like this. Many of them are without husbands now, those women who are climbing the political ladder. They don't have enough experience, and they get blamed for things that men don't. That's why we decided to form this Women's Parliament.

At our first meeting, when we were discussing different problems, I suggested that we must include culture work in our agenda. We know that many male politicians are uncultured, but it's worse when a woman lacks culture. Her behavior gets interpreted negatively. For example, a woman might get more emotional in an argument about passing a certain bill. She might also say, "Don't try to explain it to me; I'm a woman, after all." So women must be taught to work effectively with foreigners, and local partners, and in business, and so on. They have to be prepped, because we need many more women in government. After all, 54 percent of the world's population is women. Women live longer than men. To me this means that there should be more women than men in politics. But there aren't. Where are they? Women complain that they are kept out of office, but this is impossible to prove. Perhaps we need quotas like they have in some countries.[18] Whatever it takes to get more women into office, but women need to be prepared for politics.

Women Activists

Although I never heard Faina refer to herself as a "feminist," she espoused a forceful discourse of equal rights and women's empowerment that set her apart from many other activists in Ukraine. Many NGO activists have sought to advance women's, children's, and family interests through a rhetoric of women's special caring natures, their roles as "moral leaders of the nation," and their natural place behind the scenes in NGOs instead of in official politics, a narrative that perpetuates the reassertion of patriarchy in the Ukrainian political sphere, and women's ongoing marginalization from the political process. When I first heard about Faina and contacted her for our initial interview, I expected her to be grandmotherly, and, as an elderly woman, to have "traditional" ideas about gender roles, and the respective proper personalities and responsibilities of men and women that are so commonly espoused in Ukraine. As it turned out, of the eleven female NGO leaders who participated in my research, Faina showed the greatest commitment to women's rights (as opposed to children's or family rights) in all spheres of life. Her tireless work enriched the lives of many women, and dispelled many of the stereotypes I held as a Western feminist researcher interested in women's issues in Ukraine.

Faina: Preparing for Death

After I moved here as a young woman, for a time I lived near Fastiv, where there's a train station—it's about 60 kilometers from Kyiv, in the direction of Vinnytsia. I lived with a family, and I was really surprised when the grandmother said to me, "Grandfather and I have already prepared our coffins; they are up in the attic, along with everything else they'll need to bury us." You know, as a girl of fourteen, in the seventh grade, I thought it was horrible when I learned that they had ordered their own caskets and put together the clothes and the material for their own burial. They must be crazy! Why torture themselves that way? But as time went on, I realized that they were very wise people, because death can come at any moment. There may be no boards available to make a coffin—there was a time like that. Or maybe the time of year will be bad—too cold. Maybe the people in the household won't have enough money. I experienced this myself, when my father died in my own home. I went to the department store, and it was closed. I needed to buy everything—those handkerchiefs they traditionally put over the hands, underclothing, and a coffin. But everything was closed for the weekend. What was I to do? I had to go around to my acquaintances: "Can you open the storehouse so I can get some things?" I had to try to get hold of the *zanachka,* a person in a shop who squirrels away deficit items. I had to find some tulle, and a pair of slippers or shoes. All that costs money. So those grandparents were very wise to prepare their own coffins, handkerchiefs, clothes, and underclothes. They even bought headscarves for the mourners. They were prepared for death, and no one would think ill about them later for placing the burden on others. Everyone should think about how to prepare for death.

Dacha

Earlier this year I was in the hospital, and the doctors barely dragged me over from "the other side." The next morning the girls came to see me. I was lying down, I couldn't stand up, and one woman sat down on my bed and asked, "Faina, how do you feel?" "Great!" (Laughs.) It is my habit to be positive, it's the way society raised me. Another woman called me and asked, surprised, "And you still go to the dacha?" I said, "Yes. No one feeds me." I have a garden plot, and I have to work there for now because I live off my garden. There is very little time but I put my heart into it. I also grow flowers there, and I love to see the results of my work. I don't use fertilizer, because I want to know what's in my food.

The Cabinet of Ministers is considering eradicating the blanket entitlements and assigning them individually. One of these is free use of public transport, which the elderly get automatically. Losing that would hang me, because I must take the bus to my dacha very often.[19] It's hard on me—I'm an ill person. I have high blood pressure, and have to take all kinds of pills for my heart. And when my blood pressure goes up my head immediately begins to hurt, and my heart hurts. And when my heart hurts it becomes hard for me to breathe, so I get arrhythmia. But first of all, I breathe easier in the country than here in the city, where I lose my breath because of all the car exhaust. Second, my produce is ripening and I have to go water it, and then harvest it—cherry plums, apricots, cabbage, squash, and my flowers and apples. I get to travel there and back for free. Last time I gathered a dozen cucumbers and three tomatoes. It's hard in this heat, very hard. But I don't have a choice. I even gather the green apples that fall, for compote. I often spend the night, because there's so much work. Yesterday Lena called me, and I said, "You know, Lena, today I feel better than

I did yesterday. If you leave me at the dacha for a month and keep me working, maybe I'll regain my health?" We joke, of course. But I travel there for free; I can't afford to pay for transport. I need that produce for my health—the berries, vegetables, fruit—they are full of vitamins. Some of them I'll can for later. I brought back some herbs that I'm drying—echinacea, and berry leaves—I'll use them for herbal tea. These are things I can't afford at the market; if they take away our free transport, they might as well slit our throats. The mayor is trying to calm people by saying, "For now, it doesn't apply to the elderly." But I told my members: "Girls, they are trying to cloud your thinking. If that resolution passes, the mayor will have nothing to say, and they'll start charging us dearly for transport."

As far as friendships go, it is difficult for me to get close to people, because it is difficult for me to part. Right now, I can't say that I have a soul-mate girlfriend. I have a very good relationship with everyone, and I communicate well with all of them. But there is a limit beyond the bounds of which I won't say more. And maybe it is bitter for me as a person, maybe I would like to, but I can't see or find that which I can share on that level. Once I had a girlfriend, Nina, who thought I had saved her life. There was a time in her life when she and her husband had problems, and she had found another man, and she thought he would marry her. But he betrayed her. After that she led me to believe that she was going to throw herself under a train, and I guess I intervened. Her daughter said, "Aunt Faina, mama owes her life to you." But she passed away already, she died. She had a lot of worries and cancer began to spread very quickly, and she didn't make it to her retirement pension by one year. So Nina is no more. Sometimes I call up her other friends, and say, "Let's go to the grave. Let's go to Nina."

Although I can't say I have very close friends, someone is always waiting for me. I have more work than I have time to do it. If I haven't enough time, I don't have a minute to think for myself, or to be bored, to wonder whether or not someone needs me. I knew what it would be like getting older, and I was prepared for that. I had to find myself some kind of niche in order not to be lonely, and to be needed. All the more so since we say, "The elderly are not needed." I say, "Not needed? Let's go. What do you want to do? What do you want to demand of yourself? Demand it." I say the same thing to myself.

• • •

It always struck me as sad that Faina seemed to struggle with loneliness, despite her very busy schedule, and constant social interaction as For Survival's director. She never seemed quite comfortable in the solitude that she both valued and regretted. Faina Neiman died at her dacha, alone, of a heart attack, on 14 May 2005. She is remembered and missed. The other women of For Survival continue their activities in Kyiv.

Notes

1. This research was supported by an IARO grant from the International Research & Exchanges Board (IREX), with funds provided by the National Endowment for the Humanities, the US Department of State, and the US Information Agency. The research was also funded by a US Department of Education Fulbright-Hays Doctoral Dissertation Research Abroad (DDRA) Fellowship. None of these organizations is responsible for the views expressed here. The life history narratives presented are drawn from multiple tape-recorded interviews, conducted with Faina Neiman from 1999 to 2005.

2. During World War II, the Soviet regime made no effort to evacuate Ukraine's Jewish population and remained silent about the Jews' persecution. Most Jews in Ukraine fell into the hands of the Nazis, who established 50 ghettos and over 180 large concentration camps in Ukraine. About 850,000 Jews in Ukraine were killed by the Nazis and their execution squads. In Kyiv at the ravine at Babyn Yar, 33,000 Jews were executed in two days alone, in September 1941 (Subtelny 1994: 468). For two more years the ravine served as a site of executions and mass burials of between 100,000 and 150,000 individuals, including Jews, Ukrainian Red Army soldiers, partisans, Ukrainian nationalists, and Roma (Magocsi 1996: 633).

3. In the Soviet Union, Jews were labeled as such in their passports under the category *natsional'nost'* (Rus.), and *nationality* is the term Faina often used to refer to her Jewish heritage. For the Soviet regime, it made no difference if a person was a Jew of Russian, Ukrainian, or Georgian background—for the state, "Jew" was the identity that superseded all others. In the Soviet Union, the Russian term *grazhdanstvo* was used to denote citizenship, "which did not necessarily carry connotations of shared cultural or linguistic identity. In contrast, the term *natsional'nost'* ... was primarily reflective of an individual's ancestry and determined independently of an individual's citizenship, and residence in a particular sub-state political entity (republic, autonomous republic, etc.)" (Wanner 1998: 11). The fixation of "nationality" in one's passport facilitated discrimination of Jews and other stigmatized nationalities (i.e. Roma, Chechens, etc.). The surveillance function of fixing one's Jewish (or other) nationality was highlighted by Faina's frequent reference to her Jewishness as her "data." For Faina as for many Soviet Jews, being Jewish was primarily an ethnic and cultural identity, rather than a religious one.

4. The area around the once-closed city of Cheliabinsk, the capital of the southern Ural region, was the site of two major nuclear disasters in the 1950s. Beginning in 1951, the Mayak nuclear plant began dumping radioactive waste into a small lake, and the dumping lasted an entire decade. In 1957, the nearby Kyshtym nuclear plant released at least seventy tons of waste due to a failure in the nuclear waste cooling system. Both disasters and the ecological and health consequences were covered up by the Soviet regime. See Petryna 2002: 9.

5. Irpin' is a city of around forty thousand located 60 kilometers north of Kyiv. Originally a village, Irpin' acquired city status only in 1956. During Soviet times, the perimeter of Irpin' was the retreat to the dachas (summer homes and gardens) of the Union of Writers of Ukraine, and some writers still have their dachas there.

6. Here Faina is referring to Yiddish.

7. By "Muslims" Faina is referring to Crimean Tatars.

8. All leaders of prominent women's organizations in Ukraine. V'iacheslav Chornovil was the former head of Rukh, the Popular Movement of Ukraine for Restructuring. In March 1999, Chornovil was killed in a car collision. At the time, he was a strong candidate in the presidential election, and many suspect that his death was no accident.

9. The ruble was the Soviet currency. After independence was achieved, Ukraine introduced its own currency as the kupon; today, the Ukrainian currency is the hryvnia (UAH). Even so, some people, especially the elderly, continue to refer to their money as "rubles." Faina's retirement pension was 75 UAH in 1999, about $15. In 2005 the minimum monthly old-age pension was set at the minimum subsistence level—332 UAH, about $66.

10. In 1990 and 1991, runaway inflation caused many in Ukraine (including Faina) to lose their entire life savings over the course of only a few short weeks. From the early 1990s until 2000, the Ukrainian economy was in shambles, with persistent declines in real GDP, and surging inflation of at least 10 percent per year—including an unfathomable inflation rate of about 10,250 percent in 1993 (Kravchuk 2002: 3). Poverty in Ukraine increased from 2 percent between 1987 and 1988, to 63 percent from 1993 to 1995 (Milanovic 1998). The country's economy worsened steadily during the 1990s, and Ukrainians were dealt a second blow in autumn 1998 by a worldwide economic dip that resulted in a devaluation of the Ukrainian currency of nearly 60 percent (D'Anieri, Kravchuk, and Kuzio 1999: 202).

11. Vakhtang Kikabidze was a popular Georgian songwriter, singer, actor, screenwriter, and producer in the Soviet Union.

12. Kyiv's main thoroughway.

13. Koziatyn and Popil'nia are small cities in Vinnytsia oblast' and Zhytomyrs'ka oblast', respectively.

14. Ivan Kotliarevs'kyi is the founder of modern Ukrainian literature, and he established the norms for the modern Ukrainian language. Kotliarevs'kyi's greatest literary work was *Eneida*, which he began writing in 1794 and finished around 1820. He is also author of the well-known operetta *Natalka Poltavka*.

15. In the last Supreme Soviet of Ukraine, women held 36 percent of the seats, and 50 percent of the seats of municipal councils (due to quotas), but the number of women in political positions plummeted during the 1990 election, which saw a steep decline of women's representation in the Verkhovna Rada to just three percent. Free elections after Ukrainian independence in 1994 produced a slight increase, with women constituting 5 percent of parliamentarians. Women's representation rose to 8 percent in the 1998 elections. In the 2002 parliamentary elections, however, the percentage of women deputies declined again to 5 percent. In a promising trend, the percentage of women representatives at the local (less-powerful) level did rise to 50 percent in 2002. The percentage of women in the Verkhovna Rada climbed slightly in the 2006 parliamentary elections, up to 8.7 percent (thirty-nine women parliamentarians).Whereas women constitute about 68 percent of the labor force in government service overall, their share in high-ranking civil service positions is only 15 percent (UNDP 2003: 29).

16. The formal name of the initiative was the Civil Parliament of Women of Ukraine, formed in 2002 by a coalition of women politicians, NGO leaders, and others. The Civil Parliament was organized to duplicate the Ukrainian Parliament—its 450 seats, with the same committees—to put pressure on the government to recognize women's issues. Major figures included Kateryna Vashchuk, then of the Agrarian Party and an

MP, and Liudmyla Suprun of the People's Democratic Party. According to Faina, eventually the group devolved into a forum for women politicians to advance their own business interests, and she withdrew her support. Unfortunately, the Civil Parliament of Women of Ukraine does not appear to have had much influence over the political process in Ukraine.

17. Currently the ministry has been reinstated; it is now known as the Ministry of Family, Youth, and Sport, with the emphasis on Sport.

18. In the Ukrainian Soviet Socialist Republic, a high percentage of women in positions of political power were guaranteed through quotas, and women deputies constituted at least 50 percent of local Soviets (councils), and 30 percent of the republican Supreme Soviet. However, in the Soviet Union, relatively few women advanced in the Communist Party, and those who did were usually given tasks associated with maternal and child welfare, low-prestige issues assumed to be most relevant to their interests. Proposals to reimplement the Soviet-era quota for women (at 30 or 35 percent) in the Verkhovna Rada have been debated by parliamentarians, but not approved.

19. Free public transport for retirees has been done away with, and the fares are constantly being ratcheted up.

Bibliography

D'Anieri, Paul, Robert Kravchuk, and Taras Kuzio. 2008. *Politics and Society in Ukraine*. Boulder, CO: Westview Press.

Kravchuk, Robert S. 2002. *Ukrainian Political Economy: The First Ten Years*. New York: Palgrave Macmillan.

Magocsi, Paul Robert. 2005. *A History of Ukraine*. Seattle: University of Washington Press.

Milanovic, Branko. 1998. *Income, Inequality and Poverty During the Transition from Planned to Market Economy*. Washington, DC: World Bank.

Petryna, Adriana. 2002. *Life Exposed: Biological Citizens after Chernobyl*. Princeton, NJ: Princeton University Press.

Subtelny, Orest. 1994. *Ukraine: A History*. Toronto: University of Toronto Press.

Wanner, Catherine. 1998. *Burden of Dreams: History and Identity in Post-Soviet Ukraine*. University Park: Pennsylvania State University Press.

CHAPTER 5

Biography as Political Geography

Patriotism in Ukrainian Women's Life Stories

Oksana Kis'

Introduction

The history of Ukraine in the twentieth century abounds in events that have altered the country's political, social, and economic landscapes, yet the part that Ukrainian women played in that history during the past hundred years is only marginally visible. The gender dimension of that entire epoch is especially important; it represents an era when Ukrainian women obtained broad rights and opportunities for self-realization in their public lives, a transformation that changed both the women and the public space. For all that, women's lives remained virtually unseen in the historical records.[1] This is a serious lapse in our study of Ukrainian history, especially in light of the fact that women are the key agents of socialization.

In a search for a more profound understanding of the ways in which post-Soviet Ukrainian women make sense of their past, this chapter examines the life stories of women from three separate regions. I seek to gain some insight into the ways in which their historical experiences have shaped their perception of the present. Through an analysis of the women's biographical narratives, this chapter will show the fundamental differences in their patriotic sentiments, as determined by their differing political loyalties—whether to the Soviet regime, or to the independent Ukrainian nation-state. I will also pay special attention to the role of early socialization and the expectations of upward social mobility as they influenced the formation of the women's attitudes toward the respective regimes.

A research project titled "20th Century Ukraine in Women's Memories,"[2] was conceived in 2002 as an autonomous branch of an international undertaking titled "Women's Memory: Searching for Lives and Identities of Women under Socialism."[3] Its main goal was to document the experiences of women in Soviet Ukraine by recording and analyzing their life stories. The theoretical basis of the project derives from the feminist idea of the distinctive character of women's historical experiences, and the special women's agency in history.[4] Women's talk (Devault 1990: 96–116) constitutes the methodological framework of this project and correlates with the narrative biographical interview process (Rosenthal 2004: 48–64). Primary analysis revealed the main thematic fields, key concepts, and the categories that frame and structure narratives.

Between 2003 and 2005 approximately thirty life stories, narrated by elderly retired women (born in the 1920s and 1930s) from western, eastern, and southern Ukraine, were recorded, transcribed, and archived.[5] The interviewees had all spent at least their adult years under state socialism; most were born in Ukraine. Interviews were conducted with minimal intervention from the interviewers in order to encourage spontaneity. Each conversation comprised four consecutive phases, beginning with a request for each woman's life story, from beginning to end, which allowed the respondents to organize the narration in their own unique way. Next, so-called internal questions, focused on the personal experiences of each individual, allowed the researcher to probe more deeply into some aspects of a life story, or to clarify certain details. The third phase consisted of so-called external probes, which broadened the interview scope with a series of carefully designed questions aimed at going beyond the life story itself by directing the interviewees' reflections toward more general issues.[6] The final stage returned them to the present, and encouraged some positive sentiments with a standard question: "Of what in your life are you most proud"? The women's narratives proved to be a rich source for exploring their reflections upon, and (re)evaluations of, the political systems under which they live(d)—an independent Ukraine or the Soviet regime. In this study, the concept of political loyalty is of special relevance, as it allows for a scrutiny of the very essence of the women's political allegiance.

Loyalty is the attitude and associated pattern of conduct of an individual taking something's side, and doing so with a specific motive: namely, one that is partly emotional in nature, involves a response to the thing itself, and makes essential references to a special relationship that the individual believes exists between her and the focus of her loyalty (Keller 2007: 21). According to James Connor, loyalty is one motivating force for human responses: it brings meaning, direction, and purpose into a person's life and unifies his/her activities. Loyalty is an emotion on a par with the likes of trust, hope, and shame. It helps to guide action and furnish identity, operates on various layers, and requires the existence of competing loyalties (2007: 51, 115). Political loyalty is defined as devotion to, and identification with, a political cause or community, its institutions, basic laws, major political ideas, and general policy objectives.

Given the totalitarian monopoly enjoyed in the USSR by the Communist Party, it appears reasonable to view political loyalty as a complex category, which includes loyalty to the party and its ideology, loyalty to its way of governance (Soviet rule), and the transformation of empire into the USSR. Indeed, one is hardly able to imagine an ordinary Soviet person (excluding dissidents) being loyal to the Communist Party and disloyal to the state, or loyal to the ideology of Marxism-Leninism and disloyal to the Soviet regime. Accordingly, for the sake of simplicity, I will use the term *Soviet regime* to mean a complex and inclusive category signifying the totality of the Soviet political realm.

In contemporary Ukraine, with its multiparty system and pluralism of political ideas, market economy, and controversial social policies, such a holistic approach to political loyalty appears somewhat problematic. I will use the term *contemporary Ukraine* to mean the formation that replaced the Soviet regime and is considered its antipode in many ways.

Some core elements of both systems, however, are comparable. The women's attitudes to the formation of a state that became known as the USSR, in contrast to an independent Ukrainian nation-state; the socioeconomic regimes and corresponding social policies, socialism versus a market economy/capitalism; and official policies on ethnicity as derived from the two predominant ideologies, Soviet internationalism and Ukrainian nationalism, might all be used as points of reference for an analysis of the respondents' political loyalties. Such a comparison is appropriate inasmuch as all three elements are inherently interrelated and their dramatic transformations took place simultaneously at the beginning of the 1990s.

For this particular study, oral history proved to be the most appropriate research tool; it tells us less about events than about their meaning. In the words of Alessandro Portelli, "Oral sources tell us not just what people did, but what they wanted to do, what they believed they were doing, and what they now think they did" (1998: 67). The women's answers to direct questions regarding the significance of the Soviet regime and Ukrainian independence in their lives, as well as their respective attitudes toward various ethnicities, provided rich material for analyzing their political loyalties and disloyalties. In examining such allegiances, one might easily draw a dividing line between the western region and the rest of Ukraine, inasmuch as the majority of women who expressed their overall approval of the Soviet regime were ethnic Russians (or Russified Ukrainians), residing in eastern and southern Ukraine, whereas the nationalistically inclined western Ukrainians openly censured the Soviet regime. A closer reading of the women's life stories, however, reveals a more complex set of contributing factors to the respondents' attitudes toward past and present.

Earlier research works, based on an analysis of the same set of interviews, led their authors to similar conclusions. For instance, Viktoria Sereda
examined the structure and regional peculiarities of historical identities, as
constructed and represented in the women's biographical narratives. This produced a claim that when women refer to certain historical personages, events,
and holidays in either a positive or negative way, it can signify allegiance to a
specific version of the past. Her data show that women from western Ukraine,
and those from the two other regions of the country, clearly identify with two
different historical narratives—Ukrainian and Soviet respectively (2007: 84).
Another study has also proven that women's evaluations of the same historical
event, in which they participated personally, differed radically—depending on
the ideology (communist or nationalist) they had interiorized in the past, and
to which they remain committed (Kis', in Carlson et al).

Two Regimes

On the surface, the focus and intensity of the responses—positive and negative—correlated with ethnic origins and regions the respondents called home.
To one extent or another, all of the women, even the most critical, conceded
some measure of good in the Soviet regime, yet they exhibited radical differences in their evaluations of its blessings. Women from the south and east
placed a high premium on social policies. They also praised Soviet discipline
and expressed a feeling of pride in belonging to a strong, world-class state as
well as an appreciation of the sense of community that a collectivist society
brings. They repeatedly stressed their approval of unity and friendship as a
basic principle of interethnic relations within the USSR, and supported the
universal use of Russian as a medium of communication.

Larissa from Crimea is a typical pro-Soviet example.[7] Her father, a physi-
cian, was repressed and condemned to ten years in the gulag. Although she
recalled with regret his pointless arrest, after a few minutes passed, she subordinated her terrible personal loss to the common good: "I consider myself a
happy person despite my troubles, despite this cruel experience. ... Irrespective of my father's ten-year sentence ... and this is my personal opinion, without such injustice many would never have had access to an education, they ...
would not be the people they are today" (US1–04: 357–68). In response to the
question, "What did the Soviet regime signify in your life?" even as she praised
the regime, the subtext of Larissa's response suggested something more am-
biguous. It was as though she was trying hard to present the Soviet era in the
best possible light—out of some sense of loyalty, or perhaps a need to refute
the harsh criticisms from western Ukrainian women:

There were pluses and minuses, but I grew up in that life. I have an education, I had a job, I earned money, and I could afford nice things. So for me personally … True, my parents' life was not so sweet, but my own was blessed. I cannot pass judgment on the years 1933 or 1937, or even later,[8] I did share those events with others. Still, as any sober-minded person understands, it is a sad fact that every war, every change, every reconstruction produces its own victims. (US1–04: 363–71, 1510–28)

Valeria, from eastern Ukraine, began her narration with reminiscences about the loss of her father when she was still a child, and the hardships which she, her mother, and her two siblings were forced to endure after his death (UK1–04: 1195–202). Nevertheless, she refused to reduce her story to one of victimization, and as if to dispel any potential charges of bias against a system that gave her so much, her testimony became more positive, as she continued: "Children's health was monitored in the schools . . . there was order. Of course, the general food situation was very bad … but children were well fed; they received dairy products, stewed fruit, a little meat. … School was exacting, the rules harsh, and marking strict; but we were taught well" (UK1–04: 110–13; 733–37, 890–92).

Valeria also recalled that, while still a young man, her husband felt free to write a letter to Stalin requesting permission to enroll in an aviation college. Her references to the dictator were charitable, quite in keeping with the positive aspects of her recollections of Soviet life, yet her body language ["she clenches her fist"], her praise, and relatively mild condemnation of Stalin suggested an ambivalent view of communist rule. "Today, I tell you, they malign Stalin, malign him terribly. There was something very wrong with him, but there was good in him too. So sift it like flour through a sieve; take the good and discard the lumps. Yes, he was cruel, but this is our [trails off] … many people today are returning to the idea that this was necessary [she clenches her fist, her voice resolute and emotional] so that people would understand" (UK1–04: 1195–202).

When asked "What was the significance of the Soviet regime in your life?" Valeria reiterated her approval of the communist system: "The Soviet regime was immensely important in my life [speaks enthusiastically]. We survived; we went to school and studied diligently. When we needed healthcare, it was provided. Could I, an orphan in any other society, have received a higher education? No! But I got it then, I worked, and always there were good people around me; when I needed something, they helped" (UK1–04: 2279–90).

In the life narratives of women from the east and south, one finds little condemnation of any limits on freedom and civil rights, as well as an insistence that the failures of the Soviet regime are grossly exaggerated. Natalie's statement is exemplary:

Simply put, my attitude toward the former regime is very positive. Education was free, healthcare was free, and as a little girl I often attended pioneer camps at little or no cost. The only thing I did not like was, you know, a kind of hypocrisy. When you submitted a report, it never reflected what you really wanted to say. There were prescribed formulas. ... Today's democracy does allow for creativity, and provides ample opportunity for expressing one's thoughts. But in principle I think that the former regime was more just. People were treated like human beings. As for Soviet repressions, I don't believe in the innocence of *everyone* who was ever punished. (US3–04: 31–46)

Valentina, another Russian woman from Crimea, was more effusive in her praise of the regime. This was a woman who once held a prestigious position in the local government, and her praise of the Soviet system reflected immense pride in her empowerment:

I cannot accuse the state for depriving me of liberties. Today it is being said that there was no democracy. I am a forthright person. I never liked to speak behind somebody's back, and I always spoke the truth at party gatherings (I was a member for more than twenty years); I was able point to people's faults or expose misdeeds. On the whole, people treated me well, even when I criticized our university. When I was a member of the city council, I was free to stand up and criticize any chairman, any deputy. And now it is claimed that our freedom was violated, that one was persecuted for a single criticism. I never experienced this. I knew that I was free to say what I thought and felt. Just like that! The Soviet regime is not always judged fairly. (US6–04: 1352–94)

All of the narratives testify to the women's awareness of the key defects in the Soviet system and the tragic consequences (Stalin's personality cult, political repressions for innocent people, massive deaths during the artificial famine, ethnic discrimination, etc.) The comments of those loyal to the Soviet regime are rarely tinged with sorrow. On the contrary, they try, if not to justify somehow the vices of the Soviet regime, then at least to question the charges against it or to diminish the appalling repercussions of Soviet policies. The women who considered the Soviet regime a cause of, or a contributory factor to, their life achievements, tended to express their loyalty. Their allegiance was articulated in the form of gratitude for the favorable conditions and special opportunities presented for personal growth and development. Those who think their lives improved substantially under the Soviets, and who consider their achievements noteworthy when compared to what they might have been without the Soviet regime, express unconditional loyalty. Some of their statements sound like a pledge of devotion that they would never betray, even after the demise of the Soviet Union. Here is how that allegiance was expressed:

I came from a poor peasant family, I grew up to become a professor, I was respected in a collective, in the city. ... I am grateful to the Soviet Union first and foremost, as I lived in it almost my entire life. I don't like many of the things in our life today—the way children are brought up, or education, or healthcare. I think one ought not to revile the former Soviet Union. There were many interesting things in it: we were great patriots, we were great internationalists, and so we remain. We loved our country; we loved it in the right way! But today [there is no] such feeling of affection for one's country, one's Fatherland. … It is declining somehow, and instead of the collective We, the individual I is moving to the fore. I never knew a regime other than the Soviet until the year 1992, and I believe that I became what I am because of it and the Soviet state. (US6–04: 1335–54)

Valentina's patriotic sentiments are obviously intertwined with her political loyalty to communist ideology (represented here by internationalism and collectivism). Tania's statement makes it even stronger, with her refusal to recognize the legitimacy of any regime but the Soviet one: "There is no other authority for me. I am a thorough Soviet person—I love it; I esteem it. Naturally I was distressed over the disintegration of our Soviet country [*sic*]. I hate to see it torn to pieces! There used to be one country, one currency, one people" (US2–04: 837–55; 908–10). It is no accident that these women express their loyalty to a country (*страна*) and/or to Soviet rule (*советская власть*) interchangeably. At the same time, however, none of the pro-Soviet women demonstrated outright their fidelity to the Communist Party, Marxist-Leninist ideology, socialism, etc.

Loyalty to the former regime does not condone simultaneous loyalty to the current one. Indeed, for them the two states and their political systems are antagonistic in many ways. They expressed considerable dissatisfaction with the current state, its social policies, economy, dominant ideological trends, and so on. In so doing, the women pointed to problems in the socioeconomic sphere: corruption and bribery, bad and expensive education and healthcare, the high cost of living and miserable pensions, complicated connections with relatives and friends residing in other post-Soviet countries, and more. When it came to making a clear statement about one's attitude toward an independent Ukraine, however, pro-Soviet women found themselves in deep water. Throughout their entire lives they had been socialized to express loyalty to a political authority, so an open display of disloyalty to any state was unthinkable.

Many of them find it difficult to articulate clearly their discontent; they feel uneasy about putting into words their negative attitudes or critical opinions to the extent that their speech appears choppy, uneven, reiterative. The pressure of deeply internalized political correctness impedes criticism, even when dissatisfaction with some aspects of former or current politics is palpable. To get out of this embarrassing situation, women apply several escapist strategies that allow them to conceal, or to soften, their negative attitude toward the Ukrainian nation-state. These strategies include: (1) refusal to answer the question or to discuss the issue in depth; (2) denial of the very existence of Ukrainian independence; (3) brief and formal recognition of a legitimate right of Ukraine—just like any other country—to sovereignty and statehood; (4) avoiding personal opinions by feigning political incompetence, lack of expertise, or failure to understand correctly the true sense of political transformations, and so forth.

For contrast, we turn briefly to testimonials from western Ukrainian women. They manifested conflicted attitudes toward the communists, but the women were markedly less sympathetic to the Soviet regime than their counterparts to the south and east. Those clearly disloyal to it reflected upon socialist times from a different angle; they were most critical of the regime and blamed it for its inherently unjust nature, which prevented their self-fulfillment and/or impeded the achievement of certain goals. The following defects in Soviet rule were emphasized most frequently: ethnic inequality, namely, disdain towards and discrimination against Ukrainians; forced Russification (the total obtrusion of the Russian language); violation of civil rights and liberties (freedoms of speech and religion, and property rights); massive political repressions; and excessive punishments for minor transgressions.

Although it is easy enough to criticize a fallen regime, the pro-Ukrainian women did their best to maintain a fair balance between a totally negative evaluation of the Soviet regime and acknowledgment of certain benefits enjoyed under state socialism. Higher education free of charge and generally full-time employment elicited the most appreciation, even among those most critical of the Soviet system. As far as education is concerned, it has special value for the women, as their life stories attest: it is viewed as a necessary cornerstone for their life success.[9]

Mykhailyna was a Ukrainian from L'viv, for whom life under the Soviets began after the war. The border between Poland and Ukraine was redrawn in 1946–47, and Ukrainians were expelled in large numbers from Polish territory to the Ukrainian SSR. Her family was forcibly resettled in a rural area outside of L'viv. Mykhailyna did not fault the Soviet authorities for this forced relocation. In her mind, the hardships of settling in a new place seemed trivial enough when compared to the Polish cruelty that her family had endured prior to their deportation. Slowly, however, her narrative shifted to the fears and pressures she felt at first contact with Soviet authorities—how she dreaded recruitment to forced labor in Russia (UL4–05: 132–40), how she was pressed to join Komsomol[10] and the *kolkhoz* (collective farm), which she managed to escape only by a fluke (UL4–05: 172–200, 578–85). She also recalled the exhausting work on state-owned fields for a miserly food allocation (UL4–05: 557–78) and the exorbitant compulsory state grain requisitions placed on collective farms. Finally, she referred to the state expropriation of the family's land (UL4–05: 535–54), which had prompted her relocation to the city of L'viv.

Perhaps what is most remarkable about her recollections, however, is the fact that there was no condemnation of the regime's overall policies. She focused instead on her contacts with authorities only as they touched her personal life. Even when she referred to her unwillingness to join either the Komsomol or the *kolkhoz*, Mykhailyna underscored her own security and health concerns over any ideological consideration, as the following attests:

> Well, for us—it was to be the *kolkhoz*. Then mother fell ill, and what was I to do in the *kolkhoz* by myself? I couldn't manage! My feet hurt so from the stubble in the field. Everybody in the village was driven to the MTS [Machine Tractor Station]. Those who agreed to join the *kolkhoz* were permitted to return home. Because my mother was old and sick, they took me instead. Throughout the night and the following day, authorities attempted to persuade us to become members. ... I told them I could not sign on! I knew that once I joined, we would never leave that village! When I worked in the village, the Komsomol District Committee kept me there; they tried to coerce me into joining the Komsomol! But I said: if I do join and am killed on the way home, what about my mother? What will become of her? Komsomol members were often murdered [by nationalist guerillas] in those days. (UL4–05: 172–83)

As she went on, Mykhailyna's recollections of the relocation began to produce progressively negative feelings toward the Soviet authorities. She stressed especially the ban on both her native Ukrainian language at the workplace (a kindergarten) and church attendance. The latter was punishable by dismissal from work (UL4–05: 240–49; 355–60; 430–41). Her narrative moved toward collective memory, as her increasing use of plural pronouns such as we, us, and our testified. Gradually her wording became more politicized, and further negative judgments of the Soviet regime crept in. Yet, paradoxically, even as she talked about the limitations on civil rights and liberties under communism, as opposed to those same liberties in a free Ukraine, Mykhailyna was still able to express a limited appreciation of Soviet social policies, although she was careful to emphasize their appalling cost: "Compared to life under the Soviets, things today have changed dramatically. Dramatically. Whether it was free speech, the right to attend church, a chance remark, or a song. You know what it was like. Yes, we were given an apartment, even though the process took its toll on our health; still—we got one. But there was no freedom; a person could not draw a free breath" (UL4–05: 525–32).

When asked about the Soviet impact on her personal life, Mykhailyna strove for objectivity. As she weighed the advantages and disadvantages of communism, her most profound feelings about what was good and what was bad created a tension that was reflected in her rising condemnation of the Soviet system:

> It is important that I enrolled in the university, and finished evening school. But that was the only good thing. The rest—that *kolkhoz*—it was torment when they forced us into it. ... that was a negative. And the low wages, no free speech, no worshipping in church. But it was easier to get a free apartment, so we got one.

> We studied free of charge, and enrolling in a university was less problematic. As for the rest … it was not good. I had no right to say anything, I was afraid they would take me away if I made a single questionable remark. And let me tell you about church; I attended even though it was prohibited. (UL4–04: 1435–48)

Nadiia, another Ukrainian woman from L'viv, offered similar testimony, although she was considerably less charitable in her assessment of life under the Soviets:

> It was important for me that I finished normal school. The major thing is that I received an education and became a teacher, so my dream came true. But life was hard. … What can I say! We had no rights, no voice in anything. Mother lived in constant fear. We stopped observing religious holidays. I remember when I was a first-year student at the vocational school, we always attended church. But then a certain teacher arrived. If she caught any of us in church, she threatened: "If I see you there one more time! What kind of teachers are you that you go to church?! You will never see a school or teach again!" UL2–04: 1179–235)

The subject of the Soviet regime first emerged in her testimony as she related the story of the Red Army entering her native town at the end of World War II, followed by the onset of Soviet rule (UL2–04: 66–71). Normal life was destroyed for her family; her father was accused of collaborating with the Nazis (he was an accountant at the post office during the Nazi occupation). He was arrested and condemned to ten years' incarceration. Her mother, left with the couple's three children, was branded a wife of the people's enemy and dismissed from her job as a school teacher. From her narrative, it appears that virtually every negative experience in Nadiia's life, except her education, was associated with Soviet rule: her childhood memories of postwar hardships, which the family barely survived (UL2–04: 134–38), her forced membership in Komsomol (UL2–04: 201–6), and the unremitting fear of persecution for any incautious criticism of the regime (UL2–04: 253–56), not to mention humiliations suffered on account of her ethnic origin. Nadiia never doubted that her Ukrainian ethnicity was the reason for discrimination and scorn on the part of Soviet authorities. Summarizing her experience, she stated: "One day, some women from Volgograd were seated in the courtyard. I greeted them in Ukrainian. Their response was: "*Banderivka* has arrived, *zapadenka* is here."[11] They had nothing but contempt for us, saying: "You're a *banderivka,* you're a *zapadenka.* Poles didn't respect us, and Russians didn't respect us. Poles called us louts, and Russians called us *banderivtsi,* and today they still refer to me as *zapadenka* or *banderivka.* This was true at school as well" (UL2–05: 1081–82, 1202–15).

The women who are disloyal to the Soviet regime (mainly Ukrainians from the west) tended to maintain their painful recollections of Soviet times. Although they did acknowledge some of the benefits of socialism, they were not prepared to forget or to forgive its serious shortcomings. Above all this applied to the limitations on civil rights, as well as the ethnic and religious discrimination to which they were subjected under Soviet rule. In other words, the women who considered the Soviet regime a key obstacle or a restrictive factor in their life achievements openly revealed their disloyalty to it.

Another remarkable aspect of the western Ukrainian appraisals of the Soviet regime was the manner in which the women expressed their negative attitude. They used pejorative terms (such as *moskali* and *soviety*) to describe the hated Soviet regime and its agents, even though they too had been Soviet citizens. Conversely, the language of those loyal to the Soviet system rarely breached political correctness. Indeed, this group used the insulting denominations (e.g., *banderivtsi, zapadentsi*) only in a few instances when recalling very personal negative encounters with Ukrainian nationalists. At the same time, neither side resorted to mutually pejorative terms outside the politically charged lexicon, such as *khokhly* for Ukrainians and *katsapy* for Russians.

Women expressed their disloyalty to the opposite regimes when they applied a specific linguistic tool: the pro-Soviet women invoked the Ukrainian term *nezalezhnist'* (not the Russian *nezavisimost'*) to name the independence of Ukraine in order to emphasize its unacceptability for loyal Soviet citizens. The pro-Ukrainian women emphasized their estrangement from the oppressive Soviet regime by constantly using its Russian variant—*soviety* (instead of the Ukrainian *radians'ki*). Research in cognitive psychology and cognitive linguistics suggests that word choices have significant framing effects on the perceptions, memories, and attitudes of speakers and listeners alike.[12] By failing to translate the name of an opposite regime into one's native language, women stressed its alien status, and in so doing implicitly denied its relevance to their own lives.

Social (In)Equality

One of the key concepts of the communist ideology to be implemented by state socialism is the theory of equality and equal opportunities for all. Contrary to this rhetoric, most of the women's life narratives contained references to social stratification and inequality (privilege and discrimination). Also noteworthy was the fact that diverse regional origins made it possible for these women to view and understand disparities in Soviet citizens in different ways. Women from the east and south underscored inequality based upon social status and material wealth, and praised the communist system as a great leveler. Valeria from Kharkiv, who frequently emphasized equality as a hallmark of the communist system, recalled two incidents from her life as a child in order to highlight the earlier social stratification and discrimination:

In the primary school, there was a female teacher who came from the nobility, and what a noble dame she was, how she disdained us poor children. There were times when I turned in a very good test, but Verochka, the daughter of a factory director, received the highest marks even though she didn't know a thing; she copied my work. I also had a friend, a weak student, who copied everything from me. ... Her father was the chief of police; he owned a car and a large house. (UK1–04: 914–35)

Valeria's positioning of a noble school teacher, a factory director, and a chief of police into a single "wealthy" category revealed the extent to which she viewed prosperity as the key factor in the inequality and social injustice she had suffered in childhood. Despite the declared elimination of differences between rich and poor under state socialism, the theme of social stratification, to which she returned repeatedly, also figured prominently in the narrative of Agafia from Kharkiv: "She [mother] brought us all up, earning a living as a seamstress for wealthy families in their homes, where they fed her. She left early each morning and returned at night. We could see that this upset her. ... Children from the wealthy families attended school with me; they were well dressed, especially the girls, and I could only envy them" (UK2–04: 24–25, 124–28).

Agafia equated affluence with high social status, an object of dreams and envy for her. It was clear that she perceived her own lack of wealth as something distressing even unfit for public discussion. Nevertheless, even though it could not be measured by prosperity, she did consider a success her life in the communist system: "Life went on. We were far from wealthy, but we lived well; we attended the cinema, the theater, vacationed in resorts, traveled and saw so much" (UK2–04: 545–46; 1869–71). Larissa echoed Agafia's sentiment: "I've got an education, I've got a profession, I had a job, I earned, and I could afford nice things for myself. True, I did not live in luxury, but I vacationed" (US1–04: 1512–16).

As far as other kinds of social discrimination are concerned, we also have here a clear indication of the ethnic prejudices represented by unequal relationships between the dominant and the colonized nations. A hierarchical scheme exemplified the imperialistic mindset of Valentina from Simferopil', a lifelong Russian language teacher. The cultural hierarchy model she constructed for herself relegated all nationalities in the USSR, apart from the Russian, to inferior status. Valentina repeatedly referred to the enlightening and civilizing mission of Russians toward the culturally backward non-Russians. At the end of the interview, in answer to the question, "What does Ukrainian independence signify for you?" She reiterated this conviction:

Russia was the foremost country. It dispensed generous assistance in every sphere—financial, cultural, the spiritual growth of national republics. We were sent to Uzbekistan, to Georgia, to Armenia, to every place in need. I know this well. All kinds of data show that before the Bolshevik revolution, the Trans-Caucasian countries, all Central-Asian regions, and even Ukraine, not to mention Moldova and the others, were in fact illiterate societies; language was under-developed, scholarship progressed slowly. The Soviets did everything possible to raise their literacy rate. (US6–04: 1476–85)

Valentina incorporated Soviet propaganda-style clichés into her own bio-graphical narration, and skewed information such as the degree of illiteracy and its geographical distribution in the Russian Empire, to conform to the dominant political discourse. Attesting to her ideological indoctrination was the fact that Russia and the Soviet Union were implicitly identified as being interchangeable.

Vira, a Ukrainian from the eastern city of Kharkiv who, with her hus-band, was sent to work in western Ukraine in 1939, expressed similar views, but she was more circumspect in her comments. She offered more justifications for the anti-Soviet attitudes in western Ukraine than her eastern Ukrainian counterparts were prepared to concede. To be sure, as an ethnic Ukrainian, she might not have felt altogether comfortable with her pro-Russian Soviet identity:

> The Central Committee of the Communist Party appointed my husband direc-tor of a school in the L'viv region. We tried so hard to treat the local population well. The regime provided rice, butter; and it sent children to pioneers' camps. What can I say? These poor people had suffered so much, under the Poles, the Austrians, the Hungarians, others. Now they trusted no one; all they wanted was independence, a free Ukraine. They didn't want [Soviets there]. ... Well, they did suffer. I understand. They suffered in Polish bondage, in Hungarian bondage. (UK3–04: 390–418)

Consciously or not, all of the respondents reflected prejudice of one kind or another, as well as often contradictory or ambivalent reactions. Applying ethnically determined social stratification paradigms, Russians and Russo-phones presented themselves as culturally superior to the backward peoples residing on the peripheries of the empire. The empire had done its work well. One of Agafia's remarks makes the correlation between the Russian language, with its elite status, and social divisions, especially clear

> There was a woman, a Kazan Tatar and her husband, a Lezghin, with three adult children. Today Sara is a pediatrician, her daughter Marianna is a midwife, and son Akliper an oil industry engineer. This is the kind of thing that the Soviet regime made possible. Just imagine, children of such illiterates, with a poor com-mand of the Russian language, trained as specialists! (UK2–04: 2245–47)

The prejudice against non-Russians is difficult to ignore here.

Language Divisions

Freedom of speech is also closely interwoven with the interviewees' native language. Language disparity is a particularly sensitive issue for Ukrainians. Supporters of the Soviet regime approved Russian as the universal language of international communication for the new Soviet "nation" [*sic*]. When the Soviet state collapsed, its adherents agonized over the loss of their radiant socialist utopia in which the Russian language had served as a unifier. Here is how Larissa and Valentina, both from Simferopil', described it:

> I was teaching various peoples: there were Tatars, Georgians, and Uzbeks in my class. ... There never was a problem with ethnicity. We paid no attention to such things. So what is considered a problem today was not an issue then. As someone, Stalin I think, said: "There is a nation—the Soviet people." (US1–04: 1529–54)

> Teaching in a multinational environment was very stimulating. Russians, Azerbaijani, Jews, Armenians, Georgians, and others all studied there. I recall with much fondness those days of no discord, no references to Jews or Azerbaijani, or Armenians. We were like one extended family. ... There were children of all nationalities, and one never heard a single reference to someone's ethnic background. The attitude toward the Russian language was marvelous; everybody aspired to learn it. (US6–04: 393–405, 432–37)

Naturally it came as no surprise to hear that "everybody aspired to learn Russian," in light of the fact that its privileged status opened so many doors to resources and careers. Its alleged benefits notwithstanding, western Ukrainians resisted this kind of national and linguistic homogenization to a far greater extent than their counterparts in other parts of Ukraine. To the former, it signified the destruction of a well-developed and cherished ethnic identity, of which language is the core. For those who embraced the Soviet existence, together with all that it exemplified, it represented the halcyon childhood days of national harmony, a return to a happier time when every ethnic group purportedly was respected as an equal.

Independence finally eradicated the two forces that western Ukrainian women hated most—a totalitarian political system and its official language. Two of these women, Nadiia and Mykhailyna, were adamant in their response to the question, "What does Ukrainian independence signify in your life?" Here again we have a clear indication of the differing sentiments that women in separate regions of the former Soviet Union expressed:

> What does it signify? At last one can draw a free breath, live in [what had once again become] our own country, on our own land. Our parents promised that one day Ukraine would be free, independent. ... And now it has become easier to breathe. Pensions are meager, but we live in our own free Ukraine. We walk freely, breathe freely, feel like human beings. (UL2–04: 1394–1400)

God grant that we preserve this independence. Let there be just bread and water, as long as we can speak freely and worship without fear; that is all we need.
(UL4–05: 1612–14).

By way of contrast, the Russophones in the east and south (ethnic Russians
or Russified Ukrainians) expressed their unconditional support of Russian as
a universal language and prestigious vehicle for international communication.
They saw no problem in its superior stature, insofar as it had never imposed
limitations or created any inconveniences for them personally. Scholars in different contexts have made similar observations when they examined the connection between national borders and mental boundaries elsewhere. Children
who grow up in the heart of large and powerful states and societies tend to
feel no restrictions (Davis 2002: 329–44.) It is as if they reside at the center of
the universe. But when circumstances change, and, as in this case, the dominant power becomes a national minority in the breakaway non-Russian states,
their perception of the language situation changes radically. Russophones
now exhibited extreme anxiety over the loss of the once-favored status of the
Russian tongue. Although Ukraine issued formal guarantees of unfettered development for the languages and cultures of ethnic minorities in the country
(and this included Russian), legal equality does not necessarily translate into
prestige, or the absence of discrimination in practice. Russophones fear being
forced to speak the official language of the Ukrainian state, although non-Russians were forced to speak Russian in the former Soviet state. Agafia expressed
her concerns by referring to her unpleasant experience in the 1960s:[13]

> I learned the Azerbaijani language with pleasure—but not Ukrainian. When we
> came to Kharkov after a long journey, we needed to learn so many languages that
> our children rebelled. At the time, children of military men were legally exempt
> from learning Ukrainian. But in Kharkov my son was humiliated in front of his
> entire class when he was told that those who consume Ukrainian bread must learn
> the Ukrainian language. I don't believe in such coercion. (UK2–04: 2282–95)

The same Russophones also equated the Russian language with the powerful Soviet state. Women from the southern and eastern parts of Ukraine now
consider independence as something destructive of their national integrity.
This notion also has triggered the kind of hostility that Natalia from Crimea
displayed toward the very notion of Ukrainian sovereignty, and it helps to
explain why she and Agafia were so nostalgic about their lost international
paradise:

> Ukraine is no sovereign country; it lacks genuine economic and political inde-
> pendence. This ill-considered independence affects us all. Our union with Russia
> is gone. As Soviets, we were not all Russians, of course. For instance, I am half
> Ukrainian because my father was Ukrainian, but I identify myself as Russian, and
> for me this represents the loss of my roots. All my life, we lived as citizens of one

state, but today we find ourselves on opposite sides of the divide. I think this was a very stupid development, and I would welcome a reunion if it should happen. Slavic nations must cling to each other. (US3–04: 884–94)

Yet the policy of forging a melting pot, in which no one was concerned with a separate ethnicity, was not successfully internalized by all respondents. The very fact that the women referred so frequently to the ethnicity of non-Russians (relatives, neighbors, classmates, colleague, and others) testified to their acute awareness of ethnic differences, all affirmations of unity to the contrary:

> I recall our Crimean class. Its composition was international: Russians, a few Ukrainians, many Jews, two Armenian boys, a Greek girl, and two Tatars. Classmates were very friendly, and there were no negative allusions to ethnicity, never. We all saw ourselves as equals, and nobody cared about ethnicity. (US3–04: 786–95).

> I was educated in the spirit of internationalism, so this was not an issue for me. This is what we were taught. (US3–04: 864–68)

> Our apartment house was international: Crimean Tatars, Lezgins, Kazan Tatars, and Azerbaijanis. There were some Russians, but basically it was a unified family, a unified family. (UK2–04: 124–26, 180–85)

This contradiction between proclaimed principles and reality is perhaps the most salient feature of the Soviet era. The similarity of the respondents' wording (in the biographical narrations and answers to direct questions) serves as additional evidence of their deep ideological indoctrination by Soviet propaganda.

Conclusion

To summarize, this study of the notion of patriotism can serve as an analytically valuable tool. Loyalty can mean a special kind of political allegiance that assumes a strong commitment to one's native land. Unlike other political loyalties, however, patriotic loyalty is normally not a question of a person's conscious choice. Various agents of socialization cultivate it.

Patriotism is all bound up with a fairly well-articulated portrayal of the beloved country, with all of its valuable features. Patriotic loyalty requires certain beliefs about its object, without necessarily being premised upon an independent judgment that such beliefs are true. As a result, Simon Keller claims, the patriot tends to make uncritical judgments about the qualities of his/her own country. That is patriotic bad faith, which is likely to play a central role in the patriot's construal of the world and the person's own moral obligations

(2007: 91–92). And it is very likely that a patriot's bad faith will have the effect of distorting thinking about other serious matters (2007: 53). The rigidity of one's political beliefs, and the distorting effect of political loyalty over one's own perception and over the evaluation of new data, is paralleled in a separate study (Przybyszewski 2004: 47–67).

This distorting quality of political loyalty (represented as Soviet patriotism) is visible in the women's attempts to deny, lessen, or justify the avowed failings of the Soviet regime. In the face of proven facts and data, they still prefer to keep their fidelity pure. Those sincerely loyal to contemporary Ukraine express their total and unconditional devotion to the independent Ukrainian nation-state, including all of its institutions, policies, and so on. And again, even an awareness of the serious shortcomings of the current politics (including corruption, economic instability, political quarrels, tensions between regions, unsolved ethnic problems, etc.) does not prevent them from explaining away these vices as temporary privations of transition and expressing their Ukrainian patriotism. Although their statements of loyalty do not rise to the level of a pro-Soviet-style pledge, the western Ukrainian women were bursting with enthusiasm and declared their readiness to bear any adversity for the sake of their long hoped-for and recently (re)gained country as an independent state.

Each interviewee recalled a specific past with longing. Western Ukrainians longed for their pre-Soviet way of life, only without Polish oppression. Women from the other two regions recalled with longing their Soviet reality. "Nostalgia is a sentiment of loss and displacement" explains Svetlana Boym (2001: xiii). "At first glance it represents a longing for place, but in fact it is a yearning for a different time—childhood—the nostalgic desire to turn history into a private and collective mythology, to revisit time like space, refusing to surrender to that irreversibility of time that plagues the human condition" (xv). The geography in women's memories is politically charged; it also has its temporal dimension. Thus it is impossible to overlook the east-west dichotomy that permeated the perceptions of women from opposite sides of the divide—L'viv and Kharkiv—as the best and most extreme examples in this particular study. On the women's mental maps, the regions are not only separated by geography; they belong to two different eras, and each is seen as the Other—alien and hostile.

Attitudes toward the Soviet regime versus an independent Ukrainian state, on the part of women from the three discrete regions in this study, reflected more than their territorial affiliations. They were each products of the discrete communities in which respondents were born and raised. The women's respective historical experiences shaped the constructs of the past in their narratives. Women from western Ukraine were born under a nontotalitarian social order (although they did know a measure of ethnic discrimination), and their early socialization was not impacted by communist propaganda. Before the Soviets arrived in the 1940s, their families were not subjected to the terrible Stalinist repressive machinery. Even if life for Ukrainians in Halychyna (Galicia, or western Ukraine) during the interwar period was anything but unproblematic, they had dodged all of the atrocities of Stalinist-style communist construction. They remembered their pre-Soviet lives, and developed a critical attitude towards Soviet-era discriminations. During the entire phase of their incorporation into the Soviet Union, they lived in a kind of spiritual exile. Not unexpectedly, they regarded the collapse of the USSR as a restoration of historical justice, and their own liberation a true return to their once-lost homeland.

The women's longing for a Soviet-free existence was tantamount to the nostalgia for the Soviet era on the opposite geographical and ideological divide, on the part of those who never knew a regime apart from the Soviet, any ideological order other than communism. Some of them admitted that had their socialization begun under other circumstances (as it did for the western Ukrainians), they might have evaluated socialism in more rational terms (UK3-04: 1325-28). Under the circumstances, however, how else could they perceive the collapse of this empire than as both a collective and a personal defeat? The disintegration of the USSR meant the crumbling of an entire value system in which they had placed their trust, their faith, their being. They had lost their homeland—the USSR—and thereafter were destined to feel like refugees in an independent Ukraine, a country that they were never able to love.

Loyalties to the two different political systems are indissoluble from the two state formations—the USSR and independent Ukraine—which represent for the women two incompatible objects of patriotic sentiments. Some comprehension of the origins of their respective attitudes toward both Russia and independent Ukraine would go a long way toward eliminating their respective prejudices, perhaps even lead to a mutual understanding and reconciliation of the past and, even more important, of the future.

Notes

1. In the history of Ukraine, women's studies became an actual field of research only in the 1990s. For a detailed overview of recent developments of women's and gender history in Ukraine, see Oksana Kis' 2010, and 2004: 291–302.

2. The project was conducted at the Institute of Ethnology, National Academy of Sciences of Ukraine, and was supported by a research grant from the Canadian Institute of Ukrainian Studies, University of Alberta.

3. For more information about this cross-national venture, its goals, methodology, chronology, etc. see http://www.womensmemory.net.

4. Gluck 1977: 3–13; Sangster 1994: 5–28; Gluck and Patai 1991. For a further discussion on gender differences in historical memory see Leydesdorff 1996.

5. Eight interviews in L'viv, ten in Kharkiv, and ten in Simferopil' were recorded by the end of 2005.

6. The external questions were: (1) What does the Soviet regime mean in your life? (2) What do you think about people of various ethnicities living next to you? (3) Identify the historical events which have had the most influence on your life. (4) What is the significance of Ukrainian independence in your life? (5) What was most helpful for overcoming hardships in your life?

7. The policy of anonymity precludes the inclusion of interviewees' personal data (including names, date and place of birth, current address, etc.). Each interview was assigned a special code: the first letter U means the country, the second (L, K, or S) indicates the city where the interview was recorded, the subsequent digits identify the interview's number; the numbers after a dash refer to the year of recording, and the figures after the colon refer to the number of lines excerpted from the transcript.

8. In 1932–33 between 4.5 and 8.1 million Ukrainians died as a result of the famine engineered by Stalin; the year 1937 is known for mass political repressions throughout the USSR.

9. For a detailed analysis of this issue, see: Kis' 2009: 337–52.

10. Komsomol—abbreviation for *Komunisticheskyi Soiuz Molodezhi* (Communist Union of Youth), the youth subdivision of the Communist Party of the Soviet Union.

11. *Banderivka, banderivtsi* are followers of Stephan Bandera (1909–1959), leader of the Organization of Ukrainian Nationalists, and a key figure in Ukraine's national liberation movement of 1930–1950. He was murdered by a KGB agent in Munich. *Zapadenka, zapadentsi* are people from western Ukraine. These designations are associated with the nationalist struggle against the Soviet regime, together with its Russification policy, and generally carry negative connotations. Also known as *Petliurivtsi*—followers of Semen Petliura (1877–1926)—Ukrainian politician, statesman, and one of the commanders in the "Directory of the Ukrainian People's Republic," which opposed the Bolshevik regime between 1918 and 1920.

12. Kahneman and Tversky 1981: 4553–58; Hutton 2001.

13. It was during "Khrushchev's thaw" and Shelests's Ukrainianization agenda in the late 1960s.

Bibliography

Boym, Svetlana. 2001. *The Future of Nostalgia*. New York: Basic Books.

Connor, James. 2007. *The Sociology of Loyalty*. New York: Springer.

Devault, Marjorie L. 1990. "Talking and Listening from the Woman's Standpoint: Feminist Strategies for Interviewing and Analysis." *Social Problems* 37 (1): 96–116.

Gluck, Sherna Berger. 1977. "What's So Special about Women? Women's Oral History." *FRONTIERS: A Journal of Women's Studies* (2): 3–13.

Gluck, Sherna Berger, and Daphne Patai, eds. 1991. *Women's Words: The Feminist Practice of Oral History*. New York: Routledge.

Hutton, W. 2001. "Words are really important, Mr Blunkett." *Observer* (16 December), 7.

Kahneman, D., and Amos Tversky. 1981. "The Framing of Decisions and the Psychology of Choice." *Science* (211): 453–58.

Keller, Simon. 2007. *The Limits of Loyalty*. Cambridge: Cambridge University Press.

Kis', Oksana. 2004. "L'approche de genre dans les recherches en histoire et éthnologie Ukrainiennes." *Éthnologie Français* (1): 291–302.

———. 2009. "Osvichena zhinka; osvita iak tsinnist' ta mirylo zhyttievoho uspikhu v avtobiografiiakh zhinok Urainy." In *Identychnist' i pamiat' v suchasnii Ukraini." Identity and Memory in Contemporary Ukraine*. Myroslava Antonovych, ed., 337–52. Kyiv: Dukh i Litera.

———. forthcoming. "(Re)constructing the Women's Histories in Ukraine: Actors, Agents, Authors, Narratives." *Gender, Politics and Society in Ukraine*. Olena Pevny and Anstasiya Salnykova, eds. Toronto: University of Toronto Press.

———. 2011. "Telling the Untold: Representations of Ethnic and Regional Identities in Ukrainian Women's Autobiographies." In *Orality and Literacy: Reflections across Disciplines and Cultures*. Keith Carlson et al. eds., 280–314. Toronto: University of Toronto Press.

Leydesdorff, Selma et al., eds. 1996. *Gender and Memory: International Yearbook of Oral History and Life Stories* (4).

Portelli, Alessandro. 1998. "What Makes Oral History Different." In *The Oral History Reader*. Robert Perks and Alistar Thomson, eds., 63–74. London: Routledge.

Przybyszewski, Krzysztof. 2004. "Cognitive Consequences of Political Loyalty." *Journal of Political Marketing* 3(2): 47–67.

Rosenthal, Gabriel. 2004. "Biographical Research, in Qualitative Research Practice." *Qualitative Research Practice*. Clive Seale et al., eds, 48–64. London: Sage Publications.

Sangster, Joan. 1994. "Telling Our Stories: Feminist Debates and the Use of Oral History." *Women's History Review* (3): 5–28.

Sereda, Viktoria. 2007. "Regional Differences in Historical Identities: Gender Aspect." *Bulletin of Odessa National University. Sociology and Political Science* 12 (6): 78–88.

Shutova, Olga. 2000. "Ustnaia I gendernaia istoriia v sviete antropologizatsii istoriografii." In Irina Chikalova, ed., 55ff., *Zhenschiny v istorii: vozmozhnost' byt' uvidennymi*. Minsk.

Yuval-Davis, Nira, and Marcel Stoetzler. 2002. "Imagined Boundaries and Borders: A Gendered Gaze." *European Journal of Women's Studies* 9 (3): 329–44.

CHAPTER 6

Chronicle of Children's Holidays

Construction of Gender Stereotypes in Ukrainian Preschools and Elementary Education

Victoria Haydenko

Gender typing can be explored from different angles: psychological, sociological, cultural, educational, and philosophical. The objective of this study is to show how the gender marker is embedded into education by means of children's holidays; how preschool and elementary school curricula influence its development/distortion and contribute to the construction of gender stereotypes. Three common issues are essential for understanding the formation of such stereotypes—gender-oriented games, mother, and father as role models—to bring together all the scripts. My research indicates that the feminization of primary education, a clear differentiation between masculine and feminine roles, and the predominance of maternal images all conspire to create gender stereotypes. Some of the few existing attempts, or early intervention, to deconstruct and challenge the existing views on gender (alternative narratives, course syllabi, and educational activities) will be discussed.

Education, Stereotyping, and Child Development

As E. Reimer posits, "Schools in all nations ... combine four distinct social functions: custodial care, social role selection, and indoctrination, and education is usually defined in terms of the development of skills and knowledge" (Levy 1972: 6). This makes schools an effective and powerful instrument of social control. Paradoxically, although schools make a show of supporting an ideology of equality and diversity while developing open-mindedness, the fact is, according to Levy, their teaching is reduced to shaping conformity and stunting critical thought (1972: 8). Despite Ukraine's best efforts to distance itself from its Soviet heritage (politics, ideology, education, holidays, etc.), it remains bound by it and continues to repeat its shortcomings. If we define ideology as a system of beliefs referring specifically to a social and/or political structure, we can argue that it advocates the predominance of certain views and eliminates the potential for alternatives; hence ideology and power intersect. Without the presence of unifying beliefs, it would be difficult to maintain power and to construct its screws, or to use Foucault's words, docile bodies.

A number of studies conducted on child development present evidence of the presence of gender stereotyping in early childhood (Kohlberg 1996: 82–173; Thomson 1975: 339–47). As an example, four-year-olds are highly conscious of cultural stereotypes that define their own sex, but less certain of stereotypes that pertain to the opposite sex. Between the ages of three to five, for instance, children's toy choices are influenced by gender-based reasoning; they use gender labels to guide their own preferences and meet the expectations of others (Martin, Eisenbud, and Rose 1995: 1453). Gender stereotyping is intensified by class—children from lower socioeconomic classes are more likely to hold strong prejudices, because they lack opportunities to observe a greater variety of adult role models and are subjected to more impoverished learning experiences than their peers in more affluent and more prestigious economic environments (Stroeher 1994: 101). Such segregation during the early stages of socialization contributes to gender-typing behavior. Other contributory factors include treatment of individual children by their parents, teachers, and friends.

Education theorists use the term *hidden curriculum* to indicate the existence of a set of attitudes, rules, language structure, etc. that are subconsciously absorbed by children. They form the ideological basis of certain educational procedures (including special observances) that support gender stereotypes. The hidden curriculum also serves to control children's behavioral practices through such measures as influencing what they wear, and how they interact with each other in the classroom and after school activities. In addition, the process of interiorizing stereotypes is facilitated by officially approved readings—textbooks and children's storybooks. Taken together, all such factors create constraints that force children into socially acceptable patterns of behavior for each sex. This chapter will examine such patterns in Ukrainian schools, as well as ways in which instructional materials are developed in professional journals, in order to stereotype classroom activities such as special children's holidays.

Sources and Methods

As a member of the faculty at the Khmelnytsky Humanities and Pedagogical Institute in Ukraine from 2001 to 2006, I supervised and evaluated student teaching practices in various kindergartens and primary schools. This allowed me to accumulate data on teaching methods and their impact on the socialization of young children. In addition, I have examined journals—primarily western—and conducted a survey of the few existing Ukrainian journals for preschool and primary-school teachers. The list comprises: *Biblioteka vchytelia* (Teacher's Library 2001); *Pochatkova osvita* (Beginning Education 2005, 2005b, 2005c); *Pozaklasny chas* (After School Time 2004, 2005); and *Rozkazhit' onuku* (Tell It to Your Grandson 2001, 2002, 2003). To date, they are virtually the only practical guides to planning classroom activities and organizing patriotically oriented celebrations available in Ukraine. All have been approved by the Ministry of Culture and Education, a national requirement since the country's educational system follows a universal regimen and the curriculum is identical for every school. There is some flexibility for teachers to determine how intensively the mandated materials will be used, but an annual report of all activity acts as a control mechanism that ensures at least basic universal compliance.

Gender Chronicle of Children's Holidays Observed in Schools

I have chosen to examine all of the above-listed materials for their suggested approaches to conducting special observances or holidays in Ukrainian schools. These most recent publications came out between 2002 and 2005. They contain the greatest number of directions for planning classroom activities and patriotically oriented observances, in accordance with the guidelines established by the Ministry of Culture and Education. Like so many other activities, classroom observances have a ritualistic nature. Each such routine can be understood as having its own rules: verbal and nonverbal expressions, repeatable actions, and anticipated results. In the words of P. McLaren: "Rituals may be perceived as carriers of cultural codes (cognitive and gestural information) that shape the pupils' perceptions and ways of understanding" (1986: 3). For instance, celebrating the same holidays in the same way from preschool to high school automates the activities, depersonalizes the words, and transforms the event into simple formality. This has a mechanical effect on children, inasmuch as the main stock phrases, with corresponding biases, are already recorded, or encoded, in their consciousness. The captured symbolic meanings of gender roles direct children's knowledge, form attitudes towards life, and inform subsequent activities.

It is important for us to understand the clear gender dimension of female-oriented celebrations, known as Mother's Day, International Women's Day, and Celebration of Spring holidays, and the only male-oriented observance, Army Day, all of which are built into their own special observances. Taking into consideration the frequency with which certain issues are raised, I have elected to pay special attention to the following topics as they relate to ritualistic observances or exercises in the schools in order of apparent importance for effective acculturation to socially held values: the mother image, gender socialization, and the father image.

The Mother Image

This appears to be the most pervasive symbol in children's activities, as evidenced by the number and kinds of observances ritualized in the schools. Some examples include: "Mother's Day;" "Our mother;" "We sing about mother;" "A Mother's waltz;" "A little embroidered towel for mother;" and more. The phrase "*ma-ma my-la ra-mu*" (mama washed a frame) is a typical sentence in an ABC book, which has served as a beginning primer for generation after generation of school children. The mother image occurs in one ABC book ninety-two times (Haydenko and Predborska 2006: 139). This testifies to the fact that the nation itself identifies primarily with the mother figure. She accustoms children to their native language (the Ukrainian language is your mother tongue). The mother is popularly known as Berehynia,[1] representing a nurturing woman, guardian of the now-symbolic domestic hearth, and embodiment of moral principles. She brings up children, is a good cook, and embroiders shirts for the family. For instance, the conclusion of many governmental speeches for International Women's Day was, and still is, an exaltation of Berehynia, whose task it is to help men in the realization of their ideal of national sovereignty. Matriarchal tendencies reanimated by a patriarchal world come to light in children's festivals. They are sharply defined in at least three events: International Women's Day, Family Celebration, and Mother's Day.

The cult of motherhood reached its ludicrous apotheosis in school when a teacher, M. Mashovetz, in a script entitled "Teach a child to love his/her mother," introduced the notion of "vitamin A"[2] as a product with magical properties, and presented it as a well-known term of psychology (*Doshkil'ne* 2005: 28–29). She pronounced Vitamin A a product imbued with the maternal, physical, and emotional energy necessary for a child's healthy growth—in other words, maternal love.

Portraying the ideal maternal image, educators trace in detail all of the tasks and responsibilities of a mother. Since the term *woman* is replaced by that of *mother*, all maternal functions also are represented as natural women's duties. This image serves as an example of femininity to be internalized by both boys and girls, in accordance with which they will model their behavior and adjust their gender expectations. Insofar as the internalization of gender roles occurs in a school—an institution with power and authority in the child's life—the stereotypes are intensified.

Closeness to National Roots and Nature

The characteristics of motherhood can be illuminated by reviewing the following categories:

Mother is like bread and human kindness, native language, destiny, and sacred truth:

> International Women's Day: We are mother's helpers (*Pozaklasnyi* 2004: 107)
>
> Spring Fairy Tale "March 8." Spring is coming—mother's holiday is approaching. Bless me mother in welcoming spring (*Rozkazhit'* 2002: 24, 31).

Infinite love and devotion:

> A mother is like a gentle dove who takes us under her wing of love (*Doshkil'ne* 2005: 28–29)
>
> A riddle: Who is the dearest and sweetest, caresses us and is always with us? My dear mother (*Rozkazhit'* 2002: 23)

The word *mother* itself can carry exceptional connotations, as we see in the verse "A Beautiful Word," by K. Perelisna, since it is capable of solving problems:

> Mother, mother is such a beautiful word.
> Just say the word and everything is done.
> Mother, I want some hot cereal [kasha]! Here you are.
> Mother, I want a cup of tea!—Poured out.
> Mother, I want to sleep!—Already undressed
> And covered with a blanket ...
> Mother, tell me a story (Leshchenko 1986: 15)

Hardworking

Hard work describes a mother's daily existence. She is multitask oriented, responsible for housework and the education of children. If we look at the statistics from 2002, 54.8 percent of Ukraine's families were headed by women. What can be said about the fact that 88.5 percent of Ukraine's families have no father present, whereas only 5.1 percent are without mothers? The new post-Soviet socioeconomic circumstances created an atmosphere of pressure and competition that complicated everyday life, making it difficult to survive; this led to certain changes in gender relations. For instance, M. Kiblitskaya describes the "symbolic castration" of men who fail to live up to what many regard their masculine duty (2000: 103). Conversely, mothers are portrayed as being there, fulfilling all obligations, holding the household together:

> Mother, like a bird at first light, awake since dawn,
> She moves silently about the house, so as not to waken me.
>   A Family Observance: Mother as Berehynia (*Rozkazhit'* 2003: 8)

> I kiss your hands ... drained of so much strength.
> Family Celebration:
> "Mother's hands smell of bread" (*Pozaklasnyi* 2005: 42)

> Mother has been cleaning all day,
> Mother has magical hands that sew, cook, plait, knit and sew (*Pozaklasnyi* 2005: 47–48)

> Mother's Day:
> Our sweetest mothers (*Pozaklasnyi* 2005: 44–46)

> The sun smiled and I woke up.
> Mother has worked hard already.
>   Popular children's song for Mother's Day

Mother's Day is also an occasion when children address their grandmothers as: "my dearest grandmother, my mother's mother" while ignoring the figure of the father's mother. The line "women, grandmothers, and mothers are our eternal Berehyni" emphasizes, yet again, the woman's essentialist role (*Pozaklasnyi* 2005: 37–40).[3]

Nation as Mother

Inasmuch as the mother image embodies the finest national ideals, identification of *mother* with the Ukrainian nation is not surprising: a number of riddles indicate that *mother* and *Ukraine* are synonymic notions—Discover Motherland in yourself, and Ukraine is my mother. Although in Ukrainian the word for *Motherland* is actually *Fatherland* (*bat'kivshchyna*), deriving from the word father (*bat'ko*), the image of Ukraine in primary-school textbooks is always female. Russian researcher G. Fedotov explains this apparent paradox by pointing out that the interaction of maternal-feminine and paternal-masculine underlies every nation's being. Paternal and maternal consciousness can be seen as love for Motherland and for Fatherland alike. Motherland and maternity are expressed in the language, songs, and fairy tales, in references to national roots. Fatherland is linked to obligations, law, and sentient existence (Fedotov 1991: 252). Although in Ukraine, the love of one's nation is expressed in maternal terms, the love of Motherland and Fatherland alike is implicit. The scripts on patriotic education ("Love and Know the Cossack (*Kozak*) Land" and "Cossack Entertainment") usually choose the boys as central characters since they imply endurance, strength, and speed, while the girls are considered mainly spectators (*Rozkazhit'* 2001: 24; *Doshkil'ne* 2003c: 20–23). The image of the mother (singing lullabies, twining a wreath) is present also in patriotically oriented activity: "I am a little Ukrainian girl" (*Rozkazhit'* 2001: 9).

Identifying Teachers with Mothers

Particular emphasis is placed on this in learning-related celebrations (Book Fest; Good Bye ABC; Farewell Preschool; Day of Knowledge). During the early stages of learning, especially, children acknowledge the teacher's maternal role. The well-known saying emphasizes this: "Your teacher is your second mother." Woman's ability to nurture is considered an innate feminine characteristic, whereas the diversity of women's experiences is ignored. The feminist approach, as some authors suggest (Grumet 1988; Hauser 1998), can illuminate all of the different facets of motherhood, as well as the historical and social sources of the conceptual identification of female teachers with mothers, and in such a way contribute to redefining the teachers' commitment to the care and education of children.

International Women's Day, a socialist holiday, is also observed as a mother's day. It was transformed in the Soviet Union, and subsequently in contemporary Ukraine, into a special woman's day—a day honoring mothers, grandmothers, and girlfriends. Mother's Day is also celebrated as a separate holiday, but without all of the pomp and circumstance that surround International Women's Day, and children are often heard to say:

> Let mother always be; together with mother.
>   (Rephrase of the Soviet children's song:
>   Let the sun always shine). (*Rozkazhit' onuku* 2002: 33)
> March 8 is our dear mothers' holiday; give your mother a fairytale (*Doshkil'ne* 2005: 29–30)

During the Soviet era, the celebration of International Women's Day was one of the ways to hide the real gender-based relations of (male) domination. International Women's Day was officially recognized as a day of rest for women, and generally the only day in the year when they received gifts from men (and other women), as well as so-called official acknowledgment of their significance in society. At present in Ukraine, women are greeted with flowers and wished beauty and a smiling face. Often the decorations for the event are quite similar to the ones for Valentine's Day in the west: red ribbons, flowers, and hearts inscribed with "to the loveliest." It is incredible how the school contributes to this mystification by suggesting sometimes ridiculous classroom activities that have nothing to do with the original idea of the event itself. None of the scripts makes even a casual mention of women's struggle for emancipation, nor do they mention prominent women in history. The traditional female image—the ideal of a mother—is offered as virtually the only aspect of true femininity. To paraphrase Taras Shevchenko, Ukraine's most famous poet who wrote in the nineteenth century: There is nothing better in our earthly paradise than a young mother with a baby (*Pozaklasnyi* 2004: 107). Authors of such scripts are known to maintain that the universal perception of International Women's Day is simply a Day of Women. Children throughout the world celebrate it (*Doshkil'ne* 2003: 28–31). There is little doubt that by focusing on motherhood in this way, women's accomplishments beyond the domestic sphere remain unnoticed, and Ukrainian children grow up without learning about the important public roles that women play worldwide.

Gender Socialization

All celebrations examined above share a clear goal: gender socialization by means of transmitting the allegedly correct concepts of femininity (mother, nurturer, and guardian) and masculinity (father, warrior, and defender) through gender-differentiated games. To celebrate the school holidays, the following games are chosen: We are also mothers; Laundry; Teach a brother; Dance with a mother; Daughters-Mothers/ Sons-Fathers (Sokovina 1967: 19–20, 28–29; *Sviata* 1961: 40, 88; *Pochatkova* 2005a: 23–24). In a metaphorical way, children absorb the ideals of courting and gentlemanly manners by playing games such as "Flowers Marriage:"

> A periwinkle [masculine] pays compliments to a violet [feminine] while proposing: "Your plait is waist-long; your face is like a little apple, your eyes like black pools, your eyebrows like a fine thread, will you marry me"? (*Pochatkova* 2005: 10–12)

It is not surprising that the named activities are gender differentiated and family oriented: Ukraine can be viewed as a country where the family plays a significant part in upbringing and socialization and the roles for mothers and fathers are clearly defined—in the prevailing discourse, that is. But there is a severe disconnection between rhetoric and reality. As we saw above, 88.5

percent of the Ukrainian families have no father present. At the same time, results of a survey conducted by the Ukrainian Institute of Social Research demonstrate this paradoxical situation; in the context of human values, the family scored 96 percent (friends and acquaintances scored 86 percent; work, 81 percent; leisure time, 65 percent; and so forth).[4] As for marriage itself, it is still viewed as an important step in a woman's career. Out of four thousand brides each year, one quarter are between eighteen and twenty years old.[5]

What is the relationship between gender socialization and sex education in Ukrainian preschool and elementary instruction? At first glance, sex education might appear to function as a daily exercise, with teachers discussing forbidden issues with their pupils. In point of fact, it does not go beyond traditional descriptions of gender segregation. It includes information about how to take care of a baby, the meaning of one's name, and boy's and girl's interests. Unfortunately, basic information about anatomical differences is not part of such an education. Time and again only family-oriented topics are addressed in these discussions.

The Father Image

Whereas maternal images are numerous and prominent in all celebrations, paternal images are largely underrepresented. The father is present only in special events like Family Celebrations and Army Day, and his rare images tend to relate to leisure and entertainment, cultural activities, sports, and agriculture:

> My father is my best friend. … We share an ice-cream cone,
> and attend the cinema (*Rozkazhit'* 2001: 3)
> Together we build a birdhouse; plant an apple tree (*Rozkazhit'* 2001: 15)

A father represents true masculinity because he is considered to be strong, courageous, and noble; he teaches us to grow wise while a mother caresses us. His motto is "Knowledge is power," and he has knightly manners (*Biblioteka* 2001: 31–32).

To emphasize further the gender dimension of holidays, the school offers Army Day as a way to celebrate Father's Day. Military service for men provides proof of their masculinity, and women view it as insuring safety and protection for them. For children the father image is somewhat different. A Soviet children's song (still popular) reflects the stereotypical image of a father in its declaration that "father can do anything, except be a mother." This implies that even though he fulfills his masculine obligations, the father is somehow not quite the equal of the mother. Although, structurally speaking, Ukraine is basically a patriarchal society, its constant references to itself as matriarchal renders it culturally matriarchal, so we cannot refer to hegemonic masculinity in conjunction with the nation's men. Paradoxically, what emerges in reality is a portrait of the stereotypical male who is soft, even infantile (even if he is capable of somehow living up to his socially prescribed masculine nature), underscoring the cultural perception of a powerless father image. Once again, we have the example of the serious disconnection between rhetoric (and socialization as discussed here) and reality (or perception of that reality). There is, therefore, a certain contradiction in the intense cultivation of the matriarchal image in Ukraine. The absence of a father reaches the extreme in a textbook where one can see only a stork and the mother in the idyllic parental home. Generally speaking, although the idea of fatherlessness is undergoing some positive cultural transformation, this has not yet been reflected in children's textbooks or celebrations of special holidays. Men are often represented as trying to offset their lack of involvement in family life by bringing gifts as compensation. Psychological stress is frequently given as a justification for men avoiding family responsibilities. Such stereotyping is damaging to the entire concept of socially mandated masculinity, and it leaves young boys with no positive role model for their own behavior. All rhetoric about gender-differentiated family values to the contrary, the same stereotyping leaves young girls with a negative impression of what it means to be a male.

Attempts at Destereotyping: Early Intervention

My research has shown how powerful pre- and primary-school education is for the construction of culturally patterned gender relations. R. Bigler and L. Liben make a convincing argument when they point out that teachers should learn how to teach children about nonsexist criteria, rather than simply exposing them to counterstereotypical images—that is to say, representing inversions of typical gender-specific roles—in the expectation that such exposure will ameliorate the stereotypes (1990: 1440). An antibias curriculum offers yet another approach: we should not only be talking about difference, but rather, we need to "make children consciously inhabit a world of difference" (Boldt 1996: 122). As one of the methods of intervention, Katz and Walsh recommend watching a video, with peers performing cross-gender tasks (1991: 346–47). The scripts for girls might include a model acting out a commercial for a toy robot transformed into a car or plane, or playing with a basketball, while occupational scenarios can show a female model demonstrating the activities of a carpenter or a sports announcer. Comparable activities for boys would involve commercials for Cabbage Patch dolls or a dollhouse. Occupational tasks for boys might be associated with a fashion designer, or some aspect of home economics. For the proposed reinforcement, each scenario would involve either a child or an adult coming over to the model doing the demonstrating, after she is finished, and make some positive remarks about her actions.

An overview of professional journals for the years between 2001 and 2005 has shown basically three works available to Ukrainian teachers with suggestions for early intervention: the syllabus for "Formation of Gender Equality of Primary School Children" (*Pochatkova* 2005: 2–8); a text devoted to International Women's Day: "Life Lives through Woman" (*Pozaklasnyi* 2004: 106); and a fairy tale for New Year's Day, "A Trip to Divmalia" (*Pochatkova* 2005: 10–13). There is little doubt that professional publications should also include more material on innovations in teaching. The existing deficiency reflects a number of contributory factors: inertia in pedagogical thinking; teachers' lack of initiative and interest (one of the reasons is that they are so underpaid); lack of required support from educational authorities (even though an official directive on increasing gender awareness in general does exist);[6] and the commonly held view that gender issues are not a problem in Ukrainian society.

A course proposal entitled "The Formation of Gender Equality among Primary School Children" has been developed by Y. Potots'ka to promote pedagogical innovation. Its subheadings include: My Family and I; My Rights; Gender and Gender Equity; Feelings of Equality; My Baby (How to Educate a Boy or a Girl); Success in a Career; My Profession; Justice and Partnership (*Pochatkova* 2005: 2–8). The course is designed to be interdisciplinary; it integrates knowledge from business, jurisprudence, medicine, sociology, and psychology. The prescribed program represents a kind of psychological training that includes games, readings, and drawings, where the main goal is to create a feeling that "we are all together and equal." A positive element is its linkage of children's and gender rights, so that it serves as a preventive mechanism against any discriminatory practices that a child might encounter. This course is an important step forward, but the problem is how to integrate it into the Ukrainian system. In order to introduce this, or any other course, a detailed plan must be submitted to the proper authorities months in advance, and approved by both the local education board and the Ministry of Education (this practice is a Soviet relic). Admittedly, some attempts have been made to implement this plan in certain experimental classes with more flexible curriculum requirements. Making a clear distinction between *gender* and *sex* also remains a problem in Ukraine, but this would be a subject for a separate study.

The text "Life Lives through Woman" (*Pozaklasny* 2004: 106), written for International Women's Day, is the only narrative available to teachers in an official periodical that introduces the notion of emancipation by suggesting the multiple possibilities open to women in today's world (engineer, scientist, etc.). The goal of this publication is to illustrate the lives of exceptional women throughout Ukrainian history, thereby enhancing their image and raising their status in the eyes of children before prejudices can be fully formed.

A fairy tale for the New Year titled "A Trip to Divmalia," written by V. Badovs'ka, represents a narrative that deviates from the typical by describing a beautiful life under gender equality in a country for girls and boys:

> Far away, in a green meadow, surrounded by high mountains, there is a country called Divmalia, where girls and boys live. All of the girls wear bows of different hues, and the boys wear shorts that come in different colors. They play soccer together, embroider in cross-stitch, all are friends and always help each other. Every morning upon awakening they wash, brush their teeth, exercise, and leave to take care of the essential matters of the day. No girl in Divmalia would defer to a boy in her workplace, and no boy would defer to a girl in his workplace. They are all one family, with equal rights and responsibilities (*Pochatkova* 2005: 10–13)

After reading the fairy tale, the children are asked to draw the country Divmalia. One of the drawings shows the children's perception of this unconventional story. Two activities are presented in which girls and boys participate equally—a shared experience in a soccer game, and building a house (a traditionally male occupation) in a variety of vibrant colors, as acceptable undertakings for both girls and boys. Although the tale is about gender equality, it does not avoid certain entrenched stereotypical male/female images: girls are portrayed with bows of different colors (presumably to match their traditional attire—dresses), while boys wear shorts. There is no evidence of girls in shorts. The girls' bows are a carryover from the Soviet era, when their mandated school uniform was a brown dress, a white apron, and a fluffy white bow in the hair—a style singularly unsuited to the kinds of activities being promoted in the painting. This leaves us with the impression that the purpose of Divmalia is to portray a utopia with a happy ending; "guys, let's live in peace and friendship," as Cat Leopold, a character in a Soviet cartoon proposed, rather than any serious attempt to change gender stereotyping. This alone suggests how far the educational system still has to evolve before it can address gender biases in any meaningful way.

Australian feminist educator J. Gore noted that pedagogies that operate as regimes of truth "produce particular political regimes of the body" (1993: 60). If Soviet pedagogy aimed at creating a well-rounded personality, a new human being, Ukrainian pedagogy is interested in creating an independent Ukrainian citizen. The problem lies in the fact that educators forget to include critical thought in the notion of "independent." The school's hegemonic function deprives children of any possibility of critical thought. These young Ukrainians have few choices for developing their personality, beyond the gender-marked images of a mother or a warrior.

Moreover, as important as these and other such endeavors are in promoting sexual equality, feminist work cannot be limited to these cross-gender images, theoretical research, or alterations in the higher-education systems, as is the current general trend in Ukraine. Some serious changes are required in the nuts and bolts of education, preschools and primary schools in particular. Children are acculturated to gender stereotyping early in life, as I have attempted to show. This pattern itself is the product of a prejudicial cycle—parents and teachers who have been socialized to traditional value patterns pass this experience on to their offspring at home and their young charges in the educational system. Such an approach perpetuates the cycle of gender marking. By the time children reach adulthood, in most cases it is virtually too late to alter the internalized perceptions of socially constructed gender differences. Those who have managed to transcend such traditional gender biases, however, can most effectively transmit these ideas by turning more of their attention to young children, who, as researchers have shown, are the most receptive to new ideas.

Notes

1. Attempts to create, through reviving national myths and ancient rituals, a new meta-narrative of woman's natural domain started with Vasyl' Ruban's *Berehynia,* which popularized the patriarchal fantasy of an allegedly ancient Ukrainian matriarchy. The ideal of Ukrainian women, namely Berehynia, was referred to in the twentieth century by, among others, Kateryna Motrych, who wrote: "The Ukrainian woman has a responsible mission (she is perhaps the only woman in the world, emancipated from her very inception, who never waged a battle for equal rights with her husband, but always fought instead for equal rights and the liberty of Ukraine. …) Like the Blessed Virgin, the Ukrainian woman must give birth to the Ukrainian Savior. … The salvation of our nation is a Woman. … To her we must return her sacred mission, encompassing that of the Blessed Virgin and Berehynia." Men (and many women) also tend to situate her on the moral high ground, which enables them to argue that feminism has always been an integral part of Ukrainian culture (quoted in Rubchak 1996: 319). Researchers have found such evidence of Ukraine's ancient matriarchal culture in material dating to the Trypillian (named after the village of Trypillia in ancient Ukraine) culture of the fourth to the early third centuries CE, and female figures of stone from the Scytho-Sarmatian period of the sixth to the twelfth centuries CE. Scholars have focused on the high status of Ukrainian women, even in medieval times, when female freedoms tended to shock the neighboring Muscovites. At that time, Ukrainian society was matrilocal and matrilinear—a mother's property could be inherited by her daughters alone. A husband might appeal for use of his wife's immovable property, but was obligated to take very good care of it. In reanimating the Berehynia mythologem today, researchers and popularizers of Ukrainian culture emphasize this matriarchal cult, which is also associated with motherhood and housewife.
2. That is retinol, which, from a medical standpoint, allegedly is responsible for good vision, normal bone and tooth development, reproduction, and the health of skin. It is also seen by many as an antiaging compound.
3. http://abetka.ukrlife.org/independ.htm.

4. http://www.zn.kiev.ua/nn/show/437/38054/.
5. Findings showed that eighteen is considered an acceptable marriageable age by a significant percentage of females (less so by males). Public opinion makes young people feel inferior if they remain single and/or childless. It is possible that they are trying to conform to this agenda in order to achieve social status. Age twenty is viewed as the optimum age for bearing the first child.
6. The resolution of the Cabinet of Ministers, "On a National Plan Concerning the Improvement of Women's Status and Introduction of Gender Equality in Society for 2001–2005," 6 May 2001; a Presidential Decree "On Improving the Functioning of Central and Local Executive Authorities Regarding Equal Rights and Opportunities for Men and Women," 25 July 2005; the law adopted by the Verkhovna Rada, "On Securing Equal Rights and Opportunities for Men and Women," 8 September 2005; Parliamentary hearings, "On Equal Rights and Opportunities in Ukraine: Realities and Perspectives," 21 November 2006.

Bibliography

Biblioteka vchytelia. 2001.

Bigler, Rebecca S., and Lynn S. Liben. 1990. "The Role of Attitudes and Interventions in Gender-Schematic Processing." *Child Development* 61, no. 5 (October): 1440–52.

Boldt, Gail Masuchika. 1996. "Sexist and Heterosexist Responses to Gender Bending in an Elementary Classroom." *Curriculum Inquiry* 26, no. 2 (Summer): 113–31.

Fetodov, Georgiy P. 1991. "Novoe otechestvo." *Sud'ba i grekhi Rossii,* 2. St. Petersburg: Sofia.

Gore, Jennifer. 1993. *The Struggle for Pedagogies: Critical and Feminist Discourses as Regimes of Truth.* London: Routledge.

Grumet, Madeleine R. 1988. *Bitter Milk: Women and Teaching.* Amherst: University of Massachusetts Press.

Hauser, Mary E., and Janice A. Jipson, eds. 1998. *Intersections: Feminism/Early Childhood.* New York: Peter Lang.

Haydenko, Victoria. 2005. "The Formation of Gender Differences among the Young during the Post-Communist Transition in Ukraine." In *Feminists Contest Politics and Philosophy,* edited by Claudia Leeb et al., 189–202. Brussels: Peter Lang S.A. Presses Interuniversitaires Europennes.

Haydenko, Victoria, and Iryna Predborska. 2006. "Gender Stereotyping in Ukrainian Primary Textbooks." In *Multiple Marginalities: An Intercultural Dialogue on Gender in Education across Europe and Africa,* edited by Justina Sempruch et al., 135–50. Königstein: Ulrike Helmer.

Katz, Phylis A., and Vincent P. Walsh. 1991. "Modification of Children's Gender-Stereotyped Behavior." *Child Development* 62, no. 2 (April): 338–51.

Kiblitskaya, Marina. 2000. "Once We Were Kings: Male Experience of Loss of Status at Work in Post-Communist Russia." In *Gender, State and Society in Soviet and Post-Soviet Russia,* edited by Sarah Ashwin, 55–70. London: Routledge.

Kohlberg, Lawrence. 1996. "A Cognitive-Developmental Analysis of Children's Sex-Role Concepts and Attitudes." In *The Development of Sex Differences,* edited by Eleanor E. Maccoby, 82–173. Stanford, CA: Stanford University Press.

Leshchenko, Z., ed. 1986. *Mamyn den': virshi ta opovidannia dlia molodshoho shkil'noho viku*. Kyiv: Veselka.

Levy, Betty. 1972. "The Schools' Role in the Sex Role Stereotyping of Girls: A Feminist Review of the Literature." *Feminist Studies* 1, no. 1 (Summer): 5–23.

Martin, Carol Lynn, Lisa Eisenbud, and Hilary Rose. 1995. "Children's Gender-Based Reasoning About Toys." *Child Development* 66 (5 October): 1453–71.

Martin, Karin A. 1998. "Becoming a Gendered Body: Practices of Preschools." *American Sociological Review* 63, no. 4 (August): 494–511.

McLaren, Peter. 1986. *Schooling as a Ritual Performance: Towards a Political Economy of Educational Symbols and Gestures*. London: Routledge.

Pochatkova Osvita. 2005; 2005b; 2005c.

Pozaklasnyi Chas. 2004; 2005.

Rozkazhit' Onuku. 2001; 2002; 2003.

Rubchak, Marian. 1996. "Christian Virgin or Pagan Goddess: Feminism versus the Eternally Feminine in Ukraine." In *Women in Russia and Ukraine*, edited by Rosalind Marsh, 315–30. Cambridge: Cambridge University Press.

Sokovina, Elena, ed. 1967. *Mamin prazdnik. Pesni, stikhi, igry, instzenirovki dlia mladshego shkol'nogo vozrasta*. Moscow: Muzyka.

Stroeher, Susan K. 1994. "Sixteen Kindergartens' Gender-Related Views of Careers." *Elementary School Journal* (1 September): 95–103.

Thompson, Spencer K. 1975. "Gender Labels and Early Sex Role Development." In *Child Development* (46): 339–47.

CHAPTER 7

Gender, Language Attitudes, and Language Status in Ukraine in the 1990s

Laada Bilaniuk

Introduction

In the mid-1990s, when I mentioned to a Ukrainian colleague my plan to study gender as a factor shaping language use, he wrote me that most other linguists in Ukraine would see this research question as "something exotic, American gimmicks, or the contrivances of oversatiated imperialists." Nevertheless, in recent years interest in gender studies has begun to grow in Ukraine (e.g., see Petrenko, Isaiev, and Petrenko 1999; Aheieva and Oksamytna 2001; Zhurzhenko 2001; and *Feminnist' ta maskulinnist'* (Feminism and Masculinity) 2003).[1]

Transformations in discourses and practices of gender and language have played a major role in the changes underway in Ukraine and other post-Soviet societies. Numerous studies have documented each factor separately (on language: Arel 1993; Laitin 1998; Bilaniuk 2005; Kulyk 2006; Taranenko 2007; on gender: Bohachevs'ky-Chomiak 1998; Pavlychko 1996; Rubchak 1996). In this article, however, I examine the interrelationship between language and gender in Ukraine. My analysis focuses on gender differences in language ideologies and attitudes. To explain the gendered patterning, I consider how socialization and cultural ideologies of women's relationship to language shape the documented attitudes. I also consider how differences in possibilities for social power and advancement that are linked to language use lead men and women to benefit from different strategies in using and valuing language. I show that, while sociocultural and political/economic forces reinforce each other in some cases, in others they are in contradiction, with individual economic motives prevailing over cultural paradigms of traditionalism.

Although this study is unique in the post-Soviet context, it builds on research conducted elsewhere on the linkages among gender, language, and social status with a focus on attitudes and language/dialect choice in multilingual/multidialectal contexts (Gal 1979, 1998; Woolard 1989, 1996). Here I compare the gendering of ideologies of the different labeled languages (Ukrainian, Russian, and also English), as well as attitudes toward variation within these languages, by considering evaluations of purity and proximity to standard. I examine the psychological forces that shape language use and underlie constructions of gender and ethnic identity. I analyze both conscious and subconscious language attitudes, which I studied by means of survey questions and a matched-guise language attitude test in 1995 in various areas in Ukraine. A matched-guise test is based on the premise that people take on a different guise when speaking a different language, and that they associate certain qualities with a language itself. The survey and test responses document enacted attitudes, evidence of stances by which people align themselves in communities of practice. These stances may have since shifted, but the patterns I found shed light on the social forces that have been shaping language use and other symbolic behavior.

Research in language and gender has revealed a widespread tendency for women to adhere more to overtly prestigious language forms, while men tend to use more vernacular or low-prestige forms; women have also been shown to be more progressive in linguistic innovation (Labov 1990). These tendencies (and exceptions to them) are rooted in the social, cultural, and economic conditions that affect the different valuation of linguistic resources and people's strategic choices in using them. Here I examine the extent to which these tendencies are evident in the turbulent linguistic situation in post-Soviet Ukraine in the 1990s, where language laws and socioeconomic changes were transforming language use.

In seeking to explain the gendered variation in language, I draw on the analysis put forth by Penelope Eckert in her studies of midwestern US schoolchildren. Eckert suggests that women's social positions are defined more through symbolic means than by their skills or activities, which leads females to seek more symbolic capital via language use (1998). This is also argued by Bourdieu (1991).[2] This argument is developed further in studies that show that women's status and social/ethnic identity is more dependent on display of community membership and social interaction than is men's status (Eckert 1989; Woolard, 1996). This is not to say that men are free from symbolic definition; it remains to be shown whether, in a given case, men are less constrained by symbolic capital than women are, or if differences in language use reflect differences in how language forms are valued by each gender, depending on the symbolic construction of social opportunities.

I begin with an overview of the context of language politics and gender in post-Soviet Ukraine. Next, I explain my approach in analyzing language and gender, based on data gathered during fieldwork in 1995. In my first analysis, I consider people's stances of linguistic criticism and how these are shaped by gender, ethnicity, and urban/rural background. Then I examine the subconscious associations of languages with personal qualities, as documented by my matched-guise test. I analyze how both the gender of respondents and the gender of the readers being evaluated affect linguistic attitudes. The data show remarkable consistency in gendered patterning, for which I propose explanations linked to the social and ethnic tensions in a rapidly changing society.

The Language Situation in Ukraine: Ethnicity

Ukrainian was officially designated the state language of Ukraine in 1989. The legislation making Ukrainian official was one of the first legal steps toward de-Sovietization and independence of the country in 1991. This legal step went against a long-established diglossic relationship between Ukrainian as a "low, peasant" language, and Russian as the "high, cultured" language. This change in language policy accompanied other social and political changes and served to disrupt linguistic values in general.[3]

During my fieldwork, I found that the correctness of words and pronunciations had become hotly contested in interactions as people negotiated authority. Language choice and language quality became foci of discussion in newspapers, on television and radio, and on the street. Books, brochures, and television and radio programs attacked what they defined as incorrect usages and promoted "correct" forms (Lenets 1993; Serbens'ka 1994, Hanitkevych 1995). Interviews reported in newspapers sometimes commented on the incorrectness of the language of those interviewed (Halabudra-Chyhryn 1995). Once, at an outdoor arts-and-crafts market in L'viv, I was surprised to hear two women arguing not over the price of a necklace but over the proper word for silver in Ukrainian—*serebro* or *sriblo* (the latter is considered standard Ukrainian, while the former is closer to Russian, although it was pronounced according to Ukrainian phonology). These disputes constituted a struggle over social authority. The books and television programs aspired to define a prestigious Ukrainian language, while in daily discussions people struggled to assert their social position by demonstrating control of the "correct" language. In these processes, the legitimacy and value of various linguistic forms were being redefined, and thus access to power was being reconfigured.

To understand the significance of the change in language values, we need to consider the history of language politics in Ukraine. Under the Soviet regime, Russian was imposed forcefully and also attracted people by the privileges associated with it, as it was required for access to good education and decent jobs. Ukrainian predominated in rural areas, but even there, everyone had to study Russian in school, and Russian tended to be highly regarded. Some people told me that they resented the high status of Russian—but they all agreed that in the Soviet era, Ukrainian was publicly held in low regard. People used Ukrainian at home and in rural areas, but there was a widely held view that it had no future and would die out as Russian ascended to its destiny as a world language.

Now that the Soviet Union has disintegrated, the future spread and dominant role of Russian are no longer secure. Nevertheless, Russian is still a politically powerful presence, a lingua franca of the post-Soviet regions, and its cultural prestige remains strong—a situation that the Russian government is trying to maintain (Taranenko 2003: 46–47). There is also some concern that English might replace Russian as the lingua franca. Russian is no longer an obligatory subject of study, and many schools in Ukraine no longer teach the Russian language at all (Bilaniuk and Melnyk 2008).

As I will show, the different historical and demographic trajectories in various regions of Ukraine have led to differing language ideologies. I will compare data from L'viv, Kyiv, and Dnipropetrovs'k. L'viv, in the western part of the country, did not experience as severe repression of Ukrainian language as did the central and eastern regions, since it was never within the Russian tsarist empire and it did not become part of the Soviet Union until after World War II. Since independence, western Ukraine has witnessed vigorous public support for the Ukrainian language. Kyiv, as the capital of the country and the seat of government, was both the focus of intense Russification during the Soviet era and more recently under much scrutiny as to the implementation of laws promoting the official status of Ukrainian. In Dnipropetrovs'k, in the eastern, highly industrialized part of the country, a relatively greater proportion of ethnic Russians and ethnic Ukrainians considered their native language to be Russian, and there was more overt resistance to the promotion of Ukrainian language. During my fieldwork in 1995, it was rare to hear Ukrainian speakers in the Dnipropetrovs'k urban area who were not clearly from rural areas.

"Ukrainian" and "Russian" are categories that encompass much complexity, reflecting regional, demographic, and other factors, as well as specific influences in people's personal histories. Both "Ukrainian" and "Russian" refer to standardized languages, and there is speech that falls close to a standard and is unequivocally labeled. However, there are also speech practices that blend features from both standards (see Bilaniuk 2004, 2005; Strikha 1997; Trub 2000). Languages that people perceive as being mixed or impure are called *surzhyk*, generally a derogatory term. Today the term *surzhyk* is not limited to regularized mixed forms (syncretic language varieties developed as Ukrainian-speaking peasants moved to urban areas and tried to speak Russian). People also use the term to criticize someone who might borrow a term from Ukrainian into Russian, or who speaks with an "accent." This negative label is often used as a weapon in the symbolic struggle for validity and correctness (Bilaniuk 2005, 2009).

The attention to correctness reflects a growing concern with purity in language. The resurgence of purism is likely a response to the ambivalence of having a previously peasant language become a state language. With a focus on purity, people can separate a valuable variety of Ukrainian from "debased" forms. If Ukrainian were to become a highly prestigious language, it would have to be a *pure* Ukrainian. As a professor of journalism in L'viv stated in an interview, "We need a King's Ukrainian," just as there is a King's English. Impure forms of Ukrainian and mixtures with Russian are relegated to low status. But what exactly gets considered pure and impure leaves room for debate, making language ideology a field of contestation.

Gender and Language in Ukraine

Soviet ideology perpetuated the idea of equal access to all jobs for men and women and the responsibility to work outside the home for both sexes, but in practice this did not result in equality (Pavlychko 1996; Gal and Kligman 2000). Even in Soviet ideology and symbolism, women were frequently relegated to secondary, more backward roles. A good example is a famous Soviet sculpture that genders the components of Soviet insignia by depicting a woman holding a sickle (symbolizing agriculture and peasantry) next to a man holding aloft a hammer (a symbol of industry and progress).

Postwar labor needs, along with the communist ideology of gender equality and all persons working to the best of their abilities, pushed most women to work outside the home. Even so, by and large women continued to carry the responsibility for doing most of the work inside the home (Rubchak 1996: 329–30; Wanner 1998: 112; Gal and Kligman 2000: 48). There are certainly exceptions, but the general trend was clear. Despite some token success stories, women tended to be excluded from more prestigious jobs, under the assumption that their real duty was to bear children, manage the home, and care for their husbands. Generous provisions for maternity leave made bosses reluctant to hire women for important, better-paying jobs (as stated in my interviews; see also Gal and Kligman 2000: 49). Women's weak position in the labor market became exacerbated by the post-Soviet economic crisis (Pavlychko 1996: 312).

A general return to traditionalism in the 1990s defined women's responsibility as homemaking, and men as providers (Lissyutkina 1993; Wanner 1998: 66, 112–18; Gal and Kligman 2000: 84–85). The symbolic linkage of women

with motherhood and domestic responsibilities was elaborated in national ritual and education in independent Ukraine (Wanner 1998: 66, 112–18). In the
1990s, women were suffering more in losing jobs and pay (Hockstader 1995;
Pavlychko 1996: 312; Gal and Kligman 2000: 73), but many women embraced
the ideology that excluded them from paid employment and social power
(Verdery 1996: 81; Gal and Kligman 2000: 85). However, as I show in the data
presented below, many women rejected this traditionalism in their language
attitudes and linguistic behavior.

In the return to traditionalism, women were seen as responsible for maintaining linguistic and cultural traditions (Pavlychko 1996; Rubchak 1996; Gal
and Kligman 2000: 26). Leaders of women's associations in Ukraine embraced
this ideology in statements that they must first liberate the nation before they
liberate women, and that it is women's role to revitalize the "moral spirit" of
the Ukrainian people in order to save the nation (Rubchak 1996: 317–18).
Preservation of the Ukrainian language was a central part of these endeavors
(Pavlychko 1996: 308). Language also figured in the post-Soviet mythology
of Berehynia, the "hearth-mother" who is "the perfect Ukrainian woman, the
spirit of the Ukrainian home, the ideal mother, who played an important role
in Ukrainian history, the preserver of language and national identity" (Pavlychko 1996: 311). This ideology was further exemplified in the epigraph of an
article (Chaban 1994) quoting Ostap Vyshnia, a writer of the 1920s: "I am often asked where I got my language. I got my language from my mother's nipple
(*tsytsi*). That is the inexhaustible well of language. Take notice of this, mothers,
and your children will never need to be Ukrainianized."

Are women accepting the cultural burden of maintaining the "authentic"
linguistic traditions and shunning what is nonstandard, or are they spurred by
the desire for status? Both these factors likely underlay the gender inequality
in an event I observed in Ukraine on 12 May 2000. At Kyiv State University,
scheduled conference proceedings were delayed in order to announce and
distribute awards for the best performance in a dictation. The "general university dictation in the Ukrainian language" (*zahal'no-universytets'kyy dyktant
ukrains'koi movy*) was part of a new effort to monitor and reward knowledge
of the Ukrainian language. Ukrainian is a language that, like Spanish, is very
regular in the correspondence of graphemes to phonemes; thus, performance
in the dictation relied on the distinction of some close vowels, doubled con-
sonants, and proper punctuation. The rector of the university announced that
78 percent of students passed the exercise, and thirty received awards for perfect performance. Out of the thirty winners, only five were men.

This gender inequality in performance supports the idea that women
are more likely to try to perfect institutionally valued linguistic skills. In the
awards ceremony, to those who did not win awards, the rector of the university wished that they might "master this tsarina of reading/writing" (*ovolodity*

otseiu tsarytseiu hramotoiu).[4] Thus, he evoked the image of literary (written/ read) language as an elite woman to be taken control of, possessed, and mastered. In his comment, women were metonymically transposed with literary language. While women themselves might excel at the institutionally approved language, they also become embodiments of the language and tradition.

In sum, two factors are likely to create differences in how men and women use and think of language as a resource in Ukraine: the economic and the cultural. Social and economic positionings and opportunities in Ukraine are gendered, and different skills and choices in language use are also prescribed and inculcated in the cultural ideology of gender roles. The economic and cultural factors sometimes reinforce and sometimes counter one another, as I point out below in examining some of the gender differences in my data.

Language Attitude Survey and Matched Guise Test

During fieldwork in Ukraine from November 1994 to November 1995, I conducted a survey and language attitude test with two thousand people as part of my study of language politics. The purposes of the survey and test were to document conscious and implicit attitudes toward language, and to examine how these are shaped by ethnicity, gender, regional background, and other factors, in order to obtain a deeper understanding of the tensions at play in the radically changing post-Soviet society of Ukraine. I administered the test and survey in the cities and surrounding regions of L'viv, Kyiv, and Dnipropetrovs'k, which represent three areas—west, center, and east—that differ in history, demographics, and prevailing language ideologies. In this study, I analyze the responses of the high school and university students, who comprise the bulk of my sample.

I tried to obtain similar representation from each region. To collect data from high school students, in each area I conducted the research in five schools: two in the city center, one in a noncentral bedroom community, one in a village, and an additional school either in a noncentral part of the city or a nearby village. In each of the city centers, I arranged testing in one school, where the primary language of instruction was officially Ukrainian, and in one where it was Russian. The rural schools all had Ukrainian as the primary language. The total numbers of high school students tested in each region were 239 in Kyiv, 186 in Dnipropetrovs'k, and 278 in L'viv. The university students in the sample are from various disciplines in higher educational institutions in each city. In Dnipropetrovs'k, I worked with 337 university students; in Kyiv, 224 students; and in L'viv, 375 students.

The high school and university students taken together (N=1,639) were aged thirteen to twenty-seven, with a few younger and a few older students (average age 17.5).[5] When asked to write it on a blank line, 95 percent of these respondents designated their nationality as either Ukrainian or Russian. The proportions of each nationality in the sample to be analyzed here are 83 percent Ukrainians, 12 percent Russians, and 5 percent other designations.[6] I focus on the two major ethnic groups and use their ethnic self-designations as axes of comparison, resulting in a sample of 704 Ukrainian women, 651 Ukrainian men, 118 Russian women, and 84 Russian men (total N=1,557).

The research that I conducted included a matched-guise test, followed by survey questions on personal background and overt evaluations of language. I analyze data from both the test and survey here. The matched-guise test, originally developed in 1960 (Lambert et al. 1960), allows researchers to study language attitudes in bilingual or bidialectal situations. In the test I administered in Ukraine in 1995, respondents were asked to evaluate character traits of people based on their voice quality on tape recordings. The key to the test is that respondents do not know that they are evaluating each speaker twice, but in different languages. The recording that was evaluated presented six speakers, each reading once in Ukrainian and once in Russian, and one speaker reading in Ukrainian and English. The speech samples were presented in mixed order so that speaker repetition was not evident. The structure of this test allows the researcher to control for individual voice quality, which permits the study of the subconscious association of languages with character traits.

The survey that followed asked respondents to provide some background information, as well as evaluations of language quality and language proficiency. While the matched-guise test documented subconscious language attitudes, the survey questions documented conscious, overt evaluations of language. I begin with analysis of the overt evaluations before proceeding to the subconscious matched-guise test data.

Ethnicity and Gender in Language Criticism

I first consider how students answered a survey question in which I asked them, "Give a general evaluation of how people speak Ukrainian where you live (the locality or city)." This question assesses how critical or supportive respondents are of the language used around them. It solicits judgments of language *in use*—not of an idealized Ukrainian or Russian language, which might be evaluated differently.

The implications of the answers to this question can be interpreted in several ways. On the one hand, rating a language to be of better quality is tantamount to asserting the authority of that language and its associated social and political identity. Also, if the given language is symbolic of one's own ethnic group, a higher evaluation of quality can indicate more self-confidence, which plays out in an interaction to assert higher social status. On the other hand, giving a lower evaluation takes away authority and legitimacy from a language. When a respondent's identity is linked to a language, low evaluations of quality can indicate less linguistic security and low self-esteem.

In answering the question about how well people speak, respondents had to choose from five answers: very well or purely,[7] rather well, fairly, rather badly, or very badly. In my analyses, these answers correspond to a scale of one to five, with five as the most positive evaluation. The survey also included the same question regarding Russian. Here I consider the intersections of the factors of ethnicity and gender in the responses (Tables 7.1 and 7.2). I provide information on statistical significance levels in my discussion of this non-random sample for descriptive purposes only.

Table 7.1 Students' survey answers evaluating how well Ukrainian is spoken in the respondents' area of residence.

	Percentage of respondents choosing each possible answer:						
Response and value:	Very badly (1)	Rather badly (2)	Fairly (3)	Rather well (4)	Very well (5)	Mean value	Std. dev.
Category of respondents							
Russian females (N=117)	8	24	42	21	5	2.90	0.99
Russian males (N=83)	7	24	45	19	5	2.90	0.96
Ukrainian females (N=700)	2	14	49	31	4	3.20*	0.80
Ukrainian males (N=642)	3	12	37	40	8	3.37*	0.90

* The difference between evaluations of Ukrainian males and females is highly significant (F=13.4, p= 0.0003).

Table 7.1 presents the responses of students evaluating the quality of Ukrainian language in their area, subdivided by respondents' sex and ethnicity. For ethnic Ukrainians, the mean response is 3.20 for women and 3.37 for men, values that are both slightly above average and are significantly different from one another ($p = 0.0003$). The mean response for ethnic Russians of both sexes is 2.90, just below average. The difference between these two ethnic groups is significant ($p < 0.0001$). Young people of Ukrainian ethnicity show more support for Ukrainian than do Russians. Ethnic Russians are more critical, and thus less supportive of the authority of the Ukrainian language in their region. There appears to be ethnolinguistic loyalty, leading people to give a higher evaluation to the titular language of their own ethnic group (this is also confirmed in the evaluations of Russian language in Table 7.2, discussed below).

In explaining this pattern, it should be noted that Russians are not necessarily more knowledgeable about Ukrainian than are other respondents, as was evident in answers to another survey question in which Russians claimed significantly lower understanding of Ukrainian than did ethnic Ukrainians (Bilaniuk 2009). Yet the typically more limited proficiency of ethnic Russians in Ukrainian did not prevent them from being more critical of it than were ethnic Ukrainians. It appears to be not so much an issue of discerning correctness, as a political statement. By rating the quality of the Ukrainian language lower, Russians also discredit its (local) validity and authority. As I show elsewhere, in western Ukraine this constituted resistance to the new dominant status of Ukrainian there, while in eastern Ukraine it reinforced the largely unchanged lower status of Ukrainian (Bilaniuk 2009). The question was phrased specifically regarding language in the respondents' area of residence, and thus it reflected the perceived authority of the language in use in a specific city or village, and not an abstract ideal.

Table 7.2 Students' survey answers evaluating how well Russian is spoken in the respondents' area of residence.

	Percentage of respondents choosing each possible answer:						
Response and value:	Very badly (1)	Rather badly (2)	Fairly (3)	Rather well (4)	Very well (5)	Mean value	Std. dev.
Category of respondents							
Russian females (N=112)	3	4	20	51	23	3.88	0.90
Russian males (N=83)	0	1	28	54	17	3.87	0.69
Ukrainian females (N=698)	3	11	37	43	6	3.38	0.88
Ukrainian males (N=638)	4	11	36	41	7	3.36	0.91

In looking at evaluations of Russian language (Table 7.2), female Ukrainian respondents rated it somewhat higher than they rated Ukrainian (a difference of +0.18). This shows that young Ukrainian women as a group were more willing to recognize the legitimacy and authority of Russian than of Ukrainian in their region. The Ukrainian men evaluated the Ukrainian and Russian languages almost the same. Not surprisingly, Russian respondents on average gave the Russian language much higher evaluations (3.87–3.88) than they did Ukrainian, a difference of almost a whole point. This shows that Russians of both sexes were more self-confident about their titular ethnic language than are Ukrainians of theirs. Although the Russian language in Ukraine is often criticized for having nonstandard phonology, in their answers, Russians were clearly choosing to assert the value, and by extension the authority, of their language. It also appears that Ukrainians did not reject this authority, although they did not support it as strongly as did ethnic Russians.

When considering how gender affects language criticism, we found that there was little difference within ethnic groups in evaluations of the Russian language (Table 7.2). There was, however, a significant gender difference in evaluations of the Ukrainian language among ethnic Ukrainians (Table 7.1). Ukrainian women were more critical of the Ukrainian language quality than men. Why might this be so? One possible factor was that Ukrainian respondents had more at stake than Russians did in evaluating the Ukrainian language because it was explicitly associated with their ethnic identity. The status of the Ukrainian language probably had little impact on the social status of Russians living there, particularly in the immediate post-Soviet period, when their ethnic identity was still very strongly linked with Russia.[8] However, we should expect a gender difference to emerge among ethnic Ukrainians if young men and women were differently affected by language status in respect to their social power and standing.

Under the Eckert/Bourdieu model, the changing, unstable status of Ukrainian would make it a less-useful site through which women could realize their social aspirations. In 1995, when the data analyzed here were collected, Ukrainian had already been the official state language for six years, but in practice its use was still limited, and it had not shed its associations with low culture and peasantry. Meanwhile, the status of Russian had remained stable despite political changes. Although Russian is not an official language of the state of Ukraine, in the 1990s and 2000s it was and is still used by many officials, and it is the official language of Ukraine's large and powerful neighbor to the north. Throughout the former Soviet Union, Russian is still considered a language of power, high culture, and science, even though it has become more politicized as a symbol of ethnic allegiance.

While Russian has a well-established and institutionalized standard, the Ukrainian standard was poorly institutionalized in the 1990s.[9] People in positions of power often knew Ukrainian poorly. Even if they could speak it, many public officials and educators used heavily Russified Ukrainian, or nonstandard Ukrainian dialect varieties (usually learned during childhood summers in villages, since they had little opportunity to use literary urban Ukrainian). Such instances reinforced the "impure" and rural connotations of Ukrainian and undermined its legitimacy as the official state language. Furthermore, the previously limited use of Ukrainian in administrative and scientific fields left much specialized terminology to be elaborated. The development of terminology provoked many disagreements, which undermined the sense of an established standard and thus dragged down the status of the language.

If women's social positions make them more sensitive to symbolic and linguistic capital (as Eckert 1998 suggests), this should lead them to be more critical of a language of questionable status than men would be. Such an explanation is in keeping with the data presented here. Although a lower evaluation of a language can undermine its authority, this response also reflects dissatisfaction with the current state and status of the language. Even women who were otherwise patriotic could be more critical of the Ukrainian language, thus expressing their desire for a better-established and socially validated language, if it was to be linked to their social identity. Even though knowing Ukrainian has definitely become an asset, outside of western Ukraine, Russian is at least as important. Until recently, knowing Russian was a much greater mark of high status than knowing Ukrainian, since in the Soviet system, better education and better jobs were all associated with the Russian language. In addition to this political/economic explanation, the cultural milieu in which women were expected to be guardians of the purity of their language could reinforce women's more critical stance toward Ukrainian.

Gender and Urban/Rural Background

Interesting patterns emerge when the responses are broken down by the urban or rural background of Ukrainian respondents (Table 7.3). The trend of women being more critical than men in evaluating the quality of Ukrainian is twice as strong among people whose background is in villages, as opposed to those from major cities (although the trend is significant in cities as well). The trend is even stronger among those whose background is in towns or small cities that are not regional oblast capitals. Sixty-eight respondents who could not be clearly categorized have been excluded from this analysis. There were too few villagers identifying themselves as Russians to examine gender differences within this ethnic group.

Table 7.3 Ukrainian respondents by urban/rural background: Mean evaluations of Ukrainian language quality.

Respondent's Background	sex	N	mean eval. (1–5 scale)	std. dev.	mean resp. difference*	F ratio	p value
Village	Female	268	3.29	0.73			
	Male	222	3.54	0.75	−0.25	14.5	0.0002
Small Town	Female	37	3.32	0.75			
	Male	32	3.63	0.79	−0.31	2.6	0.11
City	Female	361	3.10	0.86			
	Male	357	3.24	0.96	−0.14	4.0	0.04

* Mean female evaluation minus mean male evaluation.

The response patterns by rural/urban background suggest that the gender difference in ideologies is a product of the "periphery." Following the ideas of Gal (1979) and Bourdieu (1991: 50), women in peripheral areas, especially villages, are likely to be particularly sensitive to language as a factor in social mobility. If wielding a more widely validated language gives women a major avenue of social advancement, it makes sense that women would be more critical of the local language around them. By evaluating the language of their village more positively, women would also be validating the language and prestige of their village men. The Russian language, largely an urban phenomenon in Ukraine, would not play a role in this rural dynamic.

Many factors may shape the general trend discussed here. For example, women could be evaluating language as an avenue for advancement through marriage. Why this would be a lesser option for men remains to be determined. Researchers have argued that men's status is more tied to their material wealth and occupation, and that their ethnic identity is socially more fixed and depends less on whom they associate with than does that of women (Gal 1979; Woolard 1996).

If women are more sensitive to how they are defined by symbolic capital, their more critical stance toward their local Ukrainian language is also evidence of a more active role in evaluating and shaping the quality of their language, which is reinforced in cultural ideals of women's linguistic and traditional responsibilities. One could say that women are policing the definition of the prestige variant. This interpretation directly contradicts Bourdieu's suggestion that women are simply "inclined towards docility with regard to the dominant usages" (1991: 50). The language evaluations of both men and women reflect their struggles to shape linguistic value, to claim authority and validity, to resist domination, and otherwise to establish an advantageous position in the symbolic systems of their lives.

Subconscious Evaluations of Language

Up to this point, my discussion has centered on the active and conscious evaluations of language that I documented through survey questions. Next, I shift the focus to the attitudes that are implicit in people's reactions to speech that they hear. As explained above, I collected data on these reactions by means of a matched-guise language attitude test. The following analyses examine differences in evaluations of male and female speakers, as well as differences between male and female respondents. There is striking regularity in gender patterning in these evaluations.

First I consider how the sex of speakers affects how they are evaluated, based on the Ukrainian-Russian matched-guise test. Table 7.1 presents graphs of mean evaluations of matched-guise test traits by all student respondents, broken down by speaker sex, grouping the three female speakers together and the three male speakers together. High school and university student respondents of all ethnic backgrounds are included in this analysis (N=1,639).

For all twelve traits evaluated, there is a strikingly regular trend of higher evaluation of the character traits in the Russian guise of female readers and the Ukrainian guise of male readers: One can see that pattern clearly in Table 7.1, in that the mean female values are always to the left of the mean male values (the left direction of the graphs indicates stronger association of a quality with Russian, while values more to the right on the plots are more strongly associated with Ukrainian). An examination of the data broken down by respondents' sex and ethnicity upholds the same general trend. While Russians tend to favor the Russian language over Ukrainian, regardless of who the respondent is, female speakers are always given higher evaluations in their Russian guise relative to male speakers.[10]

Since all of the traits are positive, we can ask why it is that women are more positively evaluated in their Russian guises, while men are more positively evaluated when speaking Ukrainian. This trend runs directly counter to the mythology of women as the protectors of national traditions in Ukraine. One explanation for this gender patterning is the persistence of the connotations of Russian as a prestigious, urban language for women. These symbolic connotations may be weaker for men, since even men from villages had the opportunity to learn Russian during their mandatory army service.

It is also useful to consider the specifics of individual speakers' readings.[11] Matched-guise tests are designed to control for speaker idiosyncrasies, in that the same speaker is evaluated twice, once in each language. While this assumption of control allows for the general comparison of attitudes associated with given languages, small variations in language can carry great symbolic import. Differences in the perceived purity of the language of individual speakers, as well as their tone or style of reading, can play a significant role. Particular ways of speaking may be associated with different character stereotypes in different languages. Suprasegmental features such as speed and intonation can give a reading the flavor of seriousness, levity, or some other tone that may be differentially valued as appropriate or not in different languages for speakers of different genders.

Two of the three male readers had a strong Ukrainian accent in their Russian, while one did not. The same two men read in Ukrainian with standard Ukrainian phonology. Since language with standard phonology tends to be evaluated more highly, this explains some of the more positive marks given to the Ukrainian guises of the three men taken together. The one man who read in Russian-accented Ukrainian was evaluated about the same in each language. In interesting contrast, the women tended to be evaluated more positively in Russian when both languages were equally standard, and even when their Russian was "less pure" (has the phonology typical of standard Ukrainian) than their Ukrainian reading. A possible explanation for this surprising finding is that the tone plays a role. Through further scrutiny of the characteristics of individual readings, I found that a Ukrainian-speaking woman will be received more positively if she intones colorfully and shows a desire to engage and entertain her hearers; in contrast, a flat, rushed tone is more palatable in a woman speaking Russian. This evaluation of linguistic styles corresponds to the idealized image of the Ukrainian woman as someone who is a good story-teller, not as a no-nonsense reporter of facts. For men, however, Ukrainian was positively valued even in a more-rushed reading style, even when compared with "purer" Russian speech.

The final angle of analysis concerns differences in how women and men evaluated Ukrainian versus English, in rating the reader who is a native speaker of both languages.[12] Mean evaluations showed that all categories of respondents favored English over Ukrainian in absolute terms. This association was strongest among Russians, without clear patterning by respondent gender. Russians would have the greatest reason not to support Ukrainian, which in daily life is the language most directly challenging the status of Russian. Among Ukrainian respondents, women associated all of the traits more strongly with the English language than did men. A possible explanation for this pattern can again be found in Bourdieu's theory that women rely more on symbolic capital for their social status. In this case, since the prestige of Ukrainian was not well established, women found English more attractive and valuable than Ukrainian. The reader in question was a man, and thus his voice could have evoked the image of an appropriate partner for female respondents in the student sample. If we assume a heterosexual society in which women seek to improve their status through marriage, the more positive responses of women to the speaker's English guise make sense, since English unequivocally connotes better economic opportunities. The fact that Ukrainian women tended to evaluate an English speaker more positively than one who speaks in Ukrainian shows that the paradigm of women as guardians of the Ukrainian language and traditions does not correspond to the reality of women's language attitudes. This suggests that many women did not wholeheartedly accept the ideology of women's traditionalism.

Conclusions

My research has shown that gender is a significant factor affecting language ideology in Ukraine. The role of gender is by no means clear or simple: It is a complex social construct that intertwines with the constructs of ethnicity, class, and other facets of identity. Nevertheless, the patterns of language ideology that I have found can be explained in terms of gender differences in access to social power and status, often consistent with findings elsewhere. For example, my data showing women having more positive attitudes than men toward English is consistent with Gal's (1998) findings that women are more attracted to a nonlocal language because it gives them greater opportunities for social advancement.

In this study, I found that economic and political forces sometimes appear to be reinforced by cultural ideologies of women as preservers of tradition, but sometimes these forces are in contradiction. The fact that Ukrainian women were more critical than men of the Ukrainian language could be seen as evidence of women's "policing" the purity of the language, and thus taking on the burden of maintaining authentic traditions. On the other hand, their criticism could reflect lower valuation of a language of questionable status that does not give them the kinds of opportunities for social advancement that Russian or English can. Although the status of Ukrainian had risen—as we see in the high evaluations of standard Ukrainian speakers—Russian and English had much more established prestige and provided clearer opportunities for advancement. In the mid-1990s, Ukrainian was not yet institutionally well established, while Russian still retained its connotations of urbanity, education, and social power, and English was associated with the affluent West and political and technological power.

Why would Ukrainian women be more likely to pursue the benefits accorded by Russian and English than men, as is suggested by their attitudes? According to Eckert (1998) and Bourdieu (1991: 2), this is the result of a stronger linkage of women's status to symbolic and linguistic capital, while men's status depends more on material capital and occupation. This leads women to be more critical of a language of questionable status than men would be. If men's status is defined less by symbolic capital and more by what they have and do, they are in a better position than women to take risks in supporting a less-prestigious language; furthermore, support for Ukrainian is a way for Ukrainian men to claim power away from Russians (and Russian speakers) who have disproportionately been in control of administrative structures in Ukraine. It is to the advantage of Ukrainian men to strive to have others value the Ukrainian language, since this supports their own local power. The myth of Ukrainian women as protectors of language and traditions ultimately serves to uphold the power of local Ukrainian men in the current patriarchal system and to limit women's social mobility away from the local male sphere of control. The gender difference in evaluations was most pronounced in villages, where women were most critical of the local language, corresponding to Gal's (1989) theory that women in peripheral areas are more sensitive to language as a factor in social mobility. At the same time, my data showed that village men were more supportive of their local language, which served to boost their own local authority.

After examining the direct evaluations of language, I analyzed language attitudes that are implicit in reactions to speech, as documented by means of a matched-guise test. Analysis of the gender of the readers in this test revealed that women were evaluated more positively in their Russian guise, while men were evaluated more positively in their Ukrainian guise. It appears that women were socially rewarded more for using Russian than for Ukrainian. This makes sense given the persistence of the connotations of Russian as a prestigious, urban language for women. The prestigious connotations of Russian were likely weaker for men, since even men from villages had had the opportunity to learn Russian during army service. By examining the connotations of the specifics of individual readings, I found further explanation for the variation. For example, a very literary and colorfully intoned recording was more likely to gain approval for a woman in Ukrainian than was a flat, fast reading. Although perceived language purity appeared as the main factor shaping evaluations of men, the issue of purity was overridden by enacted personality traits in the case of some women when these did not fit a feminine ideal.

Women have a subordinate position in Ukrainian society, excluded from most political and economic positions of power and disproportionately burdened with household and family responsibilities. The Soviet rhetoric of gender equality had only allowed a few token women advancement into prestigious public social positions, and many of the post-Soviet trends further advocated women's return to traditional domestic roles. In this context, it is likely that women relied more on symbolic capital for social advancement, while men depended more on their occupation and material capital (consistent with Eckert 1998). This is not to say that men are not concerned with symbolic capital—indeed, they have the most impetus to support their titular ethnic language inasmuch as it will bolster their claims to authority. Meanwhile, mythologies of idealized womanhood depict women as responsible for upholding Ukrainian language and traditions. Women's more critical stance toward language quality corresponds to a concern for purity and also recognition of the limitations of the Ukrainian language as an avenue to social power. It is strategically wiser for women to support languages of more-established status, since they risk more in identifying themselves with a language of low prestige. Thus, Ukrainian women showed relatively more support than do Ukrainian men for languages of world status such as English and Russian. Although cultural ideologies play a role in shaping dispositions and behaviors, my data suggest strongly that language attitudes in Ukraine are shaped by people's strategies for establishing and maintaining higher social status, and their effort to shape the linguistic values around them.

Notes

This is an abbreviated version of Bilaniuk, Laada 2003. "Gender, Language and Language Status in Ukraine." *Language in Society* 32. I am grateful to Alicia Beckford Wassink, Ben

Fitzhugh, Jane Hill, Celia Lowe, and two anonymous reviewers who provided invaluable critique of this article, and to Bohdan Azhniuk, Volodymyr Dibrova, Oleksander Halenko, Assya Humesky, and Larysa Masenko for their advice and generous assistance with linguistic analyses. I am indebted to the many people in Ukraine who helped me organize and participated in this research. This article is based on fieldwork that was supported by a DOED Fulbright-Hays Doctoral Dissertation Research Abroad Grant, a National Science Foundation Grant (no. SBR-9419338), and an International Research and Exchanges Board Research Residency (with funds provided by the National Endowment for the Humanities, the US Information Agency, and the US Department of State). I thank these agencies for their support.

1. On feminism in independent Ukraine, see Bohachevs'ky-Chomiak 1998, Pavlychko 1996 and 2002, and Rubchak 1996. The development of gender studies in Ukraine is supported by institutions such as the Kyiv Gender Studies Institute and Kharkiv Center for Gender Studies. http://www.las.iastate.edu/wsp_kcgs_partners/english/Project_Activities.htm.

2. Bourdieu 1991 uses the term "symbolic capital" to denote resources such as knowledge of prestigious forms of language, ease with cultural behaviors that denote high social status, and prestigious institutional associations (such as academic degrees). Symbolic capital maybe converted to other forms of capital, such as a university degree giving access to a high-paying job, or a certain way of talking leading to acceptance and support by a particular social group. According to Bourdieu, men are judged more heavily based on their economic capital (their material wealth and their profession), while women are judged more heavily based on their symbolic capital (how they wield language and their appearance).

3. See Bilaniuk 2005, Taranenko 2007, Bilaniuk and Melnyk 2008, and Laitin 1998 for further examination of language politics in Ukraine since 1989.

4. While my English gloss for Ukrainian *hramota*—"reading and writing"—is often referred to as *literacy* in English, there is a different word in Ukrainian, *hramotnist'*, which translates more closely to *literacy*. Literacy refers to a degree of skill in reading and writing; *hramota* refers to the actual phenomena of reading and writing.

5. The exclusion of the seven individuals whose ages fall outside of the thirteen to twenty-seven-year-old range does not affect the data patterning analyzed.

6. According to the 2001 census data, Ukraine had a population of 48 million, with 78 percent identifying themselves as Ukrainians, 17 percent as Russians, and 5 percent other ethnic groups (http://www.ukrcensus.gov.ua/eng/results/). The difference between my sample and the census figures may reflect sampling procedures as well as differences in the form and context in collection of this information.

7. The wording of this response is designed to reflect the equation of purity and quality, which is pervasive in current linguistic discourse in Ukraine. See Bilaniuk 2009 for further discussion.

8. Even if this was the case in the early post-Soviet period, this may change once Ukraine has been independent for a longer period of time. See Laitin 1998 for discussion of forces affecting ethnic assimilation of Russians in Ukraine.

9. As noted earlier, there is an accepted standard Ukrainian language, although some aspects are disputed and knowledge of Ukrainian grammar rules is limited. Indeed, some interviewees told me that there is nobody who speaks pure Ukrainian, or even that there is no such thing. Disputes over terminological developments also led to the

perception by nonspecialists that Ukrainian was not fully standardized. In my analysis, I refer to widely held social perceptions of the language, as I encountered them during my fieldwork.

10. The only exceptions were evaluations by Russian women of happiness and propensity to joke, and here the mean evaluation values were extremely close (within 0.03 points).

11. For a more detailed analysis see the full version of this article, see Bilaniuk 2003.

12. Although most of the respondents likely did not know English, they were told that the last reading was a translation of the same text as heard before.

Bibliography

Aheieva, Vira, and Svitlana Oksamytna, eds. 2001. *Gender i Kultura*. Kyiv: Fakt.

Arel, Dominique. 1993. "Language and the Politics of Ethnicity: The Case of Ukraine." PhD diss., University of Illinois at Urbana-Champaign. Ann Arbor: University Microfilms International.

Bilaniuk, Laada. 1997. "Matching Guises and Mapping Language Ideologies in Ukraine." *Texas Linguistic Forum* 3: 298–310.

———. 2003. "Gender, Language and Language Status in Ukraine." *Language in Society* 32: 47–78.

———. 2004. "A Typology of *Surzhyk*: Mixed Ukrainian-Russian Language." *International Journal of Bilingualism* 8 (4): 409–25.

———. 2005. *Contested Tongues: Language Politics and Cultural Correction in Ukraine*. Ithaca, NY: Cornell University Press.

———. 2009. "Criticism, Confidence, and the Reshaping of the Linguistic Marketplace in Ukraine." In *Contemporary Ukraine on the Cultural Map of Europe*, edited by Larysa Onyshkevych and Maria G. Rewakowicz, 336–358. New York: E. Sharpe and Shevchenko Scientific Society.

Bilaniuk, Laada, and Svitlana Melnyk. 2008. "A Tense and Shifting Balance: Bilingualism and Education in Ukraine." *International Journal of Bilingual Education and Bilingualism* 11 (3/4): 340–72.

Bohachevs'ky-Chomiak, Martha. 1998. "Tender dovkola gender." *Krytyka* 3 (5): 21–23.

Bourdieu, Pierre. 1991. *Language and Symbolic Power*. Cambridge, MA: Harvard University Press.

Chaban, Mykola. 1994. "Iak z'hortalasia ukrainizatsiia na prydnipriv'yi." *Borysfen* 10: 40. (Dnipropetrovs'k monthly journal).

Coates, Jennifer, ed. 1998. *Language and Gender: A Reader*. Oxford: Blackwell.

Eckert, Penelope. 1989. "The Whole Woman: Sex and Gender Differences in Variation." *Language Variation and Change* 1: 245–67.

———. 1998. "Gender and Sociolinguistic Variation." In *Language and Gender: A Reader*, edited by Jennifer Coates, 64–75. Oxford: Blackwell.

Feminnist' ta maskulinnist'. 2003. (Special issue of the Ukrainian journal *Yi*, no. 27. http://www.ji.lviv.ua/n27texts/27-zmist.htm.

Gal, Susan, 1979. *Language Shift*. New York: Academic Press.

———. 1998. "Peasant Men Can't Get Wives: Language Changes and Sex Roles in a Bilingual Community." In *Language and Gender: A Reader*, edited by Jennifer Coates, 147–59. Oxford: Blackwell.

Halabudra-Chyhryn, Mariika. 1995. "Miunkhens'ki 'kadry' zahadkovoho rezhysera." *Ukrains'ka Hazeta* 8, no. 73 (13 April): 3.

Hanitkevych, Yaroslav. 1995. *Slovnyk Rusyzmiv u Movi Medykiv.* L'viv: L'viv State Medical Institute.

Hockstader, Lee. 1995. "For Russian Women, New Era Means More Sexism." *International Herald Tribune,* no. 34, Frankfurt, 2–3 Sept, 995.

Kulyk, V. 2006. "Constructing Common Sense: Language and Ethnicity in Ukrainian Public Discourse." *Ethnic and Racial Studies* 29 (2): 281–314.

Labov, William. 1990. "The Intersection of Sex and Social Class in the Course of Linguistic Change." *Language Variation and Change* 2: 205–54.

Laitin, David D. 1998. *Identity in Formation: The Russian-speaking Populations in the Near Abroad.* Ithaca, NY: Cornell University Press.

Lambert, W., R. Hodgson, R. Gardner, and S. Fillenbaum. 1960. "Evaluative Reactions to Spoken Language." *Journal of Abnormal and Social Psychology* 60: 44–51.

Lenets, Kateryna, 1993. *Chy pravyl'no my hovorymo?* Kyiv: Exlibris.

Lissyutkina, Larissa. 1993. "Soviet Women at the Crossroads of Perestroika." In *Gender Politics and Post-Communism,* edited by Nanette Funk and Magda Mueller, 274–86. http://ejw.sagepub.com/cgi/reprint/8/1/29.pdf?ck=nck.

Pavlychko, Solomea. 1996. "Feminism in Post-Communist Ukrainian Society." In *Women in Russia and Ukraine,* edited by Rosalind Marsh, 305–14. Cambridge: Cambridge University Press.

———. 2002. *Feminizm.* Kyiv: Osnovy.

Petrenko, O. D, E. Sh. Isaiev, and D. O Petrenko. 1999. "Mova cholovikiv i zhinok iak odynytsia sotsiolinhvistychnoho doslidzhennia." *Movoznavstvo:* 164–70.

Rubchak, Marian. 1996. "Christian Virgin or Pagan Goddess: Feminism versus the Eternally Feminine in Ukraine." In *Women in Russia and Ukraine,* edited by Rosalind Marsh, 315–30. Cambridge: Cambridge University Press.

Serbens'ka, Oleksandra, ed. 1994. *Anty-Surzhyk.* L'viv: Vydavnytstvo Svit.

Strikha, Maksym. 1997. "Surzhyk," *Berezil'* 3–4: 135–42.

Taranenko, Oleksandr. 2003. "Movna sytuatsiia ta movna polityka v suchasnii Ukraini." *Movoznavstvo* 2–3: 30–55.

———. 2007. "Ukrainian and Russian in Contact: Attraction and Estrangement." *International Journal of the Sociology of Language* 183: 119–40.

Trub, V. M. 2000. "Iavyshche 'surzhyku' iak forma prostorichchia v sytuatsiyi dvomovnosti." *Movoznavstvo,* no. 1: 46–58.

Verdery, Katherine. 1996. *What Was Socialism, and What Comes Next?* Princeton, NJ: Princeton University Press.

Wanner, Catherine. 1998. *Burden of Dreams: History and Identity in Post-Soviet Ukraine.* University Park: Pennsylvania State University Press.

Woolard, Kathryn A. 1989. *Double Talk: Bilingualism and the Politics of Ethnicity in Catalonia.* Stanford, CA: Stanford University Press.

———. 1996. "Language and Gender in Urban Catalonia." In *Gender and Belief Systems: Proceedings of the Fourth Berkeley Conference,* edited by N. Warner et al., 767–73. Berkeley: University of California, Berkeley, Women and Language Group.

Zhurzhenko, Tatiana. 2001. "(Anti)National Feminisms, Post-Soviet Gender Studies: Women's Voices of Transition and Nation-Building in Ukraine." *Osterreichische Osthefie* 43: 503–24.

CHAPTER 8

Feminizing Journalism in Ukraine
Changing the Paradigm

Mariia Tytarenko

The history of mass journalism goes back to the eighteenth century, at which time it was a strictly male domain. Women began to appear in print only in the nineteenth century (many of them under male pseudonyms, such as George Sand, George Eliot, and Marko Vovchok in Ukraine). In an article entitled "Na skloni viku," Ivan Franko, a prominent Ukrainian writer and journalist, offered an overview of the state of human emancipation in various spheres during the nineteenth century, in the form of a conversation among three individuals. One of them, a woman named Eufrosinia, is cast as a judicious mediator in a conversation between two male protagonists—the optimist Ilarion and the pessimist Zenon. She summarizes their discussion as follows: "In a man and a woman nature created neither two races, nor two separate nations, but two separate parts functioning as one whole."[1] The fact that women are associated with emotion and nurturance, while men represent intellect and rationality, and the two complement each other, is a widely argued concept in Ukraine.[2] Journalism and fiction often mimic this union of two parts in a single whole, in a synthesizing interdisciplinary process. Such synthesizing is associated with the "new journalism,"[3] which gained currency in the west in the 1960s and 1970s and is now a feature of Ukrainian women's writing.

The present chapter will probe the implications of such unions, while investigating feminized journalism. Currently *feminized poverty* is a popular term for describing the women's economically disadvantaged situation in the transitional Ukrainian society, but the rapidly growing feminization of journalism has the capacity to supplant it as an important discursive topic. Journalism not only reflects what is happening in society, it is a powerful force for shaping it, for acting as a medium in the creation of positive female role models. This model is especially important for Ukrainian girls, who might be aspiring to any career in the public sphere. In the present chapter I will examine journalism's role in constructing such a useful female paradigm. This chapter will also investigate the newest form of communication, the blogging space or blogosphere, which functions as an interactive web site for ongoing chronicles of information posted by journal bloggers, a process currently giving rise to a new breed of reader known as *homo legens* (one who reads).[4]

The first studies of gender specificity in the mass media and journalism were conducted in the late 1960s and early 1970s, in conjunction with gender research in other fields. That was a time when women started a full-scale offensive in all developed countries against editorial policies prejudicial to women, as well as other existing gender inequities. The result was an increasing presence of women in the profession. It was especially evident on TV and the radio, where female voices and faces influenced the audience and increased ratings of the programs in which they appeared, yet did surprisingly little to change the overall negative gender stereotyping throughout the media.

During the world conference on women held in Beijing in 1995, the international community conducted its initial study of the media's gender breakdown.[5] The first international conference Women and the Mass Media also took place that year in Toronto, under the aegis of UNESCO. Six years later UNESCO and the International Federation of Journalists (IFJ) launched another survey of gender representation in the community of journalists. The results demonstrated gender discrimination in almost every country, but research also indicated a modest move toward a resolution of this imbalance.[6] In 2006 the Gender Council of the European Federation of Journalists (EFJ) conducted research on gender equality in journalism. It contained credible evidence that feminization of the profession had occurred in Estonia, Latvia, Serbia, Slovakia, and Finland, with female journalists then in the majority.[7] In the USSR during the first years of the Soviet regime, women in journalism in all of the countries constituted 10 percent of the total number of authors; in the 1960s the figure rose to approximately 25 percent; in the 1970s women numbered almost a third; and in 1993 the percentage of women had risen to thirty-seven.[8] Ukrainian figures roughly paralleled this trend.

One can observe an analogous situation in the overall Ukrainian media market: for example, in 1999 there were only ninety-nine female print media sources (sixty-nine newspapers and thirty magazines) in the entire Ukrainian press (0.7 percent);[9] by 2005 that figure had grown to 16.8 percent.[10] Moreover, according to a survey by the All-Ukrainian Advertisement Coalition, the women's press outlets became the largest sector of growth in the print media. In 2005, their market capacity comprised a total of $22 million, and in 2006 it rose to $29.2 million (a 15.6 percent increase).[11] Today the Ukrainian women's media addresses practically all the age, professional, and national categories of Ukraine's female population. This kind of sustained growth has been observed in other sectors of the industry as well, especially in editorial staffs and student enrollment in higher education, where communication offerings are constantly expanding. The Department of Journalism in L'viv's Ivan Franko National University recorded the following data for the 2008–9 academic year: eighteen males of a total 144, or 12.5 percent, are first-year students; twenty-nine of 152 or 19 percent are males in their second year of study; twenty-one of 141, or 14.9 percent, are third-year journalism students; twenty of 133, or 15 percent, are male candidates for a baccalaureate; and sixteen of 126 or 12.7 percent are pursuing a master's degree. This averages out to just 14.8 percent of males per year.[12] As we are already aware, at the moment this gender imbalance is not being translated into a majority female presence in the profession, but our data offer persuasive evidence that women continue to gain ground.

One can advance a number of convincing arguments to explain this rise in the number of females in journalism and journalism-related fields. Among them is the expansion of women's emancipation, resulting in their greater acceptance in the public domain and an increase in their marketability. Female psychology is yet another reason; it is argued that women are more flexible and more creative with a superior ability for social interaction, all of which makes them better mediators. Although these attributes are not lacking in males, socialization seems to be developing such traits in women to a higher degree. Added to this is what has been described as women's increasing business acumen, which propels many of them to the highest administrative posts in the mass-media market as well.[13] In a speech to the EFJ about gender problems in the mass media, Nadia Azhgikhina provides numerous examples, based on statistical data, of the feminization of journalism as a world tendency.[14]

Journalism places its female practitioners in positions of influence to an extent that is virtually unheard of in other professions. It can be an effective medium for constructing positive images of women and shaping public opinion in the women's favor, yet despite its positive potential for increasing women's influence and the numbers of women in journalism, women continue to suffer prejudicial treatment and second-class status in virtually every other sphere of public engagement. For example, in the Ukrainian parliament there are thirty-six (or 8.2 percent) women among some 450 parliamentarians[15] and only three head regional administrations. They comprise 30 percent of the individuals in business, but are generally found in its lower ranks.[16] Finally, the average salary of women in Ukraine is 68 percent of the men's earnings.

This naturally begs the question: if journalism is so influential, with so many successful women in its ranks, why are female journalists not promoting more vigorously the issues of gender equality and elimination of negative stereotyping? A response to that highly charged question is a subject for a separate study. This chapter will remain focused on the positive achievements of Ukrainian female journalists. The most outstanding success stories are those of Yulia Mostova, Larysa Ivshyna, and Natalia Ligacheva.

Ukraine's leading journalist, with a highly developed sense of ethics, is Yulia Mostova. Along with two colleagues,[17] she declined to accept the "Best Journalist of the Year" award (for which she was nominated three times), in protest against the alleged murder of fellow journalist Georgii Gongadze.[18] She was, however, a recipient of the "Person of the Year" award. Along with her father, Volodymyr Mostovy, also a journalist, she founded the weekly trilingual newspaper *Dzerkalo Tyzhnia* (Mirror of the Week), published in Kyiv and currently ranked as one of the most respected newspaper in the country.[19] Mostova has been working as its editor since the newspaper's inception in 1994. She specializes in US, Ukrainian, and Russian foreign policy. In an interview she once accentuated her credentials by noting: "The average woman tends to focus on her appearance and issues like obesity, whereas I devote myself to news about the Black Sea Fleet, the gas supply, and the tender platform."[20]

Larysa Ivshyna is founder and chief editor of the daily bilingual (English and Ukrainian) newspaper *Den'*. She holds the title of "Honored Journalist of Ukraine" and is both the creator and editor of the newspaper's Library Series of book publications, which has already issued eight substantial works: *Viiny i myr* (Wars and Peace, 2004), in Ukrainian and Polish; *Dvi Rusi* (Two Rus's, 2004), and *Ukraina Incognita* (Anonymous Ukraine 2004), in both Ukrainian and Russian; *Den' i vichnist' Dzheimsa Meisa* (The Day and Eternity of James Mace 2005), in Ukrainian and English; *Pochemu ON NAS unichtozhal?* (Why Did HE Attempt to Destroy US? 2007), in Ukrainian and Romanian; as well as her own book, *Moi universytety* (My Universities 2006).[21] Ivshyna, a journalist with an extremely positive outlook is known as a "collector of talented people," who supports the concept of mutual help and is averse to controversy. In her mind, society is already oversaturated with what she calls "catastrophism." She accuses journalists of failing to find the joy inherent in Ukraine's greatness, even though the country and the times offer such remarkable opportunities for this.[22] Instead, they allow the mundane to overwhelm them. By way of example: let us think about our freedom and what we, as individuals, might accomplish with it, she suggests. Ivshyna maintains that women can "introduce society to so much that is new and different, without giving up the past." It is a truism that people without a past have no future. The world should know a good deal more about our country than the exploits of its renowned soccer team, she insists.[23] Transitional Ukraine is still a contested space, where tradition and modernization intersect. Currently, the mounting interest in women's issues presents a unique opportunity for modernizing the country, something that women should be pursuing. The task is a daunting one to be sure, especially as Ukrainian culture tends to resist change, even the destruction of old prejudices and negative stereotyping.[24] Someone like Ivshyna, with her powerful female voice, is in a formidable position to promote positive change. Gender justice is a much discussed topic today. Ivshyna can help to expand discourse which emphasizes women, to include the role that Ukrainian journalism can play in propagating an all-inclusive gender policy. She also argues for the urgency of pursuing such a course by adding "responsible, courageous, noble, and generous" male voices to the discourse.[25]

Natalia Ligacheva, our third journalist in this trio of exceptional female "media activists," is the corporate head and chief editor of the media corporation *Telekrytyka* (Television Review)[26] and a member of the National Committee for the Affirmation of Freedom of Speech and Development in the Informational Space, sponsored by the president of Ukraine (Yushchenko). In 2001 Natalia received a grant ($25,000) from an American fund designated for the promotion of an independent mass media, a self-governing internet project that, she admits, also enabled her to exercise her own right to free speech.[27] In 2004 Ligacheva founded a media corporation that manages a web site and publishes *Telekrytyka*.

The list of illustrious female journalists also includes Olena Prytula, chief editor of the popular internet edition of *Ukrains'ka Pravda* (Ukrainian Truth); Olha Herasymiuk, well-known TV anchor, producer of Channel *1+1*, and member of the Ukrainian parliament; Iryna Herashchenko, legislator and former press secretary to President Viktor Yushchenko, also an editor of the News Agency UNIAN; Anna Herman, another legislator and first deputy chief of the Community Board for Freedom of Speech and Information, as well as former editor of the Kyiv office of *Radio Svoboda* (Radio Liberty), and author of *Piramidy nevydymi* (Invisible Pyramids) (2003). Finally, we have Natalia Baliuk, chief editor of the daily regional newspaper in L'viv, *Vysoky Zamok* (High Castle), and Nadiia Morykvas, L'viv writer, scholar, and editor-in-chief of the magazine *Rich* (Object).

The feminization of Ukrainian journalism can also be observed in changes to the composition of editorial staffs. For instance, there are ten female and four male editors of the Ukrainian newspaper *Den'*;[28] five women and four men in *Dzerkalo Tyzhnia;*[29] five women and one man in *Vysoky Zamok;* as well as five women and eight men in *L'vivs'ka Hazeta* (L'viv Gazette).[30] Below is a comparative table of females/males in editorial positions and those heading newspaper sections. In the interest of objectivity, I have omitted exclusively women's publications such as *Natali* with its all-female editorial staff.[31] Instead I have chosen the most widely read newspapers: two nationwide papers *Dzerkalo Tyzhnia* and *Den'*, as well as two L'viv publications, *Vysokyi Zamok* and *L'vivs'ka Hazeta*.

Table 8.1 Comparative Table of Female/Male Editors of Ukrainian Newspapers

Newspaper Editors	*Dzerkalo Tyzhnia*	*Den'*	*Vysokyi Zamok*	*L'vivs'ka Hazeta*
Chief Editor	Volodymyr Mostovy	Larysa Ivshyna	Natalia Baliuk	Vasyl Tereshchuk
Deputy Editor	Yulia Mostova	Hanna Sheremet	Halyna Vdovychenko, Askold Eriomin	Volodymyr Khrushchak
Culture	Oleksiy Kononenko	Tetiana Polishchuk	Hanna Guzio	Oksana Zhyla
Politics/law	Serhiy Rakhmanin, Oleksandra Prymachenko	Olena Yakhno	Inna Yanko	Iryna Hamryshchak
Economics	Natalia Yatsenko Alla	Oleksiy Savicky	Zenoviia Voronovych	
Society	Eriomenko Lidia Surzhyk	Oksana Mykholiuk	—	Vasyl Khudycky

As is evident from this table, female representatives in selected areas of the media are in the majority, an example of a global tendency as well.[32] Although the numbers speak well for women, they do tend to dominate in the traditionally female fields of the newspapers. Hard news, politics, and the economy were, until very recently, the exclusive domain of men, and males still gravitate to them. Even university journalism departments exhibit a tendency for female students to choose media concentrations that reflect traditional women's interests—the arts, literature, cinema, theater, music, etc., whereas male students are drawn to typically male fields such as hard news, sports, politics, economics, and photography.

Feminization has also taken over media illustrating. Today more than ever, female journalists work as photographers and caricaturists, thereby changing the traditional male paradigm here as well. "Early on, photography was considered mainly a man's profession; women joined it rarely, especially as reporters. The current boom of women in photography classes is as high as 70 percent, and the same ratio can be seen at photo exhibits and photo competitions,"[33] a clear indication that the feminization of journalism is developing on both the verbal and the visual levels.

Throughout history, journalism has been linked to literature, which has led to many thought-provoking discussions on the genesis of journalism as a profession. It has also given rise to numerous trends of integrating literature and journalism, especially among women recognized for their ability and desire to unite the two. The twentieth century saw a slowly rising number of female authors beginning to join the ranks of media journalists. Many of them brought a literary background to the field. The earlier generation includes such outstanding figures as Natalia Kobryns'ka, writer and Ukraine's first feminist—a pioneer activist in the cause of women's rights; Olena Pchilka (pseudonym for Ol'ha Kosach), writer, editor of several journals, including the first feminist almanac *Pershyi Vinok* (The First Wreath), community leader, ethnographer, feminist activist, and mother of Lesia Ukrainka (pseudonym of Larysa Kosach), herself a poet, dramatist, and role model for early feminists; writer-democrat, translator, and editor Marko Vovchok (pseudonym of Maria Vilinska);[34] poet, brilliant essayist, and anti-Nazi activist (shot by the Nazis and buried in Babyn Yar) Olena Teliha; and others.

In contemporary Ukraine, the same combination of serious literary output and journalism works well for Oksana Zabuzhko, a scholar trained in philosophy, poet, and writer of Ukraine's first best-selling novel; Oksana Pakhliovska, poet, writer, translator, art critic, literary scholar,[35] and daughter of the modern dissident poet Lina Kostenko; Liudmyla Taran, poet, novelist, essayist, and committed feminist; Natalka Bilotserkivets, award-winning poet; Klara Gudzyk, the most acclaimed Ukrainian journalist on religious themes and occasional contributor to newspaper accounts of gender issues; plus many more.

There are at least three ways of uniting literature and journalism. First—journalists publish their articles as a book of collected works: Examples include: *V konteksti nashoi doby* (In the Context of Our Epoch) (1990), by Natalka Bilotserkivets; *Enerhiia poshuku* (The Energy of Searching) (1988), by Liudmyla Taran; *Khroniky vid Fortinbrasa. Vybrana eseistyka 1990 do 1999 rokiv* (The Chronicles of Fortinbras. Selected Essays from 1990 to 1999); *Let My People Go*, and *Piatnadtsiat tekstiv pro Ukrains'ku revoliutsiiu* (Fifteen Texts on the Ukrainian Revolution) (2005), by Oksana Zabuzhko; *Apokryfy Klary Gudzyk* (Apocrypha of Klara Gudzyk) (2005), by Klara Gudzyk; *Ave Europa!* (2008), by Oksana Pakhliovska; and others. Second—prominent writers are solicited to write columns or blogs for the media. And third—journalists and writers publish their speeches or public lectures integrating literature and journalism. Most interesting perhaps is the cycle of *Arcadia Olenska-Petryshyn Memorial Lectures*, given at both the Harvard Ukrainian Studies Series, and the National Mohyla Academy in Kyiv; *Binom 'Ukraina-diaspora' siohodni: kryza i perspektyva* (Ukraine-Diaspora. A Contemporary Binomial: Crisis and Prospects) (2002), by Oksana Pakhliovska, writer, poet, and director of the Department of Ukrainian Studies at Rome's La Sapienza University; *Humanitarna aura natsii, abo Defekt holovnoho dzerkala* (The Humanitarian Aura of a Nation, or Defect of the Main Mirror) (2005), by Lina Kostenko, Soviet-era dissident and poet; *Viter z Ukrainy i nashi ekzystentsiini zusyllia* (Wind from Ukraine and Our Existential Efforts) (2006), by literary critic as well as prominent figure in the 1960s anti-Soviet movement Mykhailyna Kotsiubyns'ka.

The most important result of this synergetic combination is the fact that journalism and fiction alike transcend their respective natural domains. They enhance each other by blending new writing techniques with methodology, displaying a deepened perception of the target audience, producing expanded contents, and introducing a richer vocabulary. Their synthesis also helps to shape the readership, resulting in a newly restructured paradigm of *homo legens*. In conjunction with this, Maria Zubrytska, vice-rector of Ivan Franko National University in L'viv and critic, wrote *Homo Legens: chytannia iak sotsiokul'turnyi fenomen* (*Homo Legens:* Reading as a Sociocultural Phenomenon, 2004)); she states:

> The crucial problem for me is an anthropological one—whether the person doing the reading had changed or not. No, nothing has changed here. I did see changes in technology, vision, and tools, but *homo legens* remains the same. We need to read, if not a book then everything else around us—thus we read the world.[36]

Zubrytska also is of the opinion that in its critical mass, Ukrainian literature projects a mood of pessimism, as opposed to the light and hope which it could be conveying. By now, writing should have built bridges to the future, and created models of reality as it ought to be, or might have been, and this is a task for contemporary journalism as well. Among the many suggestions and theories that instruct us on how to educate today's reader in the chaotic information field, and how to protect him and her from the pathogenic and destructive information, is that of Nataliia Sliadnieva, who advocates the founding of so-called schools of informational survival, with an informational and analytical component in the core offerings.[37] The media ecology movement is on the rise in post-Soviet countries, including Ukraine.[38] It deals primarily with new approaches to studying the media environment, in which technology and techniques, modes of information, and codes of communication are featured.

Another avenue to be explored is the information highway created by technology, which in this instance is the blog, and its latest Twitter offshoot. Modern journalism would be impoverished without the so-called citizen/public/participatory journalism, or the blogging that we now have at our disposal. Like its parent, media journalism, a blog is also an interdisciplinary fusion of literature and journalism, but it is extrapolated onto cutting-edge technology and connected to the internet. In mass communication studies, blogging is usually known as a segue from *mass* journalism to *personal* journalism. According to historians of the profession, the source of the participatory blog is personal or monojournalism, when one or a few people are simultaneously its authors, editors, publishers, and distributors of their own product.[39] As such, this personal journalism is more subjective than mass journalism, which, since its emergence in the nineteenth century, has gradually lost its significance to clichéd writing patterns, strict editorial censorship, and "objectivity,"[40] aimed at a mass readership that so often breeds indifference.

For all its interactivity, the blogosphere is no panacea either, but it does enrich the field of journalism with its many innovative features such as hypertext, hypermedia, and interactive polylogue, along with person-to-person communication.[41] Still, its unmediated format can, and frequently does, lead to unreliable and false sources of information, as well as to a widening level of illiteracy and pathogenic content. In post-Soviet countries, the blogosphere is less developed than in Europe or the United States. One of the reasons for this is that in the transitional post-Soviet society, blogging has only limited private support and it is not stipendiary. Although it mimics western patterns of communication on the web, it lacks the resources of mammoth media companies as in the United States, which make it possible to hire prominent writers or journalists to engage in regular blogging on a given topic. This practice is just beginning to evolve in Ukraine. One example is the newspaper *Ukrains'ka Pravda* (Ukrainian Truth), which created a special web section for its bloggers.[42] It does, however, lack the gender distribution of mainstream journalism. Among its some ninety professional bloggers, there are only eighteen females (seven journalists, three writers, three singers, two scholars, two models, and one lawyer). The site also lacks the exposure found in the rest of the blogosphere. Male bloggers are not only richer and more diverse in their comments, they are five times larger in number than female bloggers, although on some media sites the number gap is narrower. This is true of such media projects as *Telekrytyka,* the blog page of which contains fifteen female participants compared to twenty-one male.[43] The overall gender-balance picture is somewhat murky, however, and hence difficult to project, because many authors prefer to use pseudonyms.[44]

Web spaces with female blog sites also exist, but most are less successful than mainstream blogging spaces in terms of visitors and advertising revenue. Such sites do represent potentially lucrative revenue streams for women, but they are still very underdeveloped. Among the most prominent female bloggers are: Larysa Denysenko (lawyer, host of a TV program on Channel *1+1,* and author of five novels); Svitlana Pyrkalo (writer, translator, editor-in-chief of TV talk show *Bez Tabu* (Without Taboo), member of the BBC Ukrainian Service Staff); and Irena Karpa (TV journalist, prose writer, and punk band singer).[45]

To conclude, since the end of the nineteenth century in Ukraine, the number of women engaged in journalism and holding high editorial appointments has grown steadily, along with other forms of women's media outlets. This trend reached its peak in the media market in 2005. The same tendency carries over to students in higher education, where the percentage of males has suffered a dramatic downturn. It is possible that in time, the study of journalism might undergo a radical restructuring, as the discipline traditionally based on philology in Slavic countries is replaced by a concentration on mass communication, demanding more technical skills. In all likelihood, such a focus would attract more male students. An accurate prediction is difficult to project, however, be it on the gender composition of future journalism students or the nature of the discipline itself. For the present, the tendency toward the feminization of journalism has its own rewards for women.

First and foremost, it opens up a new and important potential revenue source for them in a transitional environment, with its widespread debilitating prejudices against women in the workplace. In other words, journalism is contributing, albeit on a small scale, to at least a limited defeminization of poverty, substituting the feminization of journalism in its place. Second, and perhaps more important, is the fact that the media, with their long reach, are in a position to create exceedingly attractive role models for many young women. Take for instance the glamorous aura that surrounds a TV anchor woman, which offers young female viewers an idealized vision of themselves as smart, successful, sophisticated individuals, with superior communication skills, in a society still tending to undervalue its women in any role but motherhood.[46] The media is a powerful instrument for fashioning such images, and a career in journalism, for instance, or prominence as a writer à la Zabuzhko, holds out the promise of transcending the debilitating prejudices against women that relegate them to second-class status in the country's public endeavors.

Aside from benefiting on several fronts from the positive images of women projected in the media, a successful career in something so visible, or as a writer of fiction, which can bring fame, and to some, fortune, the feminization of journalism acts as a powerful barometer of social acceptance. As for the blogosphere, as Ukraine offers more and more career opportunities in journalism for women, indexed by their popularity as solicited bloggers by firms with messages to sell, eventually this too will promote a general acceptance of women as equal partners in the public domain. In sum, the negative connotations for women, which inhere in the feminization of poverty, are being transformed into positive images projected by the feminization of journalism. This provides the inspiration, encourages the will, and offers the opportunity for women to break through more glass ceilings than ever before.

On the other end of the spectrum, besides bringing more women into the process, the interdisciplinary fusion of journalism and literature in Ukraine, with its longstanding tradition in Ukraine, helps authors from each discipline to transcend and enhance their own respective fields. This synergetic symbiosis enriches journalism, especially by its expanded and deepened content, methodology, tools, and formats. It is also creating a new generation of *homo legens* in the contemporary internet era.

Finally, the positive images of women in the kind of journalism under discussion here must ultimately begin to extend to constructive images of women in the day-to-day lives of average Ukrainians. Journalism provides a unique position from which to begin eliminating antifemale discrimination and poverty "with a woman's face," for eradicating the devastating negative female stereotype that denies them decent employment in the Ukrainian economy. On a wider, all-gender note, blogging supports freedom of speech to a degree unmatched by journalism itself.[47] Unmarked by specious declarations of free speech, it truly encourages freedom of expression. This applies to both sexes, and can have only positive consequences for each.

Notes

1. Franko 1986: 298. The key point of this article is the problem of the individual's emancipation, including his/her body and soul, needs, desires, and beliefs, from all strict rules, formulae, and dogmas. Great attention is devoted to the emancipation of women in the nineteenth century as well. One of the protagonists, Ilarion, states that for him personally, "a woman is the same human being as a man, and the emancipation of men from social, political, and spiritual chains will give a woman greater freedom."

2. The idea of such a single universal being underlies Ivan Franko's famous concept of *Tsilyi cholovik* (Gestalt man). This anthropological model in Franko's prose is discussed in part by Efremov 1989: 174–180; Hundorova refers to it in Franko's lyrics, in 2006: 252–54. Tykholoz examined this model in Franko's lyrics and prose, in 1999: 32–34. One can read further about the comparative typological study of the model in my article "*Svitomodel*'" (World Model) 2006: 64–78).

3. New Journalism—sometimes defined as literary journalism, neojournalism, prose of plain fact, subjective prose, the nonfictional novel, or the literature of ideas—was the name given to a style of news writing and journalism in the 1960s and 1970s. It used literary techniques unconventional for the time. The movement was an outgrowth of the nineteenth/twentieth-century realistic-tradition novelists such as Mark Twain, Charles Dickens, William Thackeray, Jack London, Ernest Hemingway, and others. The term was codified in its current meaning by Tom Wolfe, in a 1973 collection of articles that he edited as *The New Journalism*, plus eleven collections of his own articles. In the United States, the movement became very popular; its theoretical basis was developed, and a traditional school of New Journalism emerged. It generated considerable debate among both advocates and opponents, a number of anthologies, and a series of university lectures, and it found new development in gonzo (first-person narrative) journalism. Unfortunately, the phenomenon of New Journalism has not been well researched, and remains little known to Ukrainians.

4. According to anthropological and journalism studies, new human models also have come into existence. Among them are *homo videns* (one who watches TV), *homo informaticus, and homo internetus.* Together the three formed a collective "person of the year in 2006," awarded by *Time* magazine. *Homo sapiens cyberneticus,* and *homo zapping* were also among the new forms. In her book *Homo Legens* (2004: 352), Zubrytska concentrates on structural and poststructural literary theories, but not on the actual reader

model. My article, "*Svitomodel*'" (2006: 289–301), examines a multiplex model consisting of all of these paradigms, demonstrating their advantages and disadvantages.

5. In excess of thirty thousand participants engaged in it. http://www.ruj.ru/authors/azhgihina/08016.html. Accessed 10 April 2009.

6. Somina 2001. http://www.journalist-virt.ru/mag.php?s=200608891. Accessed 10 April 2009.

7. The scale of wages for female journalists was still lower than it is for men. A glass ceiling has impeded women's promotions; their income is only 10 percent lower in Finland, Denmark, Cyprus, Sweden, and Slovakia, and 20 percent lower in Great Britain, Norway, Germany, and Russia. http://www.journalistvirt.ru/mag.php?s=200608891. Accessed 10 April 2009.

8. Svitich 2003. http://www.owl.ru/win/research/zhvzhurnalistike.htma. Accessed 15 March 2009. An analogous process might be observed in the American media, where in the 1970s women totaled 20 percent, in 1990 this figure had climbed to 34 percent, and today it too stands at 37 percent.

9. Oliynyk 2003. http://www.ji.lviv.ua/n27texts/oliynyk.htm. Accessed 10 April 2009.

10. In 2005 there was a peak in the growth of the women's press in Ukraine. A record for increasing its readership and budgets from advertisement was established that was greater by 35 percent. The statistics and the monitoring of the Ukrainian media market are available at http://www.marketing.vc/view_subsects.php?num=118.

11. Skotsyk 2006. http://mmr.net.ua/issues/year/2006/num/18/news/370/index.html. Accessed 17 April 2009. The leaders in the women's print media market in 2006 were the following magazines: *Natali*, *Edinstvennaia* (Natalie, The One and Only); *Dobrie Soviety* (Good Advice); and *Burda*.

12. The list was supplied by the dean's office of the Department of Journalism at Ivan Franko National University, in L'viv.

13. Experts conclude that the reason for this wage imbalance is the fact that women obtain fewer highly paid positions. According to a survey of the Institute of Liberal Society, discrimination against women in the job market is one of the main negative tendencies to emerge during the past few years in all eastern European countries. http://www.yurincom.com/ua/legal_bulletin_of_Ukraine/publications/?aid=574&rid=47. Accessed 17 April 2009.

14. Nadezhda Azhgikhina, "*Neskol'ko shtrikhov k kollektivnomu portretu sovremennoi zhurnalistiki: gendernyi format*" (A Few Strokes in the Collective Portrait of Contemporary Journalism). http://www.ruj.ru/authors/azhgihina/08016.html. Accessed 17 April 2009. She analyses the gender situation in Russia and other post-Soviet countries, including Ukraine, during the past twenty years.

15. It is higher than it was in the fourth Verkhovna Rada in 2002 (5.5 percent), and in the first one in 1990 (only 3 percent). In the report of the Inter-Parliamentary Union that unites parliamentarians from all over the world, in 2007 there were only two countries with a number of women in parliament fewer than in Ukraine: these were the Islamic countries of Turkey (4 percent) and Egypt (2 percent). http://www.newsru.ua/world/22aug2007/zencinu.html. Accessed 10 April 2009. More women than men work in the parliament as journalists.

16. Women predominate in small- (26 percent) and medium-scale (15 percent) businesses; in big business they comprise 12 percent (only 2 percent head industrial business enterprises). Generally, the development of females in business has been oriented toward

culture, including the media, literature, and publishing, as well as science, medicine, and the retail trade. Usually such business activity is the result of women's own initiative, not some special state program. http://www.golos.com.ua/article/1236353228 .html. Accessed 10 April 2009.

17. Two other journalists are Olha Herasymiuk, and the chief editor of the internet media site Versii.com (http://www.versii.com/) Oleksandr Yurchuk. "We are convinced that the journalism of 2000 will always be associated with the name of Georgy Gongadze," they stated in their petition while declining the award. His death forced our citizenry to move from passive complainers about governmental acts toward active protest. The country has received an opportunity to become a democratic and civilized state after recovering from a "horrible disease." Unfortunately, not only numerous politicians but also some journalists reject these changes. "Never before have journalistic ethics, freedom, and solidarity been as devalued in Ukraine as they are now. Therefore, as the representatives of three absolutely different forms of mass media, we are appealing to our colleagues to remember these values, and to think about our loss—our professionalism. It is important to preserve the trust of our readers and viewers, as well as journalistic self-respect." Later, analogous rejections were received from the top journalist of Channel 1+1 Mykola Veresen', and from the magazine *Fakty I Komentari*. http://www.perehid.kiev.ua/look/31_03_2001.phtml. Accessed 10 April 2009.

18. An investigation into this alleged murder is continuing, with President Viktor Yushchenko having joined it.

19. http://www.dt.ua/ in Ukrainian; http://www.zn.ua/ in Russian; http://www.mw.ua/ in English.

20. Desiatnikova 2008. http://sobytiya.net.ua/archive,date-2008_07_21, article yuliya_ mostovaya_normalnue_jenschin/article.html. Accessed February 20, 2009.

21. Brief reviews of each book are available on the web site of the Library Series in the daily newspaper *Den'*. http://www.day.kiev.ua/108/.

22. Larysa Ivshyna. "*Svobody slova stalo bil'she, a zhurnalistyky menshe.*" http://www.day .kiev.ua/150098/. Accessed 19 March 2009.

23. Follow this line of discussion in Herasymchuk 2006. Available at: http://www.uwf .kiev.ua/Den_article_girls_30.06.doc. This statement reflects a widespread belief in Ukrainian society that custom and tradition are paramount. They view ideas emanating from the west with considerable suspicion, arguing that these are incompatible with Ukrainian culture, with its far different past. This renders Westerners incapable of understanding the Ukrainian mindset; what works elsewhere does not resonate with Ukraine's unique cultural history, and hence has no application in the country.

24. One can read about the destruction of some of the negative stereotypes of Ukrainian women such as Berehynia (Hearth Mother), Barbie, and the Soviet Superwoman, in Oksana Kis' 2003. http://www.ji.lviv.ua/n27texts/kis.htm. Accessed 17 April, 2009.

25. *Den'*, "Editorial," *Vtrata tsiloho svitu Mykhaila Vasylevskoho.* http://www.day.kiev.ua/ 263888/. Accessed 19 March 2009.

26. http://www.telekritika.ua/.

27. Nikolaeva and Furman 2007. http://telekritika.kiev.ua/articles/162/0/8642/reklamaster _intNL/. Accessed 19 March 2009.

28. http://www.day.kiev.ua/113/.

29. Access at: http://uk.wikipedia.org/wiki/%D0%94%D0%B7%D0%B5%D1%80%D0% BA%D0%B0%D0%BB%D0%BE_%D1%82%D0%B8%D0%B6%D0%BD%D1%8F.

30. http://www.gazeta.lviv.ua/info/progazetu/.

31. All nine members of the journal's editorial board are women. http://www.natali.ua/materials/show.html?idp=0&idr=0&p=&id=167&br=2. Accessed 17 April 2009.

32. According to the latest survey on the gender component in the media, conducted by IFJ in 2007 and focused primarily on post-Soviet countries, the largest percentage of women obtaining media editorial posts was found in Ukraine, Moldova, and Estonia (20 percent), then Armenia (15 percent), and Russia (10 percent). During the Soviet era, there were no female editors-in-chief in the central media of the USSR, and very few obtained this post in the local media. Currently, approximately 90 percent of the editors-in-chief in the regional mass media are women. http://www.ruj.ru/authors/azhgihina/08016.html. Accessed 17 April 2009.

33. Among other tendencies, according to the author, the feminization of modern photography came with the advent of pocket cameras, which make photography easier, more mobile, and quicker in delivering data; photo equipment is now accessible to virtually everyone. http://photoconcept.ru/gallery/fotoblog/blog_photographers/146.html. Accessed 17 April 2009.

34. Being acquainted with European and Russian authors, and maintaining numerous contacts, Marko Vovchok founded a magazine *Pereklady naikrashchykh Evropeiskykh avtoriv* (Translations of the Best European Authors). Only women worked there—that was her unalterable position.

35. Oksana Pakhliovska is also the director of the Ukrainian Studies Department at Rome's University La Sapienza. She had been working toward the foundation of this department since 1991, and finally managed to make her dream a reality in 2000. Today, it is one of the leading centers of Ukrainian Studies in the world.

36. In: Koval' 2004. http://gazeta.quintagroup.com/www/2004/08/18/NewspaperArticle.2004–08–17.5558. Accessed 19 March 2009.

37. Sliadnieva 2006. http://www.e-journal.ru/kultura-st1–22.html. Accessed 19 March 2009. The author states that such schools should teach new methods of verifying informational sources as well analytical methodology.

38. In June 1999, an Institute of Media Ecology was established at Ivan Franko National University in L'viv. The institute attempts to integrate conceptual and theoretical ideas related to media ecology and media philosophy, as well as some practical applications of media education and media literacy. The web page of the Institute is: http://www.franko.lviv.ua/mediaeco/indexeng.htm.

39. Svitich 2003: 17–18.

40. When all is said and done, there is no such thing as objectivity. Even documents in their original form, selected for some specific use, cannot be objective. Their choice and systematizing already constitutes a preliminary form of editing, a subjective opinion. Moreover, framers of documents are themselves not objective; they produce materials to conform to some predetermined objective of their own.

41 41. One of the paradoxes of the blogosphere is that, on the one hand, it leads from dialogue to polylogue, with its incalculable number of participants and various levels of communicative interaction. On the other hand, it gives participants the opportunity of person-to-person contact on the bloggers' pages (comment/rating/trackback field), in web forums, chats, Skype conferences, etc.

42. http://blogs.pravda.com/ua/.

43. http://blogs.telekritika.ua/.

44. Slavins'ka 2008. http://life.pravda.com.ua/surprising/48bbe69786df5/. Accessed 19 March 2009.
45. http://larysa.com.ua/content/view/100/1/; http://www.glavred.info/life/ego/; http:// svitske.tv/friends.
46. Although widely referred to as matriarchal, Ukrainian society in its contemporary manifestation (and earlier as well) is structurally patriarchal. For an in-depth development of this point see: Rubchak 1996: 315–30 and 2009: 139–54; also 2009b.
47. This is evidenced, especially, by the numerous "accidents" suffered by outspoken investigative journalists.

Bibliography

Azhgikhina, Nadezhda. 2007. "Kogda Rossiei budet upravliat' Margaret Thatcher? Neskol'ko shtrikhov k kollektivnomu portretu zhenshchiny-politika v rossiiskom informatsionnom prostranstve i o samom mediinom prostranstve." *Gender Studies* 16: 6–24.
Desiatnikova Irina. 2008. "Juliia Mostovaia. Normalnye zhenshchiny dumaiut o lishnem vese, A Ia—o chernomorskom flote, postavkakh gaza i tendernoi palate." *Sobytiia,* July, 21–28.
Efremov, Serhiy. 1989. *Istoriia ukrains'koho pys'menstva.* Munich: Ukrainian Free University.
Franko, Ivan. 1986. "Na skloni viku. Rozmova vnochi pered Novym Rokom 1901." Zibrani tvory, 45. Kyiv: Naukova Dumka, 298.
Herasymchuk, Viktoria. 2006. "Zhinky mozhut' modernizuvaty suspil'stvo." *Den',* 30 June.
Hundorova, Tamara. 2006. *Franko ne Kameniar. Franko i Kameniar.* Kyiv: Krytyka.
Kis', Oksana. 2003. "Modeli konstruiuvannia gendernoi identychnosty zhinky v suchasnii Ukraini." *Ï* 27: 37–59.
Koval', Yaryna. 2004. "Kozhen iz nas ie unikal'nym portretom *homo legens.* Rozmova iz Marieiu Zubryts'koiu." *L'vivs'ka Hazeta,* 17 August.
Makars'ky, Oleksandr. 2008. "Larysa Ivshyna: Svobody slova stalo bil'she, a zhurnalistyky menshe." *Zhurnalist Ukrainy,* no. 7. http://.day.kiev.ua/150098/.
Nikolaeva, Tatiana, and Aleksei Furman. 2007. "Nataliia Ligacheva: Dlia menia zhurnalistika vsegda byla bol'she missiei, chem zarabatyvaniem deneg." *Reklamaster,* 16 February. http:/reklamaster.com/spec_projects/ppage/208/show/who_is_pro/year/2007/id/549/index.html.
Oliynyk, Natalia. 2003. "Zhinocha presa v Ukraini: mynule tasuchasnist.'" *Ji* 27: 96–110.
Rubchak, Marian J. 1996. "Christian Virgin or Pagan Goddess: Feminism Versus the Eternally Feminine in Ukraine." In *Women in Russia and Ukraine,* edited by Rosalind Marsh, 330–15. Cambridge: Cambridge University Press.
———. 2009a. "Collective Memory as a Device for Constructing a New Gender Myth." *Contemporary Ukraine on the Cultural Map of Europe,* edited by Laryssa Onyshkevych and Maria Rewakowicz, 139–154. Armonk, NY: M.E. Sharpe.
———. 2009b. "Ukraine's Ancient Matriarch as a Topos in Constructing a Feminine Identity." *Feminist Review* 92: 129–150.
Slavins'ka, Iryna. 2008. "Pid maskamy i bez: khto-khto v Interneti zhyve?" *Ukrains'ka Pravda,* 1 September.
Skotsyk, Andrey. 2006. "God razvlekatel'noi pressy." *Marketing Media Review* 18, no. 24 (30 September): 18–19.

Sliadnieva Nataliia. 2006. "Sovremennyi chelovek v virtual'nom mire: Problema Infor-matsionno-analiticheskoi kul'tury Lichnosti." *Evraziiskii Vestnik* 21, no. 30 (March). http://www.ejournal.ru/kultura-st1-22.html.

Somina, Irina. 2001. "Ravenstvo v professii: evropeiskii kontekst." *Zhurnalist* (August): 89–90.

Svitich, Luiza. 2003. *Professiia: Zhurnalist. Uchebnoe posobie.* Moscow: Aspekt Press.

———. 1998. "Zhenskii vopros nakanune XXI veka." *Data from the Round Table* (April): 27–28.

Tytarenko, Maria. 2006. "Svitomodel' Homo Informaticus ta ii paradyhmy v suchasnomu sotsiokul'turnomu dyskursi." *Miscellany of the Scholarly Research Center of Periodicals* 14: 289–301.

Tykholoz, Bohdan. 1999. "Tsilyi cholovik v etyko-antropolohichnii konseptsiyi Ivana Franka." *Slovo i Chas,* no. 2: 32–34.

Zubrytska, Maria. 2004. *Homo Legens: chytannia iak sotsiokul'turnyi fenomen.* L'viv: Litopys.

CHAPTER 9

Feminism, Nationalism, and Women's Literary Discourse in Post-Soviet Ukraine

Maria G. Rewakowicz

Feminism as a phenomenon has acquired multiple significations over the years, and while it cannot be dismissed as a sociopolitical movement for women's liberation worldwide, in the past two decades the term itself has gone well beyond the original quest for equal rights and legal reforms addressing discrimination against women. In the west, the views of feminist activists in the 1960s and 1970s yielded a number of theoretical positions on patriarchy, sexuality, gender, female subjectivity, sexual difference, and identity, to mention just a few. Rosi Braidotti went so far as to declare that "feminism is shaping up as the one possible new ethical system of postmodernism" (1988: 283). In the end, however, she modified this viewpoint:

> Not until feminism has proved its ethical passions and their constructive nature.
> Not until new forms of connections are negotiated in social and political terms.
> Until we take the time to implement these changes, history will continue its one-way race. Until changes are beginning to become apparent on a collective scale, I shall not abandon myself to lyrical celebrations of female positivity. In keeping with the rigor of the feminist defense of sexual difference, I maintain that positivity needs to be constructed and enacted, and that such a project is the historical task of the female feminist subjects. As long as the positive empowerment of difference remains unaccomplished, utopias are mere *common*places. (1988: 283)

Recent feminist theoretical propositions exhibit the plurality and diversity of women's historical and cultural experiences, and underscore the need to take under consideration their differences, be it race, class, sexual preference, or ethnicity. The notion of a universal category of "woman" is retreating. Small wonder then that when Linda Hutcheon refers to the field of literary studies, she asserts:

> It would be more accurate, of course, to speak of feminisms, in the plural, for there are many different orientations that are subsumed under the general label of feminism: images of women's criticism; canon-challenging, and women's literary history; separatist or women-centered gynocriticism; feminist "critique" of patriarchal ideology in male texts; psychoanalytic studies of female subjectivity; theories of *écriture feminine* or *parler femme*; lesbian attacks on heterosexism; Marxist-socialist contextuality; deconstructive interrogations of cultural constructs; women's perspectives on Afro-American and postcolonial experience and identity as women of color. (1988, 67–68)

A proliferation of theories and methodologies entails a plurality of differences, while at the same time it engenders increased freedom for women to construct their own gender identity, an identity unhampered either by patriarchy or essentialism. Whereas not all of the above feminist theoretical approaches have found their way into Ukrainian literary quarters, many in fact have. And even though Ukraine has its own relatively strong feminist tradition going back to the second half of the nineteenth century (Bohachevsky-Chomiak 1988), the acceptance and advancement of the contemporary Western feminist project has been a comparatively new phenomenon, a phenomenon that had its beginnings in the early 1990s.

In many ways the attractiveness of feminist theory and gender studies for women scholars in Ukraine stems from a profound need to find new reading strategies in literary criticism, after many years of stagnation and ideological constraints under the Soviet regime. Moreover, the growing intellectual exchange between Ukrainian female scholars and their Western counterparts, following the collapse of the Soviet Union, brought about an increased awareness of the problems confronting women in independent Ukraine. This dialogue, coupled with financial support from the west in the form of grants and fellowships, presented Ukrainian feminists with an opportunity to pursue not only their own scholarly projects but also a new social agenda for all women in post-Soviet Ukraine. A handful of individuals such as Solomea Pavlychko, Vira Aheieva, Tamara Hundorova, and Nila Zborovs'ka were especially instrumental in introducing new feminist discourses into Ukrainian scholarship.

Solomea Pavlychko's pioneering efforts to apply feminist theory to Ukrainian literary scholarship as one of many possible methodological strategies cannot be overstated. Her contribution to such discourses has never been questioned, and since her untimely death in 1999 it has become an object of intense veneration among her feminist colleagues.[1] Pavlychko's *Feminizm,* published posthumously in 2002, attests to the fact that in her investigations of feminist issues, she did not limit herself to literary studies alone.[2] A number of articles, some written in English and first published in the west, deal with broader aspects of the women's movement in contemporary Ukraine, including its political, social, and national dimensions. One such article, "Feminism and Nationalism" (or to be precise, a project proposal for a fellowship dated 1992) is of particular interest to me because it makes a persuasive case for the importance of understanding the connection between feminism and nationalism with regard to the intellectual history of Ukraine.[3] Pavlychko states: "One of the greatest tasks feminism faces in this decade is to understand its relationship to nationalism" (2002b: 53). Not surprisingly, Pavlychko pays tribute to her predecessor in feminist scholarship, historian Martha Bohachevsky-Chomiak (who analyzed this relationship from political and social angles) and announced her intention to venture beyond the social history of the Ukrainian women's movement by studying the history of ideas as well. Turning to the feminine and intellectual tradition in Ukrainian literature from a feminist perspective, Pavlychko argues, can provide new insights "into the larger debate on the 'Europeanization' of Ukrainian culture, and the unique voices of female writers in this respect" (2002b: 55).

The goal of this paper, however, is more modest. First, I want to investigate the extent of the interconnection (or lack thereof) between feminism and nationalism in two schools of feminist (gender) studies in Ukraine, namely those of Kyiv and of Kharkiv. Second, I want to employ the same grid—feminism/nationalism—to selected works of literature by female authors, in order to test the applicability or inapplicability of such a correlation. Finally, as a byproduct of the above discussion, I also hope to point to the direction (however sketchy it might be at the moment) assumed by women's literary discourse(s) during the past decade and a half in Ukraine.

The concept of nationalism, like that of feminism, does not conform easily to a singular definition and, depending on interlocutors, might even evoke hostile reactions. For my purpose, I will use the definition put forward by Anthony Smith, which interprets nationalism as "an ideological movement for attaining and maintaining autonomy, unity and identity for a population which some of its members deem to constitute an actual or potential nation" (2001: 9). His decision to integrate the concept of nation in his definition of nationalism means that Smith needed to elucidate what he understood by the term *nation:* "Nations ... are felt and lived communities whose members share a homeland and a culture" (2001: 12). Smith's conceptualization of nationalism entails a given community's aspirations for self-determination and independence, and once such a goal is achieved, it also calls for maintaining national unity and identity. In other words, nationalism as an ideology occupies an equally significant place in both preindependence and independence situations. Another important distinction to which Smith alerts us is the fact that two kinds of nationalisms exist, one based on the principle of a shared territory and common laws (civic nationalism), and the other on ethnicity, that is to say, on the principle of a common ancestry (ethnic nationalism).[4] When one looks at the Kharkiv and Kyiv centers of gender studies from this perspective, one is almost tempted to say that the above distinction, civic versus ethnic, lies at the heart of the divergence between these two Ukrainian feminist schools. But this conjecture needs further elaboration.

Both centers were founded in the mid-1990s, and both have come to prominence owing largely to the efforts of their leading personalities. In the case of Kharkiv, it is mainly Irina Zherebkina and her husband Sergei Zherebkin. In Kyiv, Solomea Pavlychko was the driving force, although one should add that her endeavors received substantial assistance from a talented team of literary scholars, namely, Tamara Hundorova, Vira Aheieva, and Nila Zborovs'ka. Of course, the differences between these two schools stem not only from the distinct interpretations of Ukraine's post-Soviet realities and its national agenda but also from their contrastive applications of feminist theory. The Kharkiv school foregrounds the philosophical and sociological aspects of feminism, and only occasionally ventures into the literary sphere, whereas the Kyiv school concerns itself predominantly with literary criticism and the development of new feminist methodologies in order to reinterpret Ukrainian literary classics. One should also bear in mind the fact (and it is not without significance) that the Kharkiv studies are published almost exclusively in Russian, while the works coming out of Kyiv are virtually all in Ukrainian.

Coming back for a moment to the civic versus ethnic varieties of nationalism: even though both presuppose and agree with the idea of a nation-state, they base their tenets on a different set of principles. True, ethnic nationalism can exist over time even without political sovereignty, because it draws its strength from a belief in a common culture and language. For any ethnic community, the myth of common ancestry and shared historical memories are of great importance. Yet, despite the fact that ethnic nationalism is concerned mainly with issues of cultural identity, the drive for independence or the idea of a nation-state also is implied. Smith convincingly argues that "cultural and political forms of nationalism often succeed one another, and nationalists might oscillate between them" (2001: 77). Civic nationalism entails statehood and promotes the idea of nation as a rational association of citizens bound by common laws and a shared territory. In the case of independent Ukraine, civic nationalism is clearly promoted by politicians from all factions on the political spectrum. At the same time, ethnic nationalism still has its advocates, especially among those Ukrainians who feel that their culture and language are deliberately undermined by the authorities.

When one examines closely the writings of the Zherebkins, one is struck by the absence of connectedness (territorial or linguistic) to things Ukrainian. That is, they do take up Ukrainian subjects, but do so from "without" rather than "within." The fact that Kharkiv is territorially part of Ukraine seems to be ignored by design. Their perspective on the women's movement in Ukraine, and the gender-related problematic, is clearly that of an outsider. Thus one can conclude with assurance that even the civic model of nationalism (which marginalizes ethnic 'blood-and-soil' claims) is too much for them to bear. Vitaly Chernetsky explains it forthrightly:

> In the work of the Kharkiv school, one finds a curious slippage between a sustained feminist analytical project and the strategic use of feminist terminology for invectives against the Ukrainian state and the national culture, which the school apparently views as coextensive. Similarly to many other ex-Soviet Russophones, the Kharkiv gender studies school authors seem not to have done the work of mourning for the disintegrated Russian empire, and find themselves arrested in melancholic longing for the unified Russophone cultural space. They refuse the approach of the Ukrainian language as a means of communication and regard its use as an aggressive imposition of external power. Indeed, by way of refusing to subscribe to a Ukrainian identity, apparently not only linguistically but of any kind, members of the Kharkiv school offer a bizarre latter-day confirmation of Fanon's insight: a colonial subject comes to experience the metropoly as the norm and him/herself as the Other.[5]

Irina Zherebkina's first contribution to Ukrainian feminist scholarship appeared in 1996 as a monograph entitled *Zhenskoe politicheskoe bessoznatel'noe: Problema gendera i zhenskoe dvizhenie v Ukraine* (Women's Political Unconscious: The Problem of Gender and the Women's Movement in Ukraine). It is difficult not to see this work as a response to the book published a year earlier by Martha Bohachevsky-Chomiak, *Bilym po bilomu: Zhinky v hromadians'komu zhytti Ukrainy, 1884–1939* (White on White: Women in the Public Life of Ukraine), which constituted the author's Ukrainian version of the previously published *Feminists Despite Themselves: Women In Ukrainian Community Life, 1884–1939* (1988). Zherebkina's project, thematically and theoretically much wider in scope than Bohachevsky-Chomiak's undertaking, strikes us as a hodgepodge of contemporary feminist theory, literary criticism, historical and sociopolitical ruminations, all woven together in a rather disjointed manner. She clearly benefits from Bohachevsky-Chomiak's meticulous research (judging by the number of endnotes), but disagrees with the latter with respect to the viability of presenting the women's movement in Ukraine as simultaneously feminist and nationalist. To Zherebkina, feminism and nationalism are mutually exclusive, even though, as Kumari Jayawardena indicated (1986: 1–3), these ideologies go hand in hand when it comes to communities with colonial and semicolonial status. In other words, combining the struggles for national and women's liberation is not a Ukrainian invention, but rather a paradigm for all those subjected to imperialist powers.

Zherebkina underscores the fact that the women's organizations in contemporary Ukraine are for the most part neoconservative and largely hostile to the feminist agenda.[6] She also ascribes to them a preoccupation with nationalist ideology and an attempt to construe the "Other" (in this case Russia) as the enemy (1996: 51). At the same time, both Zherebkina and her husband Sergei seem completely oblivious to the endeavors of the Kyiv feminist school and its methodological freshness and innovations. Instead, Zherebkin (1999), in his essay "Femina Postsovietica v ukrainskoi postsovetskoi literature," (Femina Postsovietica in Ukrainian Post-Soviet Literature), dwells on the misogynist tendencies in contemporary Ukrainian works by male authors. He also denies feminist credentials to Oksana Zabuzhko's *Pol'ovi doslidzhennia z ukrains'koho seksu* (Field Research on Ukrainian Sex), simply because her protagonist forfeits the construction of feminist subjectivity in favor of masculine subjectivity.

The entire discourse on feminism coming out of the Kharkiv center is considered by its adherents to be neutral, unmarked, even though its main proponents do not particularly mask their partiality with regard to the issues of nationalism in present-day Ukraine. The Kyiv school, on the other hand, is implicitly marked by supporters of the Kharkiv center as nationalistic, or at least nationally inclined.[7] The problem with such marking, however, is that it legitimizes itself only in the presence of the Other. To put it differently, the Kyiv school appears to have a national bias only because the Kharkiv center so completely lacks it. Under normal circumstances, that is to say, without postcolonial impediments, all one can say about the Kyiv feminist school is that it functions the way it should, namely, producing interesting works of literary scholarship, experimenting with new methodologies and theories. Pavlychko's unorthodox readings of early feminist writers, such as Ol'ha Kobylians'ka, Lesia Ukrainka, and Ahatanhel Kryms'kyi (1997 and 2000), were followed by the novel interpretations of Lesia Ukrainka and Kobylians'ka by Vira Aheieva (1999a), and Tamara Hundorova (2002), as well as by the collections of essays and literary criticism of Oksana Zabuzhko (1999), and Nila Zborovs'ka (1999). These works represent a wide range of feminist approaches, from feminist critique of patriarchal ideology to psychoanalytic studies of female subjectivity. With the exception of Pavlychko's monograph on Kryms'kyi, and a few essays by Zabuzhko, however, nationalist concerns do not figure prominently in the works of these scholars. What is also worth emphasizing is the fact that both the Kharkiv and Kyiv feminist schools in Ukraine seem determined to ignore each other as legitimate centers for gender studies in Ukraine. We are dealing here with two parallel worlds, each referring to the same phenomenon, yet each interpreting it from entirely different angles.

The work of the Kyiv feminist school comes in stark contrast to the overall tendencies and attitudes among Ukrainian women's organizations and the rank-and-file women as well. As Solomea Pavlychko underscored, in order to be accepted by society, many leaders of women's organizations in Ukraine emphatically insist that they are "not feminists."[8] First and foremost they are concerned with national revival issues, including the language question, ecological threats, freedom of religion, and information. Preservation of the family as the cornerstone of the well-being of a society is also high on their agenda, and is promoted chiefly via a return to ancient symbols and myths.[9] Such a climate is not particularly conducive to a flourishing of feminist positions in contemporary Ukraine in general, and in literary scholarship in particular. This reality often forces feminist scholars to take up defensive postures whenever debates about the efficacy of feminism and/or gender studies arise. I am referring here especially to a series of publications in the journal *Krytyka* in 1999,[10] and two years later to a new wave of polemics in the same journal in the September and November issues of 2001.[11] Nevertheless, despite the struggle of maintaining its authority in literary and cultural scholarship, the feminist voice in Ukraine is heard and increasingly finds its way onto the pages of numerous periodicals, both scholarly and popular.[12] But this voice is forced to compete with a number of distorted perceptions of what feminism really stands for, prevalent mostly in the mass media and some works of pulp fiction, and among ordinary citizens of Ukraine as well.[13]

In addition to a number of individual works in the field of literary criticism by scholars associated with the Kyiv Institute of Gender Studies, in 2001 the institute itself presented a concerted undertaking in the form of the internet publication entitled *Vydnokola*. This electronic journal, three issues of which have been published thus far, clearly signals a move on the part of the Kyiv center to expand the discourse beyond the narrow confines of literary studies. A number of papers included in this publication deal with the sociological, historical, and political aspects of gender issues. Still, one must concede that literary scholarship dominates simply because the team responsible for the editing of this journal comprises mainly literary critics. An effort has been made as well to include contributions from scholars representing Western points of view (Ksenya Kiebuzinski, Maxim Tarnawsky, and Vitaly Chernetsky). Whereas the central focus of *Vydnokola* is on Ukrainian topics, the journal does strive for international appeal by incorporating contributions from outside Ukraine, and by accepting articles dealing with other than Ukrainian subjects, just as long as they foreground some aspect of gender studies.

The link between feminism and nationalism in works of literature by contemporary Ukrainian female writers is even less pronounced than that in the realm of literary scholarship. By and large, women authors do not champion nationalist concerns. In this regard, Zabuzhko's novel, *Pol'ovi doslidzhennia z ukrains'koho seksu*, constitutes an exception rather than the rule. The novel skillfully underscores the parallels between the national and the personal, focusing with equal passion on both feminine and masculine points of view. The failed masculinity of Zabuzhko's male protagonist moves in tandem with

Ukraine's impotence as a nation. In this sense, *Pol'ovi doslidzhennia* goes well beyond purely feminist concerns. Zabuzhko's feminism projects itself more as a vehicle for engendering a discursive space in which both nationalist and feminist issues are taken up, rather than any ability (or desire) on her part to produce a typical feminist novel.

Often perceived as Zabuzhko's disciple, Svitlana Pyrkalo intimates her own vision of societal inner workings with regard to the women's position in contemporary Ukraine. Her short novel *Zelena Marharyta* (Green Margarita) published in 2001, in comparison to Zabuzhko's *Pol'iovi doslidzhennia*, approaches feminist and national identity issues with humor and casualness. Pyrkalo's offhand and fragmentary manner of narration, quite in line with postmodernist premises, helps her to debunk the entrenched gender stereotypes as well as allows her to parody the trivialities found in a number of women's magazines. Consider for a moment the following titles: "A Debate. How to Become a Star: A Textbook for the Businesswoman;" "The Best Makeup Foundation for Brains: Now in a New Container;" "Man as a Particularly Useful Creature;" "Mobile Telephone as a Measure of Sexual Dignity," to mention just a few. They all point to Pyrkalo's penchant for playfulness, and her mastery of handling controversial issues in a lighthearted way. At the same time, Pyrkalo's protagonist Maryna, a self-proclaimed feminist, when faced with a choice between going abroad to study or staying in Ukraine, chooses the latter, tacitly acknowledging the importance of national belonging in a postcolonial setting.[14] And yet, one must not forget to mention the interesting paradox between the author and her character—Pyrkalo now lives in London and works as a BBC journalist. It is also interesting that her second novel *Ne dumai pro chervone* (Don't Think About the Red), published in 2004, reflects that new reality.

In the sphere of poetry, Ukrainian female authors, especially those of the younger generation, shy away from a direct thematization of questions pertaining to nationalism or national identity. Having experienced a long tradition of literature fulfilling other than strictly aesthetic functions, women poets in Ukraine prefer not to engage in overly ideological themes. But implicit, interiorized responses both to feminist and national concerns are certainly there. For example, the poetry of Marianna Kiianovs'ka foregrounds female self-sufficiency and autonomy, and does not thematize woman as mother. Any inference of woman's auxiliary role in a society, or connectedness to someone other than herself—such as a spouse or a family—is not only kept out of her poetic vocabulary but is viewed as incompatible with Being: "There is I and you, and there is God's permanence" (2000: 29). Kiianovs'ka's lyrical heroine does not reject love or relationships, but subordinates them to her own subjectivity.

Mar'iana Savka, on the other hand, ironically deconstructs the patriarchal myth of women yearning to give themselves to "real" men. She also reminds her readers of the ways in which women are not understood because they remain so to say "unread": "Woman has always been/ Opened on the first page/ And left unread" (2002: 71).

Liudmyla Taran, a poet representing an older generation of female writers who is especially active in shaping feminist discourses in post-Soviet Ukraine, goes even further. She experiments with gender reversals, assumes the male gaze, and contemplates female sexuality from a mostly desirous male perspective. She uncovers and simultaneously debunks the male tendencies to treat the female body as an object, yet does not reject the possibility of a real dialogue between the sexes: "Women are the Other. Protect/ Your pensive and luscious eyes:/ In your gaze, they/ Desire to see themselves./ But you, men, are the same!/ You added laughing and calling me."[15]

In conclusion, I wish to emphasize two points. First, examining the link between feminism and nationalism, both in works of literary scholarship and those of fiction and poetry, I would venture to say that this conjunction is not particularly strong. However, contrary to Irina Zherebkina's assessment, what there is of it is neither antagonistic nor exclusionary. Second, women's literary discourse in contemporary Ukraine constitutes an island of progressive attitudes and ideas in an otherwise vast ocean of artificially engineered myths and stereotypes, which confine women to narrowly formulated prospects. In many ways, Rosi Braidotti's as-yet-unvalidated premise of feminism "shaping up as the one possible new ethical system of postmodernism" becomes an imperative for a still small, but influential and productive, group of Ukrainian women intellectuals.

Notes

This chapter was prepared, in part, under a grant from the Kennan Institute of the Woodrow Wilson International Center, Washington, DC.

1. See, for example, Zabuzhko 2003: 25; and Aheieva 2002: 5–16.
2. *Feminizm* constitutes a compilation of Pavlychko's articles written on feminism between 1991 and 1999. It also compiles all the talks and interviews she gave to various newspapers, journals, and other media. Unfortunately, the editor of this anthology (V. Aheieva) limits the bibliographical information to publication dates and does not provide the original sources of the reprinted material.
3. Needless to say, that project never was completed, but Aheieva's book *Zhinochyi prostir: Feministychnyi dyskurs ukrains'koho modernizmu* (2003) comes relatively close to Pavlychko's proposed project.
4. Smith applies the same distinction and the same "civic" and "ethnic" models to his discussion of issues pertaining to national identity. See his *National Identity* (1991: 9, 11).
5. Chernetsky 2002. See also Chernetsky 2007: 240.
6. Zherebkina 1996: 35.

7. I am referring here to Zhurzhenko 2002.

8. See, for example, Pavlychko 2002c: 189.

9. Marian J. Rubchak concentrates, for example, on the significance of the Virgin Mary and the deity of Berehynia (1996: 315–30).

10. See Taran 1999: 18–21; Zborovs'ka 1999b: 25–28 and 1999c: 27–31; and Aheieva 1999c: 22–23.

11. The September issue of *Krytyka* (2001) includes a series of articles biased against feminism and gender studies in Ukrainian scholarship, namely Mar'ian Shkorba, "Genderni dity liberalizmu" (Gender's Liberal Children), 20–23; Larysa Berezovchuk, "Pryshestia dyskursu," (The Advent of Discourse), 24–29; Inna Bulkina, "Zhinocha dohma," (The Women's Dogma), 30–31. The November issue includes a response by Vira Aheieva, "Na storozhi starozhytnostei," (On the Lookout for Antiquity), 28–29.

12. For example, such major journals and magazines as *Slovo i Chas*, no. 8–9 (1996), and no. 11 (1997); *Art-Line* (March 1998), and *Yi*, no. 17 (2000), devoted special issues to feminism.

13. Most notorious in literature for the masses is a novel *Feministka* (Feministics) (Kononovych 2002). The author caricatures not only popular notions with regard to women-feminists but also presents his parodied take on the whole trend of gender studies. On page 80: "A feminist," Mandela began patronizingly, "is a woman who hates men. Formally, this ideology transformed itself into an international women's movement, which fights for women's rights. The main characteristic of feminism is that it engenders so-called gender studies. So, if a group of women founds an institute of gender studies or any one of them publishes a book with gender in its title, rest assured that you're dealing with feminism in its pure and unaltered form." This particular work of fiction would not merit mentioning, if not for the fact that Liudmyla Taran deemed it appropriate to respond to it with a review, published in the electronic journal *Vydnokola* (2002b).

14. Liudmyla Vynohorods'ka elaborates this point in her article "Ekstravagantnyi kokteil' z ukrains'kym prysmakom. Povist' S. Pyrkalo 'Zelena Marharyta'—sproba prochytannia" (2002).

15. Жінки—це інші. Стережися/ Очей замислених і млосних:/ Вони у погляді твоєму/ Жадають бачити себе./ Але й ви, чоловіки, такі самі! /Додала ти, сміючись і прикликаючи мене. Taran 2002a: 36.

Bibliography

Aheieva, Vira. 1999a. "Na storozhi starozhytnostei." *Krytyka* 11: 28–29.

———. *Poetesa zlamu stolit'*. 1999b. *Tvorchist' Lesi Ukrainky v postmodernii interpretatsii*. Kyiv: Lybid'.

———. 1999c. "Khto bit'sia pryvodu matriarkhatu." *Krytyka* 5: 22–23.

———. 2002. "Intelektual'nyi portret." In *Feminizm*, edited by Solomiia Pavlychko, 5–16. Kyiv: Osnovy.

———. 2003. *Zhinochyi prostir: Feministychnyi dyskurs ukrains'koho modernizmu*. Kyiv: Fakt.

Berezovchuk, Larysa. 2001. "Pryshestia dyskursu." *Krytyka* 9: 24–29.

Bohachevsky-Chomiak, Martha. 1988. *Feminists Despite Themselves: Women in Ukrainian Community Life, 1884–1939*. Edmonton: Canadian Institute of Ukrainian Studies.

Reprinted in Ukrainian as: *Bilym po bilomu: zhinky v hromads'komu zhytti Ukrainy, 1884–1939*. Kyiv: Lybid', 1995.

Braidotti, Rosi. 1988. *Patterns of Dissonance: A Study of Women in Contemporary Philosophy*. New York: Routledge.

Bulkina, Inna. 2001. "Zhinocha dohma." *Krytyka* 9: 30–31.

Chernetsky, Vitaly. 2007. *Mapping Postcommunist Cultures: Russia and Ukraine in the Context of Globalization*. Montreal: McGill-Queen's University Press.

———. 2002. "Protystoiachy travmam: genderno ta natsional'no markovana tilesnist' iak naratyv ta vydovyshche u suchasnomu ukrains'komu pys'menstvi." *Vydnokola*. http://www.vidnokola.kiev.ua/Magazine/N3/Num3.htm.

Hrycak, Alexandra, and Maria G. Rewakowicz. 2009. "Feminism, Intellectuals and the Formation of Micro-publics in Postcommunist Ukraine." *Studies in East European Thought* 61 (4): 309–33.

Hundorova, Tamara. 2002. *Femina Melancholica: Stat' i kul'tura v gendernii utopii Ol'hy Kobylians'koi*. Kyiv: Krytyka.

Hutcheon, Linda. 1988. *A Poetics of Postmodernism: History, Theory, Fiction*. New York: Routledge.

Jayawardena, Kumari. 1986. *Feminism and Nationalism in the Third World*. London: Zed Books.

Kiianovs'ka, Mariianna. 2000. *Mifotvorennia*. Kyiv: Smoloskyp.

Kononovych, Leonid. 2002. *Feministka*. L'viv: Kal'variia.

Pavlychko, Solomiia. 1997. *Dyskurs modernizmu v ukrains'kii literaturi*. Kyiv: Lybid'.

———. 2000. *Natsionalizm, seksual'nist', oriientalizm: Skladnyi svit Ahatanhela Kryms'koho*. Kyiv: Osnovy.

———. 2002a. "Feminism and Nationalism." *Feminizm*, 53–55. Kyiv: Osnovy.

———. 2002b. *Feminizm*. Kyiv: Osnovy.

———. 2002c. "Women's Discordant Voices in the Context of 1998 Parliamentary Elections in Ukraine." In *Feminizm*, 189–212. Kyiv: Osnovy.

Pyrkalo, Svitlana. 2001. *Zelena Marharyta*. Kyiv: Smoloskyp.

———. 2004. *Ne dumai pro chervone*. Kyiv: Fakt.

Rubchak, Marian J. 1996. "Christian Virgin or Pagan Goddess: Feminism versus the Eternally Feminine in Ukraine." In *Women in Russia and Ukraine*, edited by Rosalind Marsh, 315–30. Cambridge: Cambridge University Press.

Savka, Mar'iana. 2002. *Hirka Mandrahora*. L'viv: Vydavnytstvo Staroho Leva.

Shkorba, Mar'ian. 2001. "Genderni dity liberalizmu." *Krytyka* 9: 20–23.

Smith, Anthony. 1991. *National Identity*. Reno: University of Nevada Press.

———. 2001. *Nationalism: Theory, Ideology, History*. Cambridge: Polity.

Taran, Liudmyla. 1999. "Pryvyd povstaloho zhinochoho dukhu." *Krytyka* 1–2: 18–21.

———. 2002a. *Kolektsiia kokhanok*. L'viv: Kal'variia.

———. 2002b. "Na pravakh antyreklamy." *Vydnokola*. http://www.vidnokola.kiev.ua/Magazine/N3/Num3.htm.

Vynohorods'ka, Liudmyla. 2002. "Ektravagantnyi kokteil' z ukrains'kym prysmakom. Povist' Pyrkalo 'Zelena Marharyta'—sproba prochytannia." *Vydnokola*. http://www.vidnokola.kiev.ua/Magazine/N2/Num2.htm.

Zabuzhko, Oksana. 2003. *Inshyi format*. Ivano-Frankivsk: Lileia NV.

———. 1999. *Khroniky vid Fortinbrasa: Vybrana eseistyka 90-kh rokiv*. Kyiv: Fakt.

———. 1996. *Pol'ovi doslidzhennia z ukrains'koho seksu*. Kyiv: Zhoda.

Zborovs'ka, Nila. 1999a. *Feministychni rozdumy na karnavali mertvykh potsilunkiv.* L'viv: Litopys.

———. 1999b. "Shevchenko v 'zhinochykh studiiakh'." *Krytyka* 3: 25–28.

———. 1999c. "Chomu v ukrains'kii literaturi nemaie liubovnykh romaniv." *Krytyka* 7–8: 27–31.

Zherebkin, Sergei. 1999. "Femina Postsovietica v ukrainskoi literature." In *Femina Postsovietica. Ukrainskaia zhenshchina v perekhodnyi period: ot sotsial'nykh dvizhenii k politike,* edited by Irina Zherebkina, 281–335. Kharkov: KhTSGI.

Zherebkina, Irina. 1996. *Zhenskoe politicheskoe bessoznatel'noe: Problema gendera i zhenskoe dvizhenie v Ukraine.* Kharkov: Kharkov Center for Gender Studies.

Zhurzhenko, Tatiana. 2002. "(Anti)national Feminisms: Women's Voices of Transition and Nation Building in Ukraine." Munk Centre for International Studies, University of Toronto (18 March). Seminar Lecture.

CHAPTER 10

Feminist (De)Constructions of Nationalism in the Post-Soviet Space

Tatiana Zhurzhenko

Feminism and gender are no longer exotic concepts in contemporary Ukraine. Universities now offer courses on gender issues, an array of conferences has already taken place, dissertations are being defended, articles and books are being published. Gender and Women's Studies centers have been established; some are more than ten years old, most notably those in Kyiv, Kharkiv, L'viv and Odessa. Their activities and publications are analyzed in this article. It is not my goal to contribute to the current discussions of whether feminism exists in the post-Soviet context, nor if the use of a Western term such as *gender* is justified in either Ukrainian or Russian, or if *zhinochi studiyi* (women's studies) is the same as gender studies. I depart from the obvious fact that in Ukraine, feminist discourse, or rather multiple feminist discourses, already exist, as do various academic gender projects. I make no attempt to judge which one of them is "truly" feminist. Other issues interest me more: for instance, how do these various feminist discourses and intellectual endeavors relate to the dominant discourse of nationalism; how do they define their position in the current situation of unfinished nation building and blurred identity; what role do they seek in the process of a national revival? Rather than exploring the question of how nationalism manipulates women's interests and distorts the feminist consciousness in Eastern Europe, I intend to examine this relationship from the opposite point of view: how do various feminist discourses participate in the process of inventing a Ukrainian nation and negotiating its borders, in constructing collective memory and national identity?

The Ukrainian constellation is unique in Eastern Europe. Not only is it unclear just what feminism means in post-Soviet Ukraine; even less apparent are its national boundaries. How much nationalism does feminism need, how much can it digest? Who, precisely, represents Ukrainian feminism? Can every variety of feminism in Ukraine be called Ukrainian? Can Ukrainian feminism be articulated in Russian? What role do Ukrainian feminists in Western diasporas play in Ukraine's domestic developments? Evidently, the national boundaries of Ukraine are not congruent with the boundaries of its national feminist discourse. This makes it an exemplary case, which demonstrates the constructedness, plurality, and mobility of such boundaries.

All schools of feminism in Ukraine, regardless of whether they maintain a critical distance from nationalism or are actively involved in the national revival, have to define their attitude toward nation building and their position on nationalism. This article will examine the strategies of such self-determination, along with the often implicit and unarticulated dependence of Ukrainian feminism on nationalist discourse.

National Feminism: A Defensive Alliance of Two Ideologies

"To paraphrase Nietzsche, at this threshold of the third millennium I will venture to assert that 'feminism is dead.' This fills my soul with sadness. The same might be said of nationalism, of which we have no lasting idea, any more than we have of what constitutes feminism." This is the pessimistic pronouncement opening Sofiia Onufriv's introduction to a special issue of the Ukrainian journal *Yi* (7: 2001), dedicated to feminist questions. It expresses the disappointment of a female intellectual with the lack of passion and moving ideas in post-Soviet politics. In the context of my article, this remark is also interesting as a typical example of the intimate connection between nationalist and feminist discourses.

And if today, as Sofiia Onufriv sees it, the golden age of nationalism and feminism is behind us, their histories remain firmly connected, especially in Eastern Europe. During the nineteenth and particularly the twentieth centuries, women's emancipation went hand in hand with the collapse of empires and the formation of nation states. The American historian Martha Bohachevsky-Chomiak, in her work on the early western Ukrainian women's movement, demonstrated that nationalism and feminism were two sides of a single process of political and social modernization (1988). Women played an active role in awakening national awareness, founding national organizations, organizing social movements, and forming political parties. The struggle for national liberation, and participation in the process of nation building, became for them a school for public and political activity; work in women's organizations prepared them to participate in "greater politics."

Nationalism is usually seen as a patriarchal ideology, which ascribes gender-specific social roles to women while at the same time portraying itself as a universal idea responsive to women's needs. Following Bohachevsky-Chomiak, nationalism appeals to women for two reasons: first, because it promises protection for the family and children, and, second, because it supports women's self-affirmation as mothers and national heroines (2003: 173). At the same time, in her view, to equate nationalism with patriarchy would be a mistake, inasmuch as democratic nationalism facilitates the liberation of women, promises them equal rights, and opens the way to participation in the public sphere. The interests of women and the nation can converge in numerous ways. That is why, during the first half of the twentieth century, Ukrainian feminists saw their task as using the democratic potential of nationalism for the benefit of women on the one hand, and on the other, employing the women's energy and capacity for nation building. Justifying the specific path of the Ukrainian women's movement, and referring to analogous experiences in Third-World countries, Martha Bohachevsky-Chomiak suggests that the concept of "pragmatic feminism" reflects the specific situation of women in stateless nations on the periphery of Europe. Today, this concept of "pragmatic feminism" is widely accepted in Ukrainian gender studies.

In the present article, I will attempt to demonstrate how the narrative assuming common historical roots of both nationalism and feminism and stressing the progressive, democratic bases of the two ideologies informs today's gender research in Ukraine. What lies behind this narrative of national feminism? It is obvious that feminism is not the most widely accepted notion in the country today. And as far as Ukrainian nationalism is concerned, it remained during the 1990s, and right on up to 2004, in the words of Andrew Wilson, "a minority faith" represented by marginal parties (1996). Exploiting elements of nationalist ideology for its own purposes, the Kuchma regime ascribed to nationalists the role of dangerous radicals, and on occasion resorted to their historical association (justified or not) with fascism. The same authorities exploited the rhetoric of gender equality for their own purposes, while feminism, in the eyes of the majority of the people, remained an alien Western product. That is why national feminism assumes that these marginalized ideologies— nationalism and feminism—need each other, albeit in different ways. While aiming at rehabilitating the nationalist ideology, national feminism refers to its democratic potential and rejects authoritarianism and patriarchy as its unavoidable consequences. Feminism, which bears no political responsibility for the atrocities of the twentieth century, can serve as a potential ally of nationalism by restoring its democratic legitimacy. In post-Soviet Ukraine, national feminism is legitimized by its loyalty to the national idea, while at the same time civilizing it and giving it a human dimension.

Feminism and nationalism appear as allies also because they both see themselves as victims of a communist ideology and a totalitarian system. According to this narrative Stalinism put an end to the Ukrainian nation-building project that, from today's vantage point, was the only democratic alternative to communism. The communist regime repressed the advocates of this endeavor, the Ukrainian intelligentsia, and used "terror by hunger" against the Ukrainian peasantry. The same antidemocratic regime declared the women's problem solved, blocked independent women's initiatives, and exploited the women's labor and reproductive capabilities for its own purposes. Thus feminism and nationalism would seem to be natural allies—their common goal is to overcome the consequences of the communist regime and Ukraine's colonial status. It is an irony of history that socialism, with its emancipatory potential, its historical ties to both women's movements and nationalism, has become marginal to feminism in Ukraine, as in the whole of Eastern Europe. Currently, socialism is associated with the repressive policy of the Soviet regime that, from today's perspective, was directed against feminism and democratic nationalism alike.

It bears emphasizing that the discourse of national feminism is not simply a synthesis of two ideologies. It emerges as a result of a demarcation between the nationalist mainstream and its inevitable thrust of women into private life, on the one hand, and on the other, the Western feminist tradition with its cosmopolitan trajectory. As we know, nationalism gives rise to a maternalist discourse, assigning to women the function of biological and symbolic reproduction of the nation as their main social role (Yuval-Davis 1997). That is why feminism usually sees its task in criticizing both maternalism and neo-traditionalism. Ukrainian national feminism accepts neither the patriarchal ideology nor discriminatory nationalist practices; it associates the birth of the nation with women's emancipation, not with a return to traditional gender roles. Consequently, it faces the task of defining its attitude toward the Ukrainian women's movement, which has been a carrier of a maternalist discourse from its inception (Hrycak 2006: 69–100). At the same time, national feminism draws in part on that maternalist discourse. While the myth of the guardian of the domestic hearth, Berehynia, and its corresponding myth of Ukraine's matriarchal culture have come under challenge from scholarly criticism, both myths continue to legitimize the allegedly authentic Ukrainian feminist tradition as it differs from the West (Rubchak 1996, 2001).

National feminism not only opposes "traditional" nationalism, it also disagrees with the Western feminist mainstream, which has been inclined to ignore the national question, at least until the postcolonial turn[2] in the 1980's.[3] Taking antimilitarist and antichauvinist positions toward their own governments, Western feminists often failed to understand the specificity of the Eastern European situation, and viewed it instead through the orientalistic lens of backwardness and danger. They internalized the dichotomy of "good"

(Western) and "bad" (Eastern) nationalism, which is widespread in the social sciences. The war in the former Yugoslavia, followed by mass crimes against women, intensified this image. That is why national feminism in Ukraine, insisting on the legitimacy of (democratic) nationalism, assumes an ambivalent position. It is compelled to present itself in two different ways: affirming the European origins of Ukrainian culture and political mentality and its common roots with Western feminism, while referring to the experience of postcolonial countries to justify its pronational stand.

The ambiguities of the national feminism paradigm are especially visible in recent women's history studies. Ukraine, independent since 1991, faces the need to create a national narrative, which establishes historical continuity of its statehood despite the recurrent ruptures, to provide a reconciliation of the opposing (regional) historical memories, and to resolve the problem of coping with the communist past. In contrast to "old nations," whose historical narratives bear the stamp of cultural and political continuity, in the history of the "new" Ukraine, tensions and breaches are glaringly evident. Here, women's and gender histories must struggle for legitimacy in light of the fact that Ukraine's right to its own history remains a subject for discussion (von Hagen 1995: 658–73), while at the same time the national history paradigm has generally revealed its limitations.

After 1991 a number of serious research works on women's history were published. Studies by Martha Bohachevsky-Chomiak,[4] Liudmyla Smoliar (1998, 1999), and Oksana Malanchuk-Rybak (2006) reconstruct the national traditions of Ukrainian feminism and the women's movements. The return to the history of the Ukrainian women's movement reflects a growing interest in its roots, and search for the historical identity of Ukrainian feminism. At the same time, women's history in Ukraine has to deal with the same ruptures, the same sore spots, as national historiography does.

First, there is the need to overcome the regional divisions in Ukrainian women's history. Women's movements on the territory of contemporary Ukraine developed under different political circumstances. They were influenced by diverse political cultures, mentalities, legal systems, etc. The special role of the Ukrainian diaspora in the West makes the picture as a whole even more complicated. Thus far, the historical studies mentioned above represent regional rather than national historical narratives. Theoretical and methodological questions of writing national women's history have yet to be resolved, but a discussion is already in progress. In an article on history of the Ukrainian women's movement, Martha Kichorowska Kebalo constructs a narrative that frames the movement as a multiphased and ideologically multistranded, as well as a transnational phenomenon (2007: 36–60).

Second, a national narrative of women's history sets a standard according to which the regional variations of women's movements are assessed. As

Malanchuk-Rybak points out, "liberal feminism in Halychyna and Bukovyna developed according to the typical European, namely Central European, model" (2006: 82, 255), while in the Ukrainian lands under Russian rule, feminism was distorted by imperial influences. As a consequence the symbolic hierarchy of a European, democratic, nationally conscious western Ukraine, and an allegedly pro-Russian, denationalized eastern Ukraine, is reproduced in women's history.

Third, an unexamined appropriation of the national history paradigm leads to an ethnicization of history (focusing on one ethnic group to the exclusion of all others). In doing so, researchers have a tendency to discount the multinational context of women's movements in Ukraine.

Last, women's history needs to scrutinize its own attitude toward the Soviet past, toward the contradictory project of Soviet modernization and its consequences of state-led women's emancipation. As women's studies and feminism in Ukraine see themselves in the role of victims of communism, they look upon their activities as a revival of an interrupted tradition, and so preclude a serious assessment of the contradictory Soviet heritage.

Additional contributions to Ukrainian feminism developed in the diaspora, especially in North America. At one and the same time they strengthened the paradigm of national feminism, yet were transnational in character. American scholars of Ukrainian origin, Martha Bohachevsky-Chomiak and Marian Rubchak were among the first Western scholars to research and disseminate feminism in Ukraine. Their studies, published on both sides of the Atlantic, became an integral part of feminist debates in Ukraine. Their contributions marked the return of an important part of Ukrainian feminism to its homeland. As such, they constituted a kind of transnational bridge between Western and Eastern feminisms. All such multiple strands of feminism play their part in the current "national feminist" dialogue.

Kyiv: Feminism as a Modernist Project in Ukrainian Culture

The Kyiv Center for Gender Studies (*Kyiivskyi Tsentr Gendernykh Studii*) was established in 1998 by a group of researchers at the Institute of Literary Studies, Academy of Sciences of Ukraine. Solomea Pavlychko, Vira Aheieva, and Nila Zborovs'ka were co-founders. Tamara Hundorova, and the well-known novelist Oksana Zabuzhko, became close collaborators. This is one of the first, and most productive, of such centers to be established in Ukraine. One should remember that the thin stratum of the Ukrainophone intellectual elite, mainly scholars in the humanities and dominantly male were, during the waning days of the Soviet era, the first "professional" carriers of a Ukrainian national identity. In the Perestroika period they formed the core of the emerging national democratic movement. As experts in Ukrainian culture, which was excluded from the mainstream and relegated to the realm of the exotic, they saw their mission in the preservation of this very culture, and adopted a conservative position on it. That explains why feminism emerged on the one hand as a result of the active engagement of women scholars in the national democratic movement, and, on the other, as a protest against the cultural conservatism of their male colleagues.[5]

As early as 1991 Solomea Pavlychko published her path-breaking article "Does Ukrainian Literary Scholarship Need a Feminist School?" This piece examines the need for feminist literary criticism in Ukraine as a precondition for the development of a "normal," fully fledged European culture, and for the first time interprets certain texts of female Ukrainian modernists of the late nineteenth and early twentieth centuries as feminist. Kyiv's literary scholars see feminism as an instrument for analyzing patriarchy in Ukrainian culture. Their research strategy—a search for the feminist roots of Ukrainian modernism and the feminist re-interpretation of national literature—is aimed at reaffirming Ukraine's European identity and overcoming the relics of provincialism and post-colonial status of Ukrainian culture.

In 1997 Solomea Pavlychko also published *The Modernist Discourse in Ukrainian Literature,* in which she started her deconstruction of the existing literary canon. In contrast to the traditional populist and "revolutionary democratic" interpretations of Ukrainian culture, uncritically adopted from the Soviet era, Pavlychko focused on lesser-known and underappreciated modernist tendencies. In her opinion, modernism, having opened new perspectives for Ukrainian culture at the beginning of the twentieth century, was oriented towards the European Zeitgeist—individualism, intellectualism, rejection of cultural taboos, but feminism above all. At the end of the nineteenth century, modernism emerged as an alternative to and opponent of populism (*narodnytstvo*), which considered literature a tool for educating the masses, with the aim of social and national emancipation. Pavlychko presented the modernism vs. populism conflict as an attempt to break out of the closed circle of colonial culture, constricted by the national idea, in order to overcome the complexes of a peripheral, stateless nation. While political and cultural populism were considered progressive by both Soviet and nationalist critics, Pavlychko saw populism as a carrier of a patriarchal ideology. Populism assumes the existence of an ideal collective (*hromada*) and allegedly high morality of the peasant soul, an idealization of the peasant way of life, the peasant family and, of course, the peasant women. In the populist tradition, literature is structured as a patriarchal space: an extended family headed by nineteenth-century Ukrainian poet Taras Shevchenko and his follower "sons." Any challenge to the established canon is seen as a betrayal of the people and of the ideal of national liberation. In her book, Solomea Pavlychko demonstrates that Lesia

Ukrainka, pseudonym of Larysa Kosach (1871–1913), and Ol'ha Kobylians'ka (1863–1942), were pioneers in Ukrainian modernist literature, and that their radical modernism was closely connected to a European cultural orientation and feminist ideas. Pavlychko presented the clash of modernism and populism in Ukrainian culture as a gender conflict, a female writer's challenge to the reigning patriarchal tradition.

Her colleagues expanded this pioneering theme. Tamara Hundorova produced a richly detailed psychoanalytical study of Ol'ha Kobylians'ka's oeuvre against the background of European cultural and philosophical currents of the time—Nietzsche, Freud, Social Darwinism, and others (2002). Kobylians'ka challenged the romantic correlation of woman and nature on the one hand, and, on the other, the Darwinian interpretation of woman as a biological being and reproductive source (Hundorova 2002: 227). Her gender utopia, according to Hundorova, was a "feminine model of high modern culture," in which the woman acts as a cultural heroine.

Vira Aheieva dedicated a special study to Lesia Ukrainka, whom she scrutinizes in the context of the fin de siècle modernist tendencies (2001). In her interpretation, Ukrainka appears as one of the few writers who defended individualistic and aristocratic values in provincial Ukrainian culture, and one of the very few to do this from a woman's perspective. Aheieva views the individualism and elitism of the poetess as the beginning of a reorientation of the Ukrainian intelligentsia—a moving away from the populist agenda of educating the people, to the agenda of forming a modern European elite for the country. In her subsequent book, Aheieva returns to the phenomenon of women's writing (2003). One of the chapters is devoted to the "mother-son" relationship in Ukrainian culture. For her, the predominant topos of despotic mothers who nurture infantilistic sons symbolizes the complexes of a colonial nation. Conversely, the theme of matricide in the stories written earlier by Mykola Khvyliovy can be read as an allegory of the nation being sacrificed to the communist ideal. Aheieva also analyzes the terrible mothers, or mother-monsters, in contemporary Ukrainian literature. For her, this tendency to a desacralization of the mother image symbolizes the loss of an authentic pre-Soviet Ukraine, the tragedy of a lost national identity.

The Kyiv school not only reinterprets the history of Ukrainian literature, it also analyzes the current cultural situation. Its representatives believe that the old colonial complexes reappear in the form of neo-populism and a utilitarian approach to literature as the "conscience of the nation," of misogyny and colonial infantilism.

Owing largely to Oksana Zabuzhko's sensational novel *Field Studies of Ukrainian Sex*, these problems were vividly discussed within the Ukrainian cultural milieu. Zabuzhko formulated her view of the gender conflict in Ukrainian culture in an informative article entitled "The Woman Author in Colonial

Culture" (2001). According to Zabuzhko, Ukraine's geocultural situation as a second-rate province, a periphery of provincial Russia, is very inhospitable to a female writer, who gets caught in the trap of the unfulfilled national idea. By focusing exclusively on women's themes, she avoids the most urgent problems of the nation and thus marginalizes herself. Assuming the role of a fighter, she finds herself repressed by a brutal masculine system of values. As the example of Lesia Ukrainka shows, colonial culture is prepared to listen to the female author's voice only if she is able to evince a masculine quality. The Ukrainian female writer is doubly marginalized: as an agent of her colonial culture and by the power of the gender hierarchy.

The attitude toward nationalism of the Kyiv feminist school can be illustrated by Nila Zborovs'ka's approach (1999). She contrasts nationalism as an ideology, required and exploited by the governing powers, with the female nationalist Utopia as a private, intimate sentiment that refuses to submit to appropriation and manipulation. Paradoxically, feminism is capable of generating an alternative to the masculine discourse of traditional nationalism—archaic, moribund, and inadequate for modern society. "Women's nationalism" is not an alien ideology, but rather a deep personal sentiment, an honest feeling of altruistic love (she sees precisely these feminine motifs in Taras Shevchenko's works). In such a reading, nationalism and feminism share the same marginal position; they both oppose imperial-cosmopolitan thinking and state patriarchal discourse.

Odessa: The Return of the Woman to National History

The Odessa Center for Women's Studies (*Odes'kyi Naukovyi Zhinochyi Tsentr*) achieved its reputation largely through the efforts of Liudmyla Smoliar (1958–2004), in her role as pioneer of women's history in Ukraine. Her monograph titled *The Past for the Sake of the Future* (1998) is a groundbreaking study on the women's movement in the Ukrainian lands under imperial Russian rule; it complements the research of Bohachevsky-Chomiak, who concentrated on women in western Ukraine. Basing her book on a wide array of archival materials and illuminating in detail the regional developments, Smoliar's study includes a class-specific analysis of the legal status of women in Ukraine and their economic standing in various occupations, an overview of the demographic situation, and a critical account of public education for women.

Smoliar's history of the Ukrainian women's movement is constructed along the lines of the national history narrative. Chronologically and structurally, the emergence of the women's question was connected to the first phase of the national liberation movement. This phase is characterized by the development of ethnographic, philological, and historical research on Ukraine, and a growing interest of the local intelligentsia in its past. The women's question appeared in the process of the rediscovery of national traditions. This is particularly true of the special role women held in the Ukrainian family and society and of the traditional representation of women in Ukrainian culture.

Smoliar formulates four characteristics of the women's movement in central and eastern Ukraine. Two of them relate to the peculiarities of the Russian legal and political system: Russian absolutism meant the absence of political rights not only for women but for men as well, and women enjoyed relative economic independence due to the Russian property law, which, in contrast to the Napoleonic code, gave married women control over their own assets. The two other characteristics relate to national specificities: The tradition of gender parity in Ukrainian society sets Ukrainian women apart not only from their European counterparts but from their Russian ones as well, and, as was the case in other stateless nations, the women's movement in Ukraine emerged on the wave of a national awakening. Taken together, these four characteristics portray Ukrainian feminism in the central and eastern Ukrainian lands as a universal phenomenon, which "never fell into the extremes of a war of the sexes" (Smoliar 1998: 61). Feminism, in the opinion of Smoliar, became a component of the national liberation struggle. In a subsequent work, she takes up the concept of "pragmatic feminism," as put forth earlier by Bohachevsky-Chomiak (Smoliar 2006: 397–411).

Smoliar's concept of the Ukrainian women's movement, and her corresponding definition of the nation, are rather broad. She examines the national democratic current of the women's movement in central and eastern Ukraine, along with the liberal-democratic and the social-democratic currents. Her narrative includes not only women's and feminist movements aimed at a national revival and a break with the empire but also the movements that strove for political modernization and democratization of the Russian Empire (which did not eschew revolutionary methods). Thus she transgresses the boundaries of the national history paradigm. Her approach opens a space for a discussion of important methodological questions relevant to women's history. For example, if the Ukrainian women's movement is broader in scope than its national-democratic current, then how do we define the nineteenth-century national boundaries at a time when most of Ukraine was part of the Russian Empire? Here it becomes clear that feminist discourse, consciously or not, contributes to the definition of the Ukrainian nation and participates in the construction of its boundaries.

Smoliar seems to prefer a territorial definition of the nation, focusing on the women's movement in the Ukrainian *guberniyi* (provinces) of the Russian Empire. Any territorial definition becomes problematic as soon as one projects it into the past, however. Noble women in the Russian Empire did not possess a national identity in the contemporary sense of the word; they did not subscribe to any ethnic alignment. In the best instance, they might identify with a regional patriotism associated with their families. As we are aware from Smoliar's work, the mathematician Sofiia Kovalevskaia, and the revolution-ary activist Sofiia Perovskaia, among others,[6] had Ukrainian roots, yet they are routinely associated with Russian history. That is because the social and political activities of so many women were concentrated in the centers of the empire, Moscow and St. Petersburg. On the other hand, Smoliar's territorial definition of the nation is supplemented by an ethnic one, insofar as other national groups living on the same territory (such as Poles and Jews) are not included in her study. The separation of Ukrainian history from Russian impe-rial history poses a problem that besets Ukrainian historiography in general: how far back can one go to extrapolate such national categories?

Smoliar's version of women's history not only follows the paradigm of national history, but supplements and enriches the national historical narra-tive, and reinforces its legitimacy. In a collective volume, which she edited, titled *The Woman in History and Today* (1998) she attempts to construct a systematic and homogeneous metanarrative of Ukrainian women's history, from ancient times up to state independence. Hence she creates an immutable and monolithic historical subject—the "Ukrainian woman," marked by a vir-tually unchangeable character throughout history. In an article published in the Austrian journal L'HOMME (2006), Smoliar relies on accounts of foreign travelers to Ukraine in the sixteenth to the eighteenth centuries, in which they expressed their astonishment at the uniquely liberated status of Ukrainian women and their distinctive character. Her essentialization and even idealiza-tion of Ukrainian women is bolstered by references to the works of Yuriy Lypa, one of the leading ideologists of Ukrainian nationalism. Referring to his essay titled "Ukrains'ka zhinka" (The Ukrainian Woman)—a text that reads like a political tract—Smoliar, rather than analyzing it as an example of a specific discourse, uses it as a scholarly argument.

L'viv: From Ethnology to Oral History

In 1999 a group of young scholars founded a research Center in L'viv, "Woman and Society" (*Zhinka i suspil'stvo*). The codirector of the center, Oksana Kis', is an ethnologist with a focus on gender research.[7] Kis' was the first scholar in Ukraine to adopt, in a systematic way, a gender approach to historical and eth-nological research of national culture. For instance, she examines the process of socialization of young girls in the Ukrainian family, and the social roles of women, motherhood, and childhood in Ukrainian culture (1999: 49–55; 2000: 274–85). She also works on contemporary gender issues in Ukraine (2003a: 109–19). One of her studies focuses on an analysis of Yulia Tymoshenko as a popular political figure (2007: 121–40). Kis' explains Tymoshenko's popularity by her conscious strategy of combining elements of two models of post-Soviet womanhood—Berehynia and the Barbie doll. Lately, Kis' has moved in a new direction—concentrating on women's memories. Under her tutelage, the L'viv center participated in an international project in oral history devoted to a study of the memories of women in Eastern European countries. Kis' also was one of the first scholars in Ukraine to adopt oral history as a field of research, and perhaps the first to apply this method to gender research.

Kis''s innovative work is worthy of note because it shows the potential as well as the limits of post-Soviet ethnology for gender research.[8] Since the end of the 1980s, ethnology has been one of the most active disciplines involved in the national renaissance and the creation of new nation-states. In Ukraine, Ukrainian studies (*ukrainoznavstvo*) were institutionalized as an obligatory part of the higher-education curriculum, and Marxism-Leninism chairs were transformed into chairs for Ukrainian culture. The growing involvement of ethnological discourse in the political process also becomes visible in the emergence of new approaches claiming the status of academic disciplines, such as ethnopolitics, ethnopsychology, and so forth. This type of ethnology, which serves the purposes of nation building, is based on a concept of culture dating back to the nineteenth century. According to Nira Yuval-Davis, it is bound to "an essentialist view of 'culture' as having specific fixed 'cultural stuff' of symbols, ways of behavior and artifacts, which coherently and unproblematically constitute cultures of specific national and ethnic collectives" (1997: 41).

The emergence and development of ethnology in Eastern Europe was tied, in large part, to the evolution of national movements. According to Miroslav Hroch, "the beginning of a national revival is marked by a passionate concern on the part of a group of individuals, usually intellectuals, for the study of the language, the culture, the history of the oppressed nationalities" (1985: 22). The empires also needed ethnographic expertise to develop administrative, cultural, and economic policies toward various ethnic and religious groups living on their territories. Soviet ethnography, as Francis Hirsh demonstrated, was directly involved in the construction of the new Soviet nations and nationalities (2005). In the hands of national elites as well as in the imperial administration, ethnography functioned as an instrument for creating ethnic and national groupings.

After 1991, ethnology, appealing to tradition and culture as the essence of an ethnos, was and still is used for legitimizing post-Soviet national projects. Typically, this ethnological discourse has been constructed around a female figure—as a rule, a mother as symbol of the nation. The focus of ethnology is family and kin, customs, tradition—everything that is usually connected to the female sphere and constitutes the heart of national culture. In the words of Yuval-Davis:

Gender relations often come to be seen as constituting the essence of cultures as ways of life to be passed from generation to generation. The construction of 'home' is of particular importance here, including relations between adults and between adults and children in the family, ways of cooking and eating, domestic labor, play and bedtime stories, out of which a whole world view, ethical and aesthetic, can become naturalized and reproduced (1997: 43).

A discourse of this type directly links "gender" to the survival of the nation.

In this context, with her work Kis' not only contributes to our understanding of the woman's position in Ukrainian society of the past (for instance, she is interested in the social role of marginalized women—single and childless women, widows, and "witches"), but she also tries to use ethnological knowledge as an instrument for feminist criticism. First and foremost, the object of such criticism is maternalist ideology, stereotypes of Ukrainian women as *berehyni*, and the myth of Ukrainian matriarchy. Drawing upon rich ethnographic material, Kis' deconstructs the ideal motherhood myth, rooted in the popular mind as well as in social sciences and the humanities. The basic postulates of that myth are that the child has an absolute value in the Ukrainian family, and motherhood is a fundamental social role, giving meaning to a woman's life. Referring to the works of Adrienne Rich and Nancy Chodorow, Kis' opposes the essentialization of motherhood, and prefers to see it as a social construct (2003b: 156–72). She scrutinizes the way in which motherhood is established as the realization of a woman's destiny and is being inculcated on every level of a girl's socialization. She demonstrates that maternal functions frequently were subordinated to the economic interests of the family, and thus mothers often had an ambivalent feeling toward their newborns. Demystification of motherhood and other taboos, opposition against idealizing and romanticizing the traditional way of life—these are initial steps of feminist criticism in Ukrainian ethnology, owing largely to the efforts of Kis' (2005).

In recent years, her interests have turned to new fields of research, notably oral history. Kis' believes that this approach opens an opportunity to access subconscious, hidden, unarticulated meanings, an approach that, she claims, is especially productive for research on post-totalitarian Ukrainian society. Women, in particular, were heretofore deprived of their voice. Women's memories must now be articulated in order to incorporate them into national history. Given the lack of interest in researching the Soviet period (except for certain politicized themes) and the poor conceptual apparatus for this subject, oral history can serve also as an instrument of understanding the Soviet past through individual experiences and narratives. However, the feminist project of bringing the women's voice into history is not politically and methodologically unbiased. The woman's voice is not authentic in and of itself; it is always the researcher who selects from the interviews and develops the interpretive framework. Kis''s article "Telling the Untold: Representations of Ethnic and

Regional Identities in the Autobiographies of Ukrainian Women" is based upon interviews with two elderly Ukrainian women, representing the eastern and western regions of the country (2010). Their narratives reflect the recent past on an individual level, enabling us to look at Soviet history from a new angle. Not surprisingly, the attitudes of the woman from western Ukraine, and her counterpart from the east, toward the Soviet regime and the new Ukrainian state differ significantly. Not only is Kis"'s interpretation of women's memories shaped by the "Ukrainian west" and the "Sovietized east" dichotomy, which is so characteristic of contemporary Ukrainian discourse, it also reinforces that classification. The danger in such a division is that individual women's memories simply will be reduced to illustrations of widespread regional stereotypes.

Kharkiv: Feminism as the Deconstruction of Nationalism

The final example to be examined here is the Kharkiv Center of Gender Studies (*Kharkovskiy Tsentr Gendernyh Issledovanii*), founded in 1994 by Sergei and Irina Zherebkin. Irina Zherebkina, its permanent director, studied philosophy in Kyiv and at the beginning of the 1990's worked at the Institute of Philosophy in Moscow. The conceptual basis of feminist research of the Kharkiv center is the philosophy of poststructuralism, literary criticism, and psychoanalysis. Over the past ten years, the center has conducted an annual summer school on feminist research for participants from former Soviet republics. Russian continues to be the working language of the summer school, which takes place each year in Foros (Crimea). The center publishes a Russian-language journal titled *Gendernye issledovaniia* (Gender Research), the only periodical on gender issues not only in all of Ukraine, but in the entire post-Soviet space. The center also edits books, mostly translations of Western feminist works and monographs by Irina Zherebkina (2000, 2002b, 2003), published in recent years primarily by Aleteia, a publishing house in St. Petersburg.

Zherebkina's position differs from the projects of the other centers discussed above in that she deliberately positions herself outside the discourse of national feminism. She does not define her location or the object of her research as "Ukraine," preferring temporal categories instead: post-Soviet countries, transitional societies, or the former USSR. Zherebkina does not subscribe to Ukrainian feminism in any way. By distancing herself from its traditions, she intentionally refuses to define her position in terms of categories imposed by others: "It is important not to participate in the discursive either/or choice, whatever form it might take (globalization or localization, universal or particular, national or multicultural, and so on)" (2002a: 10). In contrast to her Ukrainian colleagues, she is skeptical of the very possibility of an independent feminist movement and gender research in post-Soviet countries, given their simulative and manipulative character.

Zherebkina's methodological preferences center on Western theorists of post-feminism such as Rosi Braidotti, Judith Butler, Zila Eisenstein, and Renata Saletzl. These authors stress the crises and paradigm shifts in contemporary feminism, which implies a transition from "feminism of equality" to "feminism of difference," criticism of classical liberal feminism, thematization of female subjectivity, and the deconstruction of binary oppositions in feminism (for example East-West). In Zherebkina's opinion, this methodology functions mainly on the level of the collective unconscious. It can be utilized effectively for analyzing the characteristics of post-Soviet societies. The questions she puts to her readers are: How does power (in the Foucauldian sense) appropriate the right to speak in the name and interest of women? How are women's interests being constructed and presented in official discourse and nationalist ideology? These questions exclude any optimistic view of Ukrainian culture as "predisposed" to feminism and challenge the rebirth narrative of the Ukrainian women's movement.

Nationalism, in Zherebkina's view, is an object for psychoanalysis rather than for sociology or political theory. Departing from Benedict Anderson's idea of "imagined communities," but interpreting this concept in the spirit of Žižek and Lacan, she insists that "loss" or "lack" is what structures the imagination. For example, the loss of territorial integrity stimulates the emergence of the myth of a single identity. Besides that, in transitional societies, due to the collapse of the old identity the symbolic becomes more important than real economic or social problems. For the disoriented masses, the persuasive new national identity acts as compensation for their daily tribulations, yet it conceals a reallocation of property and power. Thus, nationalism has in Zherebkina's eyes a manipulative character. Finally, "in the national imagination the image of the Other usually connotes the enemy" (2002a: 20). In Zherebkina's interpretation, nationalism inevitably assumes the exclusion of the Other and adopts an aggressive stance against it. This explains for her the increasing anti-female sentiment in transitional societies (2002a: 23). Clearly, this interpretation of nationalism as an ideology and politics that victimizes women remains in opposition to the discourse of national feminism.

In her book *Women's Political Unconsciousness,* published in Kharkiv in 1996 and reprinted in St. Petersburg in 2002, Zherebkina addresses directly the interaction between nationalist and feminist discourses. This book analyzes the tradition of Ukrainian feminism, but it differs crucially from the position adopted by Bohachevsky-Chomiak, Smoliar, and other authors mentioned above, from whom Zherebkina is careful to distance herself. She is of the opinion that nationalist ideology, operating according to romantic images

of "mothers of the nation" prepared to make sacrifices for their people, sym-
bolically "rapes" women by assigning to them certain social roles and inhibit-
ing their awareness of their own interests.

Drawing on a range of historical and cultural material (Ukrainian literature of the nineteenth to the twentieth centuries, histories of the women's
movement, documents of contemporary women's organizations and conferences) Zherebkina scrutinizes the transformation of traditional female images
in Ukrainian culture, as well as the historical continuity of Ukrainian feminism before and after the Soviet era, which determines the role of nationalism in women's movements. Hence, although she avails herself of the same
historical evidence as Bohachevsky-Chomiak, Zherebkina writes a history of
the Ukrainian women's movement as a failed endeavor.

Small wonder, then, that the texts of Irina and Sergei Zherebkin have been
subjected to severe criticism by advocates of Ukrainian national feminism.[9]
Criticizing their determination to present nationalist and feminist discourses
as always conflicting and hostile, as well as the "Russocentric linguistic and cultural politics of this school," opponents frequently characterize Kharkiv feminism as "imperialistic and anti-Ukrainian." Vitaly Chernetsky once observed:
"As many other post-Soviet Russophones, the members of the Kharkiv school
of gender research seem not to have done the 'work of mourning' for the Russian Empire, and find themselves caught in a state of melancholic nostalgia
for the united Russophone cultural space" (2007). A second objection of the
critics is the oversimplification of nationalism as an exclusively repressive ideology, and the identification of nationalism with Ukrainian culture as reduced
to the state's cultural politics. They have also been unanimously critical of
Zherebkina's position as an indifferent bystander or even antagonist of Ukrainian culture. Clearly, its highly critical reflection on nationalism in gender research sets the Kharkiv Center apart from other feminist schools. Nonetheless,
its distinctive "nonnational" feminist project has its limits. In structuring it in
post-Soviet rather than national categories, the Zherebkins paradoxically are
tempted to essentialize the transitional or fleeting aspects of their object. Their
self-chosen localization—in the former USSR—unavoidably loses its justification insofar as the post-Soviet space itself is in the process of disintegration.
In sum, while widely recognized in the post-Soviet states, the Kharkiv Center
plays only a marginal role in contemporary Ukrainian feminist discourse.

Epilogue

The various feminist projects examined above, which emerged within and at
various intersections of the social sciences and the humanities, represent a
range of positions on nationalism. The scope is quite extensive: from a femi-

nist reinterpretation of the national cultural canon, the invention of a national feminist tradition, the return of women to national history, to a deconstruction of the ideology and politics of nationalism. In some cases, the attitude toward nationalism is a consciously adopted political stance; in others, this attitude remains implicit, although in one way or another, the national question does impact the objectives, the paradigm, and the methodology of feminist research.

The obvious dilemma (not to mention the ideological difficulty) in defining Ukrainian feminism indicates the absence of a consensus in society on the larger question—that of defining the Ukrainian nation and its symbolic boundaries. Not every kind of feminism in Ukraine is Ukrainian, if we understand by "Ukrainian" linguistic and cultural distinctiveness. Should we therefore view feminism in Ukraine as a postcolonial and transitional phenomenon? Is it possible at all to accomplish the project of nationalization? The examples above demonstrate that despite the dominating nationcentric discourse, Ukrainian feminism is de facto a transnational phenomenon. The collisions of feminist discourses disclose a gap between the cultural-ethnic and the territorial definition of the nation and a divergence between the national and the discursive boundaries of Ukrainian feminism. The conflicts among the different feminist schools (or their demonstrative shunning of one another) reflect a struggle for cultural hegemony, for the right to appropriate the language of Western feminism, along with the postcolonial paradigm, for the purpose of validating their own academic projects and political strategies.

Translated from Russian by Marian J. Rubchak

Notes

1. Onufriv 2001.
2. *Postcolonialism* is a set of theories in literary studies, philosophy, and political science, which deal with the cultural legacy of colonial rule, in particular the dilemmas of developing a national identity in the former colonies. In the 1980s, Western feminism came under criticism for its bourgeois, Eurocentric presuppositions and its failure to acknowledge differences in ethnicity and the historical specificities of the so-called Third-World woman (Chandra Talpade Mohanty, Guyatri Spivak, and others). Contemporary feminist theories have adopted the postcolonial perspective, although its applicability to postcommunist societies remains controversial.
3. See, for instance, Kaplan 1997, where she considers both ideological positions nearly incompatible.
4. A Ukrainian translation of *Feminist Despite Themselves: Women in Ukrainian Community Life, 1885–1939* (Bilym po bilomu. Zhinky v hromads'komu zhytti Ukrainy, 1885–1939), was published in Kyiv by Lybid' in 1995.
5. See for instance Pavlychko 1992.

6. Alexandra Kollontai comes to mind.
7. Oksana Kis' defended her dissertation *Zhinka v sils'kii simyi v druhii polovyni 19ho—pochatok 20ho stolittia* (The Woman in the Peasant Family in the Second Half of the Nineteenth and Beginning of the Twentieth Century) in 2002. She also edited a thematic issue of the journal *Yi* as well as an anthology of feminist texts, and helped to popularize widely works on feminism and gender research.
8. In the post-Soviet context, the terms *ethnography* and *ethnology* are not clearly differentiated. While in Soviet times, the former represented an academic discipline dealing with the cultural characteristics of ethnic/national groups, the latter was imported in the 1990s from the west, but still concentrates on nations and ethnic groups.
9. Zherebkina's approach was criticized by Martha Bohachevsky-Chomiak, Nila Zborovs'ka, Vitaly Chernetsky, and others.

Bibliography

Aheieva, Vira. 2001. *Poetesa zlamu stolit'. Tvorchist' Lesi Ukrainky v postmodernii interpretatsii.* Kyiv: Lybid'.

———. 2003. *Zhinochyi Prostir. Feministychnyi dyskurs ukrains'koho modernizmu.* Kyiv: Fakt.

Bohachevsky-Chomiak, Martha. 1988. *Feminists despite Themselves: Women in Ukrainian Community Life, 1884–1939.* Edmonton: Canadian Institute of Ukrainian Studies.

———. 2003. "Natsionalizm i feminizm: Providni ideolohii chy instrumenty dlia z'iasuvannia problem?" In *Gendernyi pidkhid: Istoriia, kul'tura, suspil'stvo,* edited by L. Hentosh and O. Kis', 166–81. L'viv: VNTL Klasyka.

Chernetsky, Vitaly. 2007. *Mapping Postcommunist Cultures: Russia and Ukraine in the Context of Globalization.* Montreal: McGill-Queens University Press.

von Hagen, Mark. 1995. "Does Ukraine Have a History?" *Slavic Review* 54: 658–73.

Hirsch, Francis. 2005. *Empire of Nations: Ethnographic Knowledge and the Making of the Soviet Union.* Ithaca, NY: Cornell University Press.

Hroch, Miroslav. 1985. *Social Preconditions of a National Revival in Europe.* Cambridge: Cambridge University Press.

Hrycak, Alexandra. 2006. "Foundation Feminism and the Articulation of Hybrid Feminism in Post-Socialist Ukraine." *East European Politics and Societies* 20 (1): 69–100.

Hundorova, Tamara. 2002. *Femina melancholica. Stat' i kul'tura v gendernii utopii Ol'hy Kobylians'koi.* Kyiv: Krytyka.

Kaplan, Gisela. 1997. "Feminism and Nationalism: The European Case." In *Feminist Nationalism,* edited by L. A. West, 3–40. New York: Routledge.

Kichorovska Kebalo, Martha. 2007. "Exploring Continuities and Reconciling Ruptures: Nationalism, Feminism, and the Ukrainian Women's Movement." *Aspasia: International Yearbook of Central, Eastern and Southeastern European Women's and Gender History* 1: 36–60.

Kis', Oksana. 1999. "Osoblyvosti sotsializatsii divchatok v ukrains'kii sim'i XIX-pochatku XX stolit'." In *Etnichna istoriia narodiv Evropy. Tradytsiina etnichna kul'tura slov'ian,* 49–55. Kyiv: Stilos.

———. 2000. "Ukrainskaia ved'ma (eskiz sotsial'nogo portreta)." *Gendernye issledovaniia* 5: 274–85.

———. 2003a. "Modeli konstruiuvannia gendernoi identychnosti zhinky v suchasnii Ukraini." *Yi* 27: 109–19.

———. 2003b. "Materinstvo i detstvo v ukrainskoi traditsii: Dekonstruktsia mifa." In *Sotsial'naia istoria. Ezhegodnik 2003. Zenskaia i gendernaia istoria,* edited by N. L. Pushkareva, 156–72. Moscow: Russian Political Encyclopedia.

———. 2005. "Koho oberihaie Berehynia, abo matriarkhat iak cholovichyi vynakhid." *Dzerkalo Tyzhnia,* 23 April–6 May.

———. 2007. "Zhinochi strategii v ukrains'kii politytsi." In *Poshuky gendernoi parytetnosti: Ukrains'kyi kontekst,* edited by Iryna Hrabovs'ka, 121–40. Nizhyn: DS Milanik.

———. 2010. "Telling the Untold: Representations of Ethnic and Regional Identities in Ukrainian Women's Autobiographies." In *Orality and Literacy, Reflections across Disciplines,* edited by K. Carlson, K. Fagan, and N. Khanenko-Friesen. Toronto: University of Toronto Press.

Malanchuk-Rybak, Oksana. 2006. *Ideolohiia ta suspil'na praktyka zhinochoho rukhu na zakhidno-ukrains'kykh zemliakh XIX- pershoi tretyny XX st.* Chernivtsi: Knyhy XXI.

Onufriv, Sofia. 2001. "Vstup." *Yi* 17: 2.

Pavlychko, Solomea. 1991. "Chy potribna ukrains'komu literaturoznavstvu feministychna shkola"? *Slovo i Chas* 6: 10–15.

———. 1992. *Letters from Kyiv.* Edmonton: Canadian Institute of Ukrainian Studies.

———. 1997. *Diskurs modernizmu v ukrains'kii literaturi.* Kyiv: Lybid'.

Rubchak, Marian J. 1996. "Christian Virgin or Pagan Goddess: Feminism vs. the Eternally Feminine in Ukraine." In *Women in Russia and Ukraine,* edited by Rosalind Marsh, 315–30. Cambridge: Cambridge University Press.

———. 2001. "In Search of a Model: Evolution of a Feminist Consciousness in Ukraine and Russia." *European Journal of Women's Studies* 2 (2): 149–60.

Smoliar, Liudmyla. 1998. *Mynule zarady maibut'nioho: zhinochyi rukh Naddniprians'koi Ukrainy. II pol. XIX- poch. XX st. Storinky istorii.* Odessa: Astro-prynt.

———, ed. 1999. *Zhinochi studii v Ukraini. Zhinka v istorii ta siohodni.* Odessa: Astro-prynt.

———. 2006. "The Ukrainian Experiment: Between Feminism and Nationalism or the Main Features of Pragmatic Feminism." *L'HOMME Schriften. Reihe zu Feministischen Geschichtswissenscaft.* Special issue: *Women's Movements. Networks and Debates in Post-Communist Countries in the 19th and 20th Centuries,* edited by E. Saurer, M. Lanzinger, and E. Frysak, 397–411. Kohn: Bohlau.

Wilson, Andrew. 1996. *Ukrainian Nationalism in the 1990s: A Minority Faith.* Cambridge: Cambridge University Press.

Yuval-Davis, Nira. 1997. *Gender and Nation.* London: Sage.

Zabuzhko, Oksana. 2001. "Zhinka-avtor v kolonial'nii kul'turi, abo znadoby do ukrains'koi mifolohii." In *Khroniky vid Fortenbrasa,* 152–93. Kyiv: Fakt.

Zborovs'ka, Nila. 1999. *Feministychni rozdumy na karnavali mertvykh potsilunkiv.* L'viv: Litopys.

Zherebkina, Irina. 2000. *Prochti moe zhelanie … postmodernism, psikhoanaliz, feminizm.* Moscow: Ideia-Press.

———. 2002a. *Zhenskoe politicheskoe bessoznatel'noe.* St. Petersburg: Aleteia.

———. 2002b. *Strast'.* St. Petersburg: Aleteia.

———. 2003. *Gendernye 90-e ili Falosa ne sushchestvuet.* St. Petersburg: Aleteia.

CHAPTER 11

Three Conversations

The Search for Gender Justice

Liudmyla Taran

Liudmyla Taran—acclaimed poetess, literary critic, journalist, essayist, and committed feminist since early childhood—places herself in the ranks of a tiny minority of feminists in today's Ukraine. To promote her cause and compile material for a book, she interviewed a cross-section of ten women and two men for their views on gender construction. I have chosen to report on a sample from this group of three "Conversations," as she names them, to illustrate further the many faces of women in Ukraine. I also wish to end this volume on a hopeful note. The success stories of Taran's respondents in this sample highlight an important crack in the glass ceiling for a small number of women in Ukraine who are seeking gender justice in an intensely challenging transitional environment. Whether they reject the feminist label or embrace it as a self-descriptor, the accomplishments of each set them apart from the majority of their countrywomen. The respondents represent three separate sectors of public life in Ukraine. Each demonstrates her unique ability to serve as a role model for those women still struggling to survive in a hostile situation.

Gender Education—a Step toward Democracy
A Conversation with Larysa Kobel'ians'ka

The first of Taran's respondents, Larysa Kobel'ians'ka, coordinator of the UN-sponsored program titled "Gender Education in Ukraine," was among the earliest of Ukraine's reformers to use the term *gender*, well before most people even guessed what it meant. Kobel'ians'ka, an indefatigable advocate of equal rights and opportunities, has devoted many years to promoting gender equality. She trains cadres of young women throughout the country in gender issues—through programs of instruction, workshops, conferences, and focus groups. Together with like-minded activists, she also lobbies legislators to sponsor amendments to Ukraine's constitution, calling for gender parity.[1] Given the society of which she is a part, Kobel'ians'ka's views cannot be considered simply enlightened. Although by Western standards her convictions might appear relatively mild, to many Ukrainians her views might well be viewed as radical in the extreme.

                                                          Marian J. Rubchak

LT: *We speak of something called "gender democracy." What exactly does this mean? Many of our fellow citizens believe that gender issues are untimely, that such artificial concepts are undesirable external impositions.*

LK: When all is said and done, what is gender? It represents an aggregate of male/female relations that includes ideas, formal and informal rights, and norms, indicated by the position and status each sex occupies in a given society. Gender is a social construct. I would, however, challenge the notion that gender is something unnatural, in the way it is so often portrayed here. To my mind even the question is a misleading ruse to circumvent the search for gender democracy.

LT: *At first glance this seems like a preposterous notion! Who could possibly have any objections to equal rights and opportunities for both sexes?*

LK: Ukraine has pledged its integration into European structures, and now it has an obligation to proceed along that promised course. The civilized direction in which the world is moving today assumes that those who subscribe to the ideal of continuing progress will endeavor to live up to its expectations, and the global community imposes its own demands upon any government aspiring to membership. In the case of Ukraine, a declaration of support for an agreement to abide by European rules does not in and of itself inspire confidence that the nation is building a democratic society. What we need in order to live up to our obligations are mechanisms for implementing the resolutions of conferences and legislation devoted to the specific issues. We should not separate gender from social progress; both must be integrated into all aspects of our national life. We must strive to redress the gender imbalance; Ukraine's current pursuit of solutions to this problem is timely indeed.

LT: *If we are to entertain any hope of achieving this goal we need to get this information out to the public. This past year participants of the Center for Gender Studies at the T. H. Shevchenko Institute of Literature, Ukrainian Academy of Sciences, organized lectures, and a series of round tables on gender issues in several Ukrainian universities—Kharkiv, Kamianets'-Podil'skyi, Cher-*

nivtsi, Cherkassy, Chernihiv, Ternopil', Nizhyn, and L'viv. Unfortunately,
they confirmed what we already knew, most of the participants—scholars
from an array of disciplines—had never heard the term "gender," so how
could they be aware of its social implications?

LK: Yes, it is important not only to acknowledge the new ideology, but to create the conditions for understanding and adopting it. Gender needs to
be accepted in the context of carefully considered changes to the system,
as well as to the educational process. Take a subject like history. Can we
come up with at least ten names of female scholars known throughout the
world, women who have somehow impacted the evolution of the civilized
world? We have never lacked slogans about women's roles in world history, yet their contributions are still a black hole. This invites skepticism
among students, causing them to grow up doubting any women's achievements, and their rightful place in history. Throughout the entire educational stream--physics, chemistry, biology, or any other discipline—they
can find virtually no evidence of women's contributions to the sciences, or
to some major historical achievement. We know that women had no access to education until the nineteenth century. Before that, all scholarship,
all culture in general, was produced by men (or in men's names).

Beginning with the first grade, information on gender roles enters
both the consciousness and subconscious of children. Authors and primers might change with the generations, but stereotypes persist. During one
of our seminars, we examined primers from 1965 to1999. The only differences lay in the paper used for printing, and updated illustrations like
the computer, yet all were accompanied by the same old male-oriented
messages. Fathers alone were portrayed using computers, even though
this does not reflect real life in any way. Children are exposed to these
hackneyed images, implying that such practices are the norm. It might
seem inconsequential that only women are represented performing domestic tasks, but generation after generation is acculturated to the notion
of a prescribed place in society for each sex, and the mother is invariably
situated in the home. These are dangerous stereotypes, which impede the
balanced, healthy development of each sex. In today's world we need to
be aware that women and men perform diverse tasks. Who does what no
longer makes a difference; we are all equal, with the right to choice and
self-fulfillment on every level.

I would like to refer to another painful issue—men organize the structure of our education, making them the sole "engineers of human souls"
(as Stalin once expressed it). From the very inception of a child's studies,
right through completion of secondary education, however, women alone
are visible. They routinely implement the patriarchal plan, all of which
skews gender sensitivity.

LT: *You coordinate the program "Gender Studies in Ukraine." Exactly what does this mean?*

LK: The program, a constituent of the UN-sponsored Fostering Gender Parity [program], has been in effect for over a year now. It is an outgrowth of our conviction that the politics of realizing one's potential can function effectively only when the issue of equality is integrated into every fiber of society, with education the most critical component. We are hopeful that the idea of gender parity will be communicated on many levels. Our program is crucial for educating government legislators; they are the ones making decisions affecting gender. When they issue directives or implement a government program, these must reflect gender sensitivity. It cannot be denied that men and women have different needs, but well-balanced, well-considered policies will anticipate and allow for them.

Presently we are working on documents designed to integrate gender issues into education. No magic wand will be waved to advance this process. Action moves change, so we have selected the sensitization of government officials as our pilot project, with a model course on gender politics for the Ukrainian Presidential Academy of Government; it is now mandatory for future legislators. This is a noteworthy and rewarding achievement. We believe that Kyiv's Shevchenko University has also taken a giant step forward in adopting a gender policy. Gender issues have been mandated for every program in the curriculum, and gender expertise acts as a guide to their integration in all humanities syllabi. We look forward to these changes.

Special courses on gender are also scheduled for adoption. Of course, I am not so naïve as to expect that they will become part of every single curriculum immediately, but I hope that the university will at least demonstrate a willingness to incorporate them in all of its offerings in time. This also applies to other tertiary institutions—the Academy of Pedagogical Sciences, Kyiv Polytechnic University, the Ministry of Foreign Affairs Diplomatic Academy, and the Odessa State Academy of Food Technology, all of which already participate in our program. I am also encouraged by our access to the latest information technology. Kyiv's Polytechnic University provides an invaluable service to students throughout Ukraine with its web site designed to meet the needs of our program. It posts information on the importance of methodology, seminar materials, interesting presentations, personal contacts—all of this is found on the site, and is accessible to every tertiary-level educator.

One of democracy's successes in this program is that women's enrollment numbers exceed those of men in the Diplomatic Academy, which recently opened its doors to women for the first time. We can only hope that its female graduates will not end up in subsidiary diplomatic positions in this historically male preserve. To prevent this, we need to change the language of diplomacy, and the structure of assignments, as quickly as possible. It is a well-known fact that today's diplomatic language does not take women into account. Many of the current titles—director, cashier, secretary, and others—make no allowance for the fact that women might be filling these positions; this bias must be rectified immediately.[2]

LT: *How influential is the gender studies program at present?*

LK: Our UN program is not empowered to make changes on gender issues to educational or research programs. All we can do is encourage the adoption of suitable materials and methodology. In the end, the responsibility for finding the most effective means for introducing change resides with the government. Our task will be to develop an integrative course with the working title: "Introduction to Gender Theory," or "Bases of Gender Theory." This will become a requirement, just like courses labeled "Introduction to Economics" or "Introduction to Legal Studies." In other words, such an introductory course is meant to serve as a basis for developing a specific world view. Its purpose is to eradicate prejudice against the sexes in the generations to be shaped during the third millennium. Finally, introductory courses alone cannot inculcate a gender oriented worldview. The entire socializing environment needs to be imbued with ideas of gender parity, gender justice; this is what we are striving for, what we hope to achieve.

Gender Research in Sociology—the Current Situation
A Conversation with Svitlana Oksamytna

This next conversation was conducted with a self-professed feminist who admittedly came to feminism somewhat late in life, but, in her words, her commitment is that much stronger. She is Professor Svitlana Oksamytna, head of the Sociology Department at Mohyla National University, and Dean of Arts and Sciences, who has pioneered some innovative methods designed to encourage her students to think about gender issues in a positive way. Professor Oksamytna is teaching them to express their thoughts through a variety of experimental (for Ukraine) projects, which involve copious research and writing.

Marian J. Rubchak

LT: *As far as I know, gender studies and sociological analyses are both relatively new fields in Ukrainian education. In your university, what is the students' attitude toward such a program?*

SO: Our university is one of a handful of such institutions to offer these courses; they are intended for the humanities in general, as well as for future sociologists. The sociology department provides two of these courses: one is prescribed for undergraduates and the other is designed for students in our master's program. A sociology student must have a thorough knowledge of the application of gender research to sociology. Although they are difficult to teach, students find these courses intensely stimulating. Why are they so difficult? Whereas young women react to these offerings with great enthusiasm because they present new insights into what has always been taken for granted, young men view the material with ill-concealed skepticism. One way or another, new approaches cannot help but challenge established stereotypes, and men have no desire to discard the traditionally accepted persuasions of a male-oriented value system that favors them so absolutely. As the course progresses, each student is required to complete a research project on some facet of gender studies. In the course of their study, many of them become excited by this prospect because they are aware that it is likely to provide an opportunity to address something new and different, some concept that had not occurred to them up to that time.

LT: *How would you describe such a project?*

SO: An analysis of the relevant data, comprehensive interviews—and this, I repeat, on a subject which they had never before contemplated. It involves evaluating media reports and/or gender images in advertising. Here is a list of titles I have proposed: Ways in which minority views on gender issues impact society; A gender analysis of an internet segment on Ukrainian labor practices; Is an ordinary (Platonic) friendship feasible between a man and a woman? A male perspective; Use of the body for and against gender; The socialization of high school students; Female stereotypes in Ukrainian folklore.

LT: *What makes these topics so compelling?*

SO: Let me show you a paper on "Gender socialization of high school students." Tetiana Soltyk plans to write her thesis on this topic. In my opinion, the subject is unique in Ukrainian sociology. High school students were assigned an essay on "Why I would want to be a girl or boy. Why not"? Up to now such a study has never been conducted in Ukraine. Our researcher collected over three hundred responses, which clearly demonstrate the extent to which gender stereotypes are inculcated from childhood on. Boys frequently and very aggressively underscored male attributes, such as the potential for showing off their physical prowess. Girls in the same peer group overwhelmingly identified with domestic tasks and childcare. To date, no one in Ukraine has conducted a thorough study of sexual stereo-types, their dynamics, and the way they are constructed.[3] Society instills socially acceptable and gender-specific stereotypes early in life. When in-dividuals reach adulthood, it suddenly becomes evident that life offers men infinitely more possibilities and advantages than women enjoy—although technically both are equal. This is a "glass ceiling" issue, especially when it applies to female career advancement. When firms decide to downsize, for instance, women are invariably the first to go.

LT: *How do our sociological studies transmit information about this state of affairs?*

SO: Until now, virtually the entire sociological discipline has concentrated on public opinion polls, but the government budget does not provide fund-ing for any sociological surveys, to say nothing of gender studies.

LT: *So it seems that our government is not in the least bit interested in public opinion or public relations on either side of the gender issue.*

SO: Well, some programs have been endorsed, and we do have a government-sponsored Committee on Family and Youth.[4] As for the Institute of So-ciology itself—the basic center has neither a department nor a research division. Not a single project has received funding from the state budget. Take, for example, such an appropriate block of questions as those de-signed to test public opinion. Our department works closely with Kyiv's International Institute of Sociology. At present, it has two [unfunded] proj-ects concerning gender issues, upon which we draw whenever possible. Occasionally, some isolated data from public opinion polls will appear in this institute—for example, something on the status of women in society.

LT: *One cannot help feeling that gender research is limited to the domain of enthusiasts.*

SO: Yes, but this is not merely a research issue; it concerns all of society. Gen-der education is finally beginning to make some modest progress—largely owing to the efforts of the UN. But how must we go about preparing society for a change in the way it thinks? At a student conference this year, Maria Huz presented a proposal titled "Gender Stereotypes among Young Students." Incidentally, the paper was awarded second prize in the All-Ukrainian Competition for Papers by Young Students. Her research demonstrated that not even the student youth is capable of divesting him-self/herself of gender stereotyping.

LT: *Is there sufficient relevant literature to assist future sociologists in mastering gender issues?*

SO: Sources—scholarly resources that future sociologists can consult—are extremely limited. Primarily, they consist of English-language lectures. My own students have access to my personal collection—monographs and anthologies gathered while I was abroad on various grants and fellowships in the United States and Canada. They can also consult literature in Russian because our northern neighbors are way ahead of us in gender research. They have published useful dictionaries and textbooks. Ukraine's materials consist mostly of philosophical and sociological journal articles, and we do not have nearly enough of those.

LT: *Today, as a consequence of the recent parliamentary elections, fewer women than ever before find themselves in the corridors of power. What does this tell you?*

SO: Data collected from wide-ranging interviews conducted by Kyiv's Institute of Sociology included the following question: "How do you feel about the insignificant number of women in the Verkhovna Rada [parliament]?" As for gender quotas, on the whole most respondents—informed individuals in decision-making positions either in city government or in business—felt that there was nothing untoward in the present situation. Their collective opinion was that as long as the deputy is competent, the sex of the individual is of no consequence. And there are some female office holders. So what can we say, for example, about the fact that women in the third-tier election list comprised only 8 percent of all those seeking office; of this tiny number a mere 6 percent were elected?[5] Some do maintain that women are quite capable of performing parliamentary duties, at times even better than men when it comes to things like designing concrete plans for defense, or for the daily requirements of the people, but not in areas affecting trade in oil, gas, and weaponry. The majority, however, were of the opinion that women would actually be more effective as office-holders because of their ability to curb the excessive actions of male deputies. The result? Men would become less combative, more conscious of their appearance (i.e. they would wear well-pressed trousers, etc.). They would also refrain from yawning and picking fights during the parliamentary sessions, and would be less inclined to pick their noses in public, or read newspapers during the proceedings! In sum, women are needed to keep men (the "real" legislators), civilized and in line.

LT: *And what about gender quotas?*

SO: Surveys conducted throughout Ukraine indicate that the majority of people do not favor quotas, for two basic reasons. First, we all had enough of that during the Soviet era. The Supreme Soviet established a quota of 305 for women; and what did we get? The list went from dairy maids [during the Soviet era a pejorative designation for simple, unaccomplished women referred to as "*doiarky*"] actually functioned as a predetermined front for discriminatory male domination. There is no room for that sort of thing in a democratic society.

Few people are aware that Western countries sometimes establish quota systems as short-term solutions to immediate problems. A case in point is Scandinavia, where such systems stem from internal ruling-party decisions (not the result of government resolutions), adopted as temporary solutions to historical injustices. When we advocate democracy and equality for all, we must also do everything in our power to stamp out injustice. Western experience has clearly demonstrated that quotas are the single most effective instrument for achieving these goals. When quotas have stabilized a situation, equal opportunities will follow of themselves. No single party should establish quotas, however. We need to adopt the Western example, where "greens," socialists, and social democrats all work together on a quota system that will advance the goal of equality, such as that of Sweden's social democrats, who proposed a quota solution to create gender parity on which everyone agrees. And what do we do? We sit back and listen to speaker upon speaker rant against admitting women to the decision-making process, or, more cynically, propose it knowing that nothing will come of the resolution. Not only is Ukraine's sexist tradition alive and well, but female politicians, especially those in the most prominent political parties, often find themselves forced to endure crude male jokes at their expense.

LT: *In your opinion as a sociologist, why are women so reluctant to embrace the idea of gender parity?*

SO: I will begin by pointing out that every committed feminist fears defining herself as such. Why? First and foremost, our society looks upon feminists as aggressive, "masculinized" women. This is the kind of distorted negative image that is virtually absent in the West today. There, is no single overriding definition of a feminist there. A large spectrum of currents and directions—from socialist, liberal, psychoanalytical to radical—informs the definition of a feminist. Ideas of sexual inequality, the advancement of which depends upon inherited male-induced stereotypes, are entrenched in our society.

A short while back, I referred to student research that demonstrated how stereotypical labels are created and instilled in a young psyche. Traditional upbringing clearly and convincingly establishes the conventional (socially constructed) status of both sexes, and defines gender-specific roles. Inequality is not considered a negative state, but rather the norm. *Woman* is coterminous with *family, motherhood,* and *domesticity.*[6] A man fulfills himself in the public sphere, in business, and so forth. The bulk of society, especially its women, considers these stereotypes normal. It is customary to judge men alone as embodiments of the necessary attributes for a successful political career. This, notwithstanding that the Ukrainian constitution provides guarantees of equal rights and opportunities.

LT: *The prejudice you describe explains why young women today still hasten to marry, often before acquiring a good education and a profession.*

SO: Yes, compared to other European countries, the average marriage age is quite low in Ukraine. Society prepares us for such expectations. A girl needs to find a husband as early as possible, otherwise she is considered inadequate; 70 to 80 percent of our young women are married between the ages of twenty and twenty-two. Unfortunately, such early marriages impede their opportunities for a good education or development of their professional qualifications. This paradigm has been restructured in the West: first comes education, then a foundation is laid for a career path; marriage and children follow after the age of thirty. Informal rules that govern this kind of conduct are now the norm in Western societies.

There are other differences as well. Our students are also astonished when they learn that in Scandinavian countries, such as Sweden and Finland, a woman who bears a child receives 80 to 90 percent of her customary earnings. Naturally women with greater professional achievements will be compensated accordingly. The money goes toward the cost of raising a child, but can we imagine that this represents even a remote comparison with our system, which rewards mothers with 40 hryvni [about $8 at the time of the interview] a month to stay at home and raise a child?[7] Yet they are expected to do just that—to raise a child and live on that miserly sum.

LT: *There is so much talk among men about the low birth rate in Ukraine, yet these are the very men who sit around in the Parliament and establish "fair" monetary incentives to keep mothers at home with their children.*

SO: The woman is hit hard automatically. She is unable to support herself as a stay-at-home mother. But the bills still need to be paid, so she is forced to depend upon others. There are many such women in our country. Data have shown that only when women are fairly represented in the legislature—a minimum number has been set at 30 percent—can we expect lawmakers to introduce and pass decrees with this dilemma in mind. Because our parliament does not come close to meeting this quota, we cannot anticipate legislation that will provide for sufficient aid to women who choose to stay at home and raise their children. So what is the point of complaining about a low birth rate?[8]

LT: *This is a question of future productive forces for our country. The problem deserves the urgent consideration of society and legislators alike. Now—to sum up: what does your gender consciousness mean to you?*

SO: Basically, it offers an alternate view on male/female relations, and the potential for female self-fulfillment. I received a traditional education, but when, through personal initiative, I started to immerse myself in gender issues and proposed a gender course to the academy, my newfound interest was transformed into a powerful urge to change my entire worldview, and my own professional development. New vistas of knowledge suddenly opened up and beckoned to me, an unaccustomed understanding of the many hidden processes and manifestations in our culture.

From the Philosophy of a Name to the Philosophy of Life
A Conversation with Yulia Tymoshenko

This is the story of a remarkable woman, whose success we track once again through an interview conducted by Liudmyla Taran. The respondent is Ukraine's intensely ambitious, twice-deposed prime minister (now out of office after completing a third term), brilliant politician, heroine of the 2004 Orange Revolution, and, according to her own self-definition, a *nonfeminist*. Her achievements suggest otherwise. Hence, one is tempted to speculate that a disavowal of feminism is an indispensable political maneuver on the part of a very shrewd politician who navigates the shoals of a male world of Ukrainian politics with extraordinary adroitness and finesse, using every means at her disposal to draw in as wide an array of constituents as possible. By appealing to a broad spectrum of voters—in a country where men value physical beauty, she comes across as "a dish,"[9] as one journalist observed; her appeal for older women resonates with her coiled braid and frequent calls for prayer at public gatherings; a savvy sense of style resonates with the younger crowd—although here her support is less certain. Young women still tend to be conflicted when it comes to their self-determination, and she presents a challenge as a role model that not all young women are prepared or able to meet. At the same time, however, she does have the power to motivate those who aspire to leadership in the public sphere—in industry, commerce, or government. In Ukraine, where the term *gender* is only beginning to gain acceptance and, although "understanding" is limited, where feminism is anathema, Tymoshenko is aware that a public declaration of support for the feminist point of view would be political suicide. The following interview opened up an avenue for speculation about her true feelings regarding the promotion of a positive political image, the impact of her public declarations on an electoral base, and aspirations for reversing the direction of a country still rife with corruption and in a state of political disarray.[10]

Marian J. Rubchak

LT: *Yulia Volodymyrivna, in one of your recent public appearances, you mentioned something about* The Philosophy of a Name, *by Pavel Florensky. Let us begin on this note.*

YT: I recall thinking as far back as my childhood that I had been given a relatively rare name, at a time when other names were so much more popular. My circle alone included three Olenkas and four Olias, but not one Yulia. I was always very proud of my name. I felt that it was so special, and all those with whom I regularly came into contact seemed to like it very much. Its origins are Roman, and as far as I know it means "well behaved and honest." I believe that we should all like our name—it is given to us for a reason and, to a certain extent, it programs our actions and our life in general.

LT: *What kind of a child were you?*

YT: From what I can remember I was a leader in every situation. To be honest, leadership came easily to me; it was an organic part of me—effortless. Also, I was always more comfortable with boys than with girls. Boys enjoyed so much more freedom, and I liked to play soccer with them, it gave me such pleasure. It is fair to say that I was intrigued by all kinds of physical activity, and that I engaged in sports as a professional athlete.

LT: *So this is where you get that amazing physical stamina, from your participation in sports! Which sport(s) did you prefer?*

YT: Gymnastics were my favorite. I exercised routinely, and this occupied a substantial part of my time. Returning to the question of my childhood, I recall that early on I was determined to be the best in all that I did. Let me give you an example: even when my mother assigned me the most mundane tasks, such as doing the dishes or cleaning the apartment, I strove for excellence. The same applied to my studies.

LT: *You were a superior student and a Komsomol* [Communist Union of Youth] *activist?*

YT: I was incapable of being a poor student, but I was no Komsomol activist. I made every effort to avoid involvement in this particular kind of ideological leadership. To be perfectly honest, I was apolitical for much of my life. When I think about it, I realize that my entry into politics was a surprise, even to me.

LT: *That is to say, through business? Perhaps you will even return to business?*

YT: I'm not interested in business anymore. I think that somehow I was thrown into it in order to prepare myself for the struggle with my serious [political] opponents today. Lacking the financial means that I have at my disposal now, I would have found myself in a much weaker position for waging this disgusting battle, and it would have made little sense to take it on. There is so much that I want to do for this country of ours. An exemplary Ukrainian life could lead to us becoming a role model for other countries.

LT: *Let us backtrack to your biography. What sort of family did you grow up in?*

YT: I was born in Dnipropetrovs'k. Circumstances were such that I grew up without a father. He abandoned my mother and me when I was born. So I was raised by a single mother, a simple woman like so many in Ukraine—a woman of integrity, diligent, and overflowing with virtue. Our family had nothing in common with privileged members of society, the party nomenclature [*nomenklatura*].[11] We could rely only on ourselves. Mother worked as a dispatcher in an auto transport enterprise. In order to earn a living, and help her own mother and her sister's family as well, she often worked a twenty-four-hour shift. I am so grateful to her—she did everything she could to ensure that I received a good education. In other words, I grew up under circumstances in which I learned the value of every kopeck, as well as the significance of injustice.

LT: *May I ask which language was spoken in your home? I notice that lately you have switched to Ukrainian.*

YT: Yes, I was determined to speak solely in Ukrainian. I surprise even myself by thinking exclusively in Ukrainian, while working on a book or writing my speeches, and praying in the Ukrainian language. It's amazing how easy I find it considering that in the beginning we spoke only Russian at home; my studies and my life outside the home were all conducted in Russian. Now I encourage my entire family to communicate in Ukrainian. All that is required is the desire; with that anything is possible.

LT: *There is an expression [in English]—"Self-made man," an inclusive term that means one who has created himself/herself. You—a woman—did you "create" yourself?*

YT: Don't imagine that I am in any way unique. Every human being is responsible for creating himself/herself.[12] Can any grown person consistently refer to some sort of "props," to being the object of someone else's influence? Everyone must take personal responsibility and build his/her own life.

LT: *What can you tell us about your daughter? After all, she did grow up in circumstances that were much more comfortable than your own. How did she react when her parents found themselves in a very precarious situation after being accused of horrific crimes? She is what—sixteen, seventeen years old?*

YT: My daughter Evheniia, Zhenia, is already fully formed; she is a mature and strong individual. Zhenia is actually twenty-one years old.[13] She has been raised in a family that habitually complicated her life. At the time [of the incident in question] she was already an adult accustomed to making her own decisions. Just before my impending arrest—I was expecting it and had already discussed it with her—I asked whether she was prepared for such a turn of events. You should know that I always consult with my family before making any decision that, to put it mildly, is bound to cause the family pain and sorrow. She assured me that she would support my choice, that she could never envision her mother running from a bad situation, hiding from persecution in some foreign country, for example.

LT: *Life tests us in various ways. Some of these tests can be unkind, even brutal.*

YT: Brutal? Not at all! In our family we always stressed goodness, generosity of soul; we were taught to love one another—lessons that have been passed on from generation to generation. For instance, my great grandmother lived near the edge of a village … all kinds of "losers," indigents and beggars knew of her extraordinary kindness. Those unfortunates were always welcome to come in and rest, have a bite to eat, to share in whatever she had. She would have "given the shirt off her back" (as the saying goes). Her acts of kindness were recounted routinely in our family circle with the greatest reverence, so I cannot imagine myself being cruel to anyone. True, I might overlook a little harshness, if that is what it took to reach a higher goal, but clear-cut actions, resoluteness, high-minded principles—these are the qualities that make for success.

LT: *So you actually reject the possibility of failure?*

YT: Yes, although, when all is said and done, in the depths of one's soul one must always make *some* allowance for such a possibility—if the pain of possible failure is to be avoided.

LT: *All told, what you say about your own qualities brings to mind the horoscope. Of course we know that this is nothing more than a game, but all signs point to you as a typical combatant—purposeful, willful, determined, diligent, uncompromising, yet these are attributes typically assigned to high-achieving males.*

YT: All I can say about this is that my objectives have always come from the neck up.

LT: *Now, a question about a luxury that few of us can contemplate: your personal psychic space, your capacity for marshalling your thoughts in private. Do you have that ability?*

YT: Thank God, I do! A person unable to think in private is diminished as a human being. Currently, I am fascinated by philosophical ideas about the evolution of humanity. I read a great deal, think about these questions, am in the process of writing a book—which, I expect to finish within the next month or so. It is about my view of the future of civilization. That is why I am immersed in the Bible, and continue to examine it so carefully.[14]

LT: *As I understand it, you are devout. What does belief in God mean to you?*

YT: Faith is a way of life. Whatever suffering we are called upon to endure, God says: "Have faith and do not fear."

LT: *In your opinion, what is the status of women today?*

YT: I will begin by noting that up to now civilization has evolved according to a male set of values. In the beginning, physical strength was king. This lasted a long time, with men in charge of all decision making (securing food, intellectual and military pursuits). Owing to their physical strength and capacity for endurance, men conducted all vital activities. Any significant loss of manpower and its resources incurred dangerous consequences. So frequently they failed to return from a hunt or a war. This created an imbalance of the sexes. Women were forced to compete for men, so they spoiled them, catered to them. This persisted for thousands of years, enabling men to cultivate their vanity. They filled themselves with egoism, and not only in attitudes toward women. Men built every system of government, every social hierarchy on the basis of this male egoism, on their monopoly, on satisfying their needs. In the end, this is how world civilization was formed; it witnessed the male appropriation of government and suffered the absence of justice and harmony. For thousands of years, women reinforced men's feeling of uniqueness. For them males personified strength and power, and this led to competition among women; it was encoded in the female psyche almost to the level of genetics. Now that the world has reached the extreme of injustice, the woman's mission is and must be to introduce harmony into society.

LT: *But it is the men who foster in women the chaos, the disharmony, and feelings of envy.*

YT: Not at all. Let me give you an example: can you imagine a woman being jealous of her own children when it comes to her husband, or the reverse? This would never enter her mind. As for the man—for him it is quite normal. The man is jealous of his own children because he holds them responsible for depriving him of his share of attention and affection. As the need for his physical strength diminished over time, the woman began to think about herself; she was now in a position to do this. However, she understood that finding her niche would necessitate a much greater expenditure of effort on her part than was required of any man. She had to be more diplomatic, wiser, more forthright, and more intelligent. Only then could she break through to those corridors of influence where the weightiest decisions are made. In the end, women surpassed men in strength and endurance. Humanity's historical evolution has brought us to the contemporary woman's preparedness to assume leadership on every level, to take hold of the mechanism of egocentricity upon which civilization has been built. But her task is to build a world based upon principles of harmony and justice.

LT: *Yet there are so few women in those spheres where the fate of a society is determined.*

YT: Most important is the fact that women must develop an awareness of their role in the present developmental stage of civilization. Only they, only women, are capable of qualitatively changing the world.

LT: *And the role of men?*

YT: Unfortunately, today women cannot count on their support. That is our reality. For thousands of years men have been developing their own lobby, enforcing their view and understanding of the world. This has brought us to a precipice—the destruction of civilization. Men have squandered their chance. They have exploited the energies of women to their own advantage, keeping them always in inferior roles. It is no surprise that even during the Soviet era, women were consistently relegated to the status of assistants, helpmeets; they served the men in their positions of leadership. This was a well-designed strategy—exploiting the formidable potential, highly developed sense of responsibility, and business acumen of "the fair sex," as women were/are called. Today men are known to oppose women's movements with extraordinary brutality. Women can rely only on themselves, on their own strengths. Illusions are out of place. Women need to help each other; every one of them has to develop a sense of solidarity, to surmount the barrier of psychological divisiveness. Changes in attitude, strategy, and tactics—these are what we need for a successful breakthrough.

LT: *Yet your own Bat'kivshchyna Party consists solely of men. It is not a women's party.*

YT: I am categorically opposed to the practice of separating the sexes in any organized institution.[15] Every woman has a father, a husband, a son—so there is no logical agenda for marginalizing the opposite sex, God forbid! The issue here is social harmony, and this is where the female mission lies. For the sake of humanity, which consists of both sexes, the women are called upon to make fundamental changes in the nature of society, not as a separate group but from within the existing structures.[16]

LT: *In the final analysis, where do we begin?*
YT: At the very least, women must exhibit unwavering faith in female candidates for parliamentary or civic office, and convince their husbands to support these much-needed contenders as well. Let us not forget that the female electorate is in the majority.

LT: *But you know how the primitive mindset permeates our society, and to what extent the media propagate the notion that women choose to go into politics only when they are unfulfilled in their private lives. In other words, a woman's dissatisfaction, her feelings of inferiority, her waning years are what prompt her to struggle for a political mandate.*
YT: One hears such comments primarily from the men, and ultimately this says volumes about their decency and intellect, isn't that so? It tells us much about why men portray women in such a light: they are fearful of losing control, they are afraid of strong, intelligent, responsible women.

LT: *I understand that you are acutely aware of your own choice, just like all women who elect to break into a sphere of decision making. But our government discourages this in women.*
YT: Every responsible individual who aspires to a respectable political career in our post-Soviet reality must rise above repression. Otherwise, it is impossible to be sincere with people. Today I feel that I am a liberated human being. For me, liberty is the ability to freely express my ideas, however inconvenient this might be for some, whether it is the current Ukrainian government, someone in the West, or our northern neighbor. I am told at times that this is a sure way to lose one's [political] rating. Well—I have paid the price for my right to say what I think. Male politicians eschew no tactical tricks and subterfuges for that right. As for me, I strive to be responsible for my every word—and that is why I call everything by its rightful name.

Translated from Ukrainian by Marian J Rubchak

Notes

1. One critical amendment was ratified in early 2006.

2. All such titles have masculine endings in the gendered structure of the Ukrainian language.
3. In her chapter in this volume, Victoria Haydenko alerts us to the way that even well-intentioned efforts to teach gender neutrality in primary schools are less than successful, owing to the potency of established stereotypes [Ed.].
4. This has been upgraded to the Ministry of Family, Youth, and Sports, with a gender subsidiary and an inequitable emphasis on sports.
5. Women's names generally appear at the bottom of any list, and since the number elected from each party corresponds to the same number of candidates taken from the list, from the top down, women lose by virtue of their position near the bottom.
6. This is one of the unmarked paradigms in today's Ukrainian society.
7. The sum changes frequently, but remains minimal.
8. Even more problematic is the lack of implementation. Good legislation does exist, some of which was passed after this interview was taken.
9. In early October, the American website "Hottest Heads of State" put her at the top of their list: http://www.isria.com/pages/ (accessed 26 October 2009). It also bears mentioning that she has garnered numerous leadership awards, and at the time of this writing is enjoying high numbers at the polls in her upcoming bid for the presidency (as of late December 2009).
10. This "conversation" with a "non-feminist" differed as much from those of the other two respondents as does the woman herself. She represents a Ukrainian paradox, a successful woman in a man's world, living her entire life by feminist precepts, yet disavowing all connections to feminism.
11. This was a small, élite subset of the general population in the Soviet Union whose members held various key administrative posts in all spheres of the Soviet life: government, industry, agriculture, education, etc. The *nomenklatura* possessed immense authority and claimed precisely the kind of privileges that any ruling class enjoyed, yet which communist doctrine denounced as a corrupt product of the capitalist west.
12. In the Ukrainian language, these endings can be neutral, thus making conversion into English possible as himself/herself; him/her, etc.
13. The "conversation" took place in 2002.
14. Her book does not appear to have been published.
15. Since her party consists of men, without Tymoshenko's "token" presence there would be a clear separation of the sexes.
16. She never did address directly the question put to her.

Notes on Contributors

Catherine Wanner is Professor, Departments of History and Anthropology, Pennsylvania State University, and award-winning author of *Communities of the Converted: Ukrainians and Global Evangelism* (AAUS prize for Best Book on a Ukrainian Subject and the Heldt prize for Best Book by a Woman in Any Area of Slavic/East European/Eurasian Studies). Her research interests center broadly on how discursive forms of ideology shape social and cultural practices in everyday life, and especially how these dynamics operate in Ukraine.

Marian J. Rubchak is a Senior Research Professor of History at Valparaiso University whose work focuses on reimagining Slavic identities in various contexts. She has written on the role of myth in shaping the identity of contemporary Ukrainian women, and the difficulties that they face in exerting agency in a transnational society with prejudices against women.

Cinzia Solari recently received her PhD from the University of California, Berkeley in the Department of Sociology and is an assistant professor at the University of Massachusetts in Boston. She has already written extensively on topics such as constructions of motherhood and nation in transnational migrations; the role of religious institutions in the settlement and transnational practices of migrants; comparative migration patterns and the gendered work identities of immigrant in-home care providers to the elderly.

Alexandra Hrycak is Associate Professor of Sociology, Reed College, and president of the American Association for Ukrainian Studies. Her numerous publications include: "Coping with Chaos: Gender and Politics in a Fragmented State," "From Mothers' Rights to Equal Rights," and "The Dilemmas of Civic Revival: Ukrainian Women since Independence." Her article "Foundation Feminism and the Articulation of Hybrid Feminisms in Post-Socialist Ukraine" placed first in the AAUS Best Article competition for 2006.

Sarah D. Phillips is Associate Professor of Anthropology at Indiana University, who won first prize (AAUS) for her *Women's Social Activism in the New*

Ukraine: Development and the Politics of Differentiation. Among her many articles are: "Will the Market Set Them Free? Women, NGOs, and Social Enterprise in Ukraine," Civil Society and Healing: Theorizing Women's Social Activism in Post-Soviet Ukraine," "Women and Development in Postsocialism: Theory and Power East and West."

Oksana Kis' is a Senior Research Fellow of Ethnology at the Ukrainian Academy of Sciences. She is a widely published scholar on both sides of the Atlantic. Her latest work is a pathbreaking Ukrainian-language monograph: *Woman in Traditional Ukrainian Culture* (2008). Kis' is one of a group of scholars who participated in an international oral history project titled "Women's Memory. Searching for Lives and Identities of Women under Socialism." She is a prolific scholar who has edited a thematic issue of the feminist journal *Yi* as well as an anthology of feminist texts and helped to popularize scholarly works on feminism and gender research.

Victoria Haydenko hails from Ukraine, where she taught gender pedagogy at Sumy State Pedagogical University. She also edited a reader on the subject, titled *Gender Pedagogy,* which was approved as a textbook for higher-education institutions by the Ministry of Science and Education in Ukraine. Her other research interests include feminism and science, and the philosophy of education. Haydenko is currently pursuing these interests as an independent scholar in California.

Laada Bilaniuk, Associate Professor of Anthropology at the University of Washington, is the author of *Contested Tongues: Language Politics and Cultural Correction in Ukraine,* winner of the ATSEEL award for Best Book in Slavic Linguistics. Other publications include "Language in the Balance: The Politics of Non-accommodation in Bilingual Ukrainian-Russian Television Shows," and "Criticism, Confidence, and the Reshaping of the Linguistic Marketplace in Ukraine." Bilaniuk's research interests include linguistic anthropology, language ideology, language politics, nationalism, popular culture, and gender.

Mariia Tytarenko is a Ukrainian scholar, recently in the United States on a Fulbright Fellowship, where she researched American new journalism and worked on Ukrainian universal publicism. She is a lecturer at Lviv's Ivan Franko University, and serves as its Chair of the Foreign Press and Information Program. Among her recent works is a volume of poetry, published in translation in *The International Poetry Review,* No. 2 (2010).

Maria G. Rewakowicz is currently a second-time Fulbright Senior Research Fellow in Kyiv. Rewakowicz is a prolific scholar and gifted poet, with four books of poetry to her credit. Her most recent collection is titled *A Green Roof*. Other publications include *Pivstolittia napivtyshi: Antolohiia poezii N'iu-Iorks'koi hrupy* [A Half-Century of Half-Silence: An Anthology of the New York Group's Poetry], "Women's Literary Discourse and National Identity in Post-Soviet Ukraine," and "Feminism, Intellectuals and the Formation of Micro-Publics in Postcommunist Ukraine" (coauthor).

Tatiana Zhurzhenko is Elise Richter Fellow at the Institute for Political Science, University of Vienna, where she is researching politics of memory in post-Soviet borderlands. Earlier she taught at V. Karazin Kharkiv National University (Ukraine) and worked at the Kharkiv Center for Gender Studies. Zhurzhenko has published widely on gender politics and feminism in Ukraine. Her recent books are *Gendered Markets of Ukraine. The Political Economy of Nation Building* (Vilnius 2008), and *Borderlands into Bordered Lands: Geopolitics of Identity in Post-Soviet Ukraine* (Stuttgart 2010).

Liudmyla Taran is a poet, journalist, prolific author of works on feminism and gender, and committed feminist. Her poetry has appeared in English, Polish, and Russian translations in anthologies on both sides of the Atlantic titled *One Hundred Years of Youth*, and *In Another Light* respectively. They were published by Litopys (L'viv) in 2000 and included her poems in both Ukrainian and in English translations. Taran's respondents are: **Laryssa Kobelians'ka,** director of the UN Program for Gender Education in Kyiv; **Oksana Oksamytna**, Dean and Professor of Sociology at Mohyla National University; and **Yulia Tymoshenko**, former prime minister, and currently leader of the opposition in Ukraine's parliament.

Index

Index note: page references with an *f* or a *t* indicate a figure or table on the designated page.